DANCE JAMAICA

DANCE JAMAICA

CULTURAL DEFINITION AND ARTISTIC DISCOVERY

The National Dance Theatre
Company of Jamaica
1962–1983

REX NETTLEFORD

FOREWORD BY EDWARD KAMAU BRATHWAITE
AND PHOTOGRAPHS BY MARIA LaYACONA

GROVE PRESS, INC./NEW YORK

First Edition 1985
First Printing 1985

Library of Congress Cataloging in Publication Data

Nettleford, Rex M., 1933–
      Dance Jamaica.

      1. National Dance Theatre Company of Jamaica—History.
I. LaYacona, Maria. II. Title.
GV1786.N26N39   1985   793.3′2′097292   84-48415
ISBN 0-394-54316-5

This book is made possible by a grant from the Ford Foundation in
commemoration of two decades of work in the dance by the National
Dance Theatre Company of Jamaica.

All photos by Maria LaYacona unless otherwise indicated.

Text design by David Miller

Manufactured in the United States of America

GROVE PRESS, INC., 196 West Houston Street, New York, N.Y. 10014

Frontispiece: The dramatic work *Court of Jah* (1975) catches the spirit
of contemporary Jamaican dance. Choreographed to reggae music
of Bob Marley, the dance explores Rastafarian religious expression in
the Caribbean.

To the artists of the Caribbean
and the mass of our people
from whom we draw creative impulse,
ancestral wisdom,
and aesthetic energy

Acknowledgments

I would like to acknowledge with gratitude the assistance of the following individuals and institutions that made the preparation and production of this book possible:

The Ford Foundation provided the basic funding for the book and will generously allow the proceeds from its sales to revert to the NDTC Development Fund. UNESCO's International Fund for the Promotion of Culture also provided valuable supplementary financial assistance toward publication expenses.

The dedicated work and sacrifice of all past and present members of the National Dance Theatre Company constitute the real substance of this volume.

General encouragement and support in writing the book came especially from Maud Fuller, Cliff Lashley, Barbara Gloudon, Wycliffe Bennett, Carl Bliss, Verona Ashman, Peggy Greaves, and Jeffrey Puryear.

Those who contributed to the book's actual production include: Alison Symes, Yvonne daCosta, Cheryl Ryman, Sheila Barnett, Tony Wilson, Alaine Grant, and Leaford McFarlane (assisting the research); Claudia Menza, Sheila Barnett, and Yvonne daCosta (reading and evaluating the draft manuscript); Joy Blake and Loretta McNeil (typing the final manuscript); Reginald Gay (editing the final manuscript); David Miller (designing the book); Janet Liu Terry (indexing the page proofs); Marjorie Whylie (providing material on the Company's music compositions); Carl Bliss (acting as financial liaison with the Ford Foundation); and Edward Kamau Brathwaite (writing the Foreword).

Besides the many photographs generously supplied by Maria LaYacona, the Company's official photographer, the following organizations and photographers are cited as sources for the remaining illustrations: API; Bruin Photographs; Bryan Studio; Syde Burke; Anthony Crickmay; Ted Cunningham; Yvonne daCosta; *Daily Gleaner*; Delmar; Kenn Duncan; Gray Studios; Errol Harvey; Institute of Jamaica; Jamaica Information Service; Jamaica School of Dance; Jamaica Tourist Board; LaMonte; *Miami Herald*; Owen Minott; Richard Montgomery; National Library of Jamaica; Johnny R. O'Brien; Amador Packer; Horst Schröder; Arthur Smith; Peter Smith; Eric Tello; Battle Vaughan; Cecil Ward; *Western Mail and Echo* (Cardiff); J. J. Wood.

The lithographs by Richard Bridgens reproduced on pages 12 and 17 were originally published in Bridgens's *West Indian Scenery, with Illustrations of a Negro Character* (London: Robert Jennings and Company, 1836). The picture on page 35 is from the book of photographs *Picturesque Jamaica, with Descriptive Text of the Island* (Kingston: Duperly and Sons, c. 1891).

Contents

Foreword

1

Several years ago when we were "coming up, coming up," in the wood-dove coo dawn of what this book gives me confidence to call our civilization, it was fashionable for certain cultural colonial administrators of a liberal orientation to characterize us as "Greek," "the tropical Aegean in the Caribbean Mediterranean." We came of course to reject these thalassic similes, but eventually would understand what the well-meaning selected Athenian metaphors meant: an atomic small-scale archipelago of fewer than ten million people (more if you add Cuba, Hispaniola, and Puerto Rico) capable of cultural explosion, with the kind of quality of intimacy which allows, on the one hand, little real privacy and, on the other, not much allowance for isolation, alienation—we can all meet each other in the marketplace and leaders can be related to with first-name familiarity, like the sons & sisters they are.

It is in fact no longer—if it ever were—quite so simple. The Caribbean Antilles, even before the death of the Amerindians, was a three thousand mile arc of a fragmented mountain range (still is!) which seems to have split off from Yucatén through south of Florida, where the Gulf was a lake, to become at last Yucaya Guanahaní, Cuba, Haiti, the Isle of Pines, Borinquén Puerto Rico, pummeling still smaller to the eastern auspices of the Virgins and the Saints, falling southward through coralline Barbados to Orinocan Trinidad and finally to Venezuela on the South American coast. This geophysical catastrophe acquired a geopsychic component over the millennia, so that each island is separated not only by saltwater blue but also by political blues: tidalwave slaveries, fragmented freedoms, historical divisions of identity & ideology, British, French, Spanish, other parts of Europe too, divided through the epidermal vein by poverty & wealth and blinding faction. In other words, whatever Greek(?) paradigm there existed was contradicted by a malindignant Babylonian implosion of "Third World problems," which ex-President Richard Nixon once said was our own fault if not our own responsibility.

What comes out of this anti/thesis is what in fact one has eyes to hear and ears to overstand. V. S. Naipaul, one of our finest (exiled) writers, saw in the early 1960s only the dread and wrote (in *The Middle Passage*) what is now practically his epigraph: "The history of the islands can never be satisfactorily told. Brutality is not the only difficulty. *History is built around achievement and creation; and nothing was created in the West Indies.*" Some say that Naipaul was lamenting, the absence of statues & temples; some say the absence of ruins! But it goes deeper than this. I mean, there is the simple(?) drum, the footstep string, bamboo fiddle, bongo violin, guitar rocksteady *cheng* which steps upon the mourning ground between wave-lip and footlight board and whirls between the manchineel and distant mountain into kumina or carnival costume. It is the tension of that dumb & drum that gives us gesture, movement, word, and grace: the poetry of Martin Carter, Walter Rodney, Kapo, Sparrow, Spree Simon's pebble sound from beaten biscuit tin and burnished oil, the pan white walking rivers: Pentecostal shepherds: Water Muma, Oropuna, Oropuche, Cooramata, Blanchesseuse, while baby mouths bawl fire from an Orange Lane, where man's neglect cracks like a dry fife stick behind the Amen Corner. Derek Walcott, another fine free Caribbean poet and playwright, wrote about it in "What the Twilight Says": root joy: yes: and exhilarating despair: "not a despair that belongs to others, but a truly tragic joy." This after twenty years laboring to conjure out of a medley of ex-colonial(?) "madmen and specialists" with "an egotism that [could] pass for genius," a dedicated dramaturge that would preserve "the awe of self-enactment as the sect gathers for its self-extinguishing self-discovering rites," moving toward our own omens.

2

Three years after the start of Walcott's Trinidad Theatre Workshop but preparing itself from about the same time, there began on the other side of the Caribbean another *responsible* movement, concerned, as the other, primordially with language: the National Dance Theatre Company of Jamaica: which in its roots, structure, and manifestations now far exceeds (though that is not the word) anything that has so far been formally attempted in the Caribbean, that is, outside the marvelous achievements of revolutionary Cuba, and which complements the work/style enterprises of the Trinidad Theatre Workshop: both—all three—refutations of the Naipaul "nothing." If Rex Nettleford's account of the National Dance Theatre Company carries with it less of the sibylline elation *and* less of the subversive despair of Walcott's "Twilight" (for Nettleford it is a developing beginning not a culmination), that has something to do with the personalities of the twinned artistic directors and with the differences—arc of miles and subtle histories—between Trinidad and Jamaica: the one (to use the "Greek" imagery one last time) Byzantine, the other Babylonian; one pleasure dome and Carnival, the other (put it simply) dread: Rasta and real estate. Trinidad, I think it is held by nearly all, has a thin brilliant anarchic infrastructure, while Jamaica—more Baptist serious and free-village-labor solid (look at the statue of Paul Bogle, national hero, outside the Morant Bay Court House)—has a cultural administrative structure that harps back to the Royal Society of Arts (1854) which became the Institute of Jamaica (1874), still extant and very active with its exhibitions, concerts, lectures, examinations, Musgrave Medals, museums, Junior Centre, art classes and gallery, and, above all, its West India reference library.

It was from the Institute of Jamaica that most cultural activities on the island have informally radiated or have been intimately connected: the Little Theatre Movement, founded by Henry and Greta Fowler in 1941, which since then was responsible for what by the mid-1950s had become, with Louise Bennett and Ranny Williams, the national pantomime, Jamaica's popular musical theater; the Jamaica School of Art (1958); the Jamaica School of Music (1962), all of which, along with a newly formed School of Drama and School of Dance, were inter-amalgamated into the Cultural Training Centre (1976), itself under the aegis of the Institute of Jamaica. What's more, many of the leading figures in Jamaica's art & cultural expression have been connected with the institute: Walter Jekyll, Tom Red-cam, and H. G. DeLisser, in the first decades of this century; Edna Manley, Albert Huie, and George Campbell in the 1930s; the novelists Neville Dawes and John Hearne as well as Nettleford himself, who have been either its directors or chairper-sons, in more recent times. Nor is it surprising that Jamaica has produced a most valuable line of cultural accounts of itself: from Frank Cundall through Philip Sher-lock to Ivy Baxter's *The Arts of an Island* (1970), Neville Dawes's *Cultural Policy in Jamaica* (1977), Nettleford's own *Caribbean Cultural Identity: The Case of Jamaica* (1978), Olive Senior's *A–Z of Jamaican Heritage* (1983), and the still largely unpub-lished research of Wycliffe Bennett.

This cultural confidence and authority has deep roots within a history of wars and struggle for respect & self-respect that goes back, as Vic Reid has been say-ing since his first novel *New Day* (1949), to the louvertures between Arawak, Span-iard, Anglican Briton, and Akan in colonial plantation Jamaica: a perspective on the meaning of freedom/liberation that has its origin in the very geological configura-tions of the place; in those Maroon communities that recognized this and in spur and Cockpit, Nanny town, and John Crow mountain; and were able to forge certain continuous disconnected continuities through slave revolt dry-gullied stony gut precipitously brown and dry and green and water-willed and Morant Bay to what at last the voice of Garvey could define; and Bedward, Rasta, reggae, Marley, Man-ley, Michael Smith. For Jamaica, as Sylvia Wynter has reminded us, had its planta-tions and its plots. The plots—poems of ground first given to the slave to stave from starve, to plant his yam and therefore plant his god *(yam: nyam: onyame)*—be-came the piece of ground whence the plots against plantations would begin. So the dialectic: cruel but creative; surrealist & underground; inchoate and grudging mutual osmosis, developing the new groundation that would abide the time and serve the day: chapel and church, "partner" and credit union, coumbite and yard and "bood," to go against and stand at last along with *Gleaner,* Commerce, Union, Party, Institute and Cultural Training Centre as a revealed and *earned* tradition: available to work with & against, consolidate & process forward the island's i/so-lated talents into something more than jingo ego monkey genius.

So that when on the morning of Jamaica's political independence (1962) Rex Nettleford and Eddy Thomas brought together, as an act of faith in past & future, a core of the island's best (and variously) trained and dedicated dancers, calling itself self-consciously and challengingly the National Dance Theatre Company, it was—we see it now—nothing more, nothing less, than one more act in the articulation of the island's sense of self-respect. Which is why it could so quickly *grounds* itself into the affection of what was becoming the nation as a whole, and why, as this book so clearly details, it set up from the outset a rigorous program of training, research-performance-assessment, followed by the reinvestment of experience back into the Company/community, and cleaved unto the "model" at the very heart and start of the Jamaica experience—the Maroon tradition—contemporaneous of course, but independent of and outside though not unconnected with "plantation." So that the National Dance Theatre Company never fell into the debt or doubt trap of government (official) subsidy, but pied its own pipers to its own tune: though since it at the same time didn't pay its pipers—and this is one of the many miracles of the Company—it didn't have to call the tune to them either, so that it has from the groundswell upward been able to develop an unpaid professional national & independent Company; thus realizing one of Walcott's dreams on the other side of the Caribbean: "imagined cities devoted neither to power nor to money but to art"— and, we might add, dyam hard diurnal work.

There was no danger, then, of the National Dance Theatre Company ever annihilating itself into the popular high-kick can-can trocadero razzmatazz that becomes so easily the first refuge of dance companies concerned with profits and which soon see their losses recouped in guilt-edged investment in each titillating sequin of the *danse tropique*. The Company, set on the cycle of its own responsibility, its own self-disciplined sense of self-respect, from the beginning set up this dialogue for three, with itself & its ancestral heritage & the society, and within this framework three clear aesthetic formulations have so far emerged: statements of *how we are/who we are* (the Company's on-going wrestle with vocabulary): *Plantation Revelry* (1963), *Two Drums for Babylon* (1964), *Kas Kas* (1965), *Mountain Women* (1972), *Street People* (1973), Eduardo Rivero's Arara–Cuban *Sulkari* (1980); statements of *why we are:* explorations of historical experience: *Legend of Lovers' Leap* (1962), *Ni—Woman of Destiny* (1976), and the magnificent *The Crossing* (1978), inspired by Alex Haley's *Roots* and Quincy Jones's music: the first major ritual enactment on a Caribbean stage of the middle passage, which in turn has bucked the Company upon the slave trade of contemporary politics: *Backlash* (1975), *Rockstone Debate* (1981), *The Visitor* (1982).

But the genre that has brought the Company by far the warmest ovations, at home and abroad, has been the celebratory *here we are* series: fusions of vocabulary disciplines and resurrections of the ancestral tradition when for the first time the whole *sound* and therefore *shape* of the Company radically altered in response to the new (ancient & modern) challenge during the 1960s, from an increasingly "conscious" society, expressed in the ital tracks provided by Toots, Cliff, and Marley; by the living scores of Marjorie Whylie, the Company's musical director, and from the presence of "real" folk drummers within the song ensemble: *Pocomania*

(1963), *Kumina* (1971), *Myal* (1974), *Tribute to Cliff* (1974), *Backlash* (1975), *Court of Jah* (1975), *Sulkari* (1980), *The Crossing* (1978), *Gerrehbenta* (1983).

3

Had it all failed, we would of course never have known it, especially since after its performance the dance is in a material sense "lost." But although twenty-one years is not too long, it is a long long time in the life of any person, animal, or artistic company, and the National Dance Theatre Company has not only been a success ("cultural ambassadors," etc.) but it has become a model of success—a model of hard-earned national success—that something *is* created here, which realization, I suspect, gives it its greatest satisfaction. This Company was born as Jamaica was re/born and has lived the stark sonorous destruction & renewal of the dream that the Caribbean has been involved in since 1962 since 1865 since 1834 since 1492. As such, it is the avatar and living monument to those countless voiceless millions dead who made their mark unmarked before this could be so. It has become the body voice: brief but enduring signatures in space: of those who footstepped crouched leapt or were hurled onto what becomes the stage and drama of this book: the record of a people's cross & crossing: creative burden of colliding conti-nents: reduced to necessary written word by this modestly masked "artistic direc-tor," who has him-singly done as much as anyone in these "blue scapes, Greek there" to articulate the pride & pain & passion brought us here, and more than most has worked far more than most toward that sense of style: vibration not missilic dictat; that cycle circle capsule contraction & release, that polyrhythmic contradic-tion we recognize as ours.

EDWARD KAMAU BRATHWAITE

Negro Dance, by Richard Bridgens. African-derived recreation
dancing grated on the aesthetic sensibilities of Europeans visiting
Jamaica in the eighteenth and nineteenth centuries. (*National
Library of Jamaica*)

1· Dance and Survival: Cultural Resistance in Caribbean Society

The creative acts of our people, forged collectively over time or by individual protago-nists, . . . have thrown up classic expressions which have in turn become prime sources of energy for that vital quest for cultural certitude. . . . All such expressions emanating from social interaction now serve as the living archives of our patrimony as well as the testament of a valid collective experience signifying the germ of a definitive civilization.[1]

It is in the nature of the times that millions of people who have been formally "set free" from the shackles of colonialism should now lay claim to a definitive civi-lization. They do so on the basis either of ancestral pedigree—as Africans and Indians perceive it—or of imminent realization—as the anglophone Caribbean populations, all creatures of colonization, would have it. These heirs of colo-nialism ferret out new or ancestrally based designs for social living and seek serviceable perceptions of themselves and of their societies emerging out of colonial rule. They forge novel and revolutionary modes of expression for con-tinued advancement toward total liberation. They also search for alternative institutions appropriate to the imperatives of decolonization and national devel-opment. This is so whether the first step on the road to that definitive civilization is through armed resistance—which happened in 1776 in the North American colonies and was repeated later in much of Latin America, including Cuba—or by means of a negotiated settlement for peaceful coexistence between the for-mer colonized and colonizer—such as the formation of the Commonwealth Ca-ribbean,[2] which during three centuries, until the independence arrangements of the 1960s, played the wily suntanned savage of a Caliban to the magisterial tutelar authority of Great Britain's Prospero.

The anguish of renewal and reshaping draws heavily on the resources of imagination and creative intellect—gifts of grace which as part of the irony of a subjugated existence served the subordinated people well. The ingenious strat-agems of imagination and intellect that allowed the slaves or the colonized peo-ples to outwit the oppressive master bear eloquent testimony to this anguished past. The history of Jamaica and the wider Caribbean area abounds in the con-sequences of such irony, and many rebellions, both individual and collective, have been lost or won through the exercise of a fecund imagination and the application of a lively intelligence. Such rebellions continue to this day, not necessarily by means of a gun but often through the resourcefulness of artistic creativity—whether the artist is poet, playwright, painter, potter, musician, actor, or dancer. As I have stressed elsewhere, "It is not by accident that the performing arts, which depend on dialogue and social interaction for their dynamic [and for collective plan and action], are the artistic cultural expressions which tend to carry greatest conviction among Caribbean people."[3]

The Creative Artist and Society

Foremost among these cultural expressions is the dance, or more accurately dance theater. In reflecting on the role and continuing force of this art form, one must consider the concept of marronnage.[4] For in a society like contemporary Jamaica the effective creative artist mirrors the style and strategies of the former Maroons. Secrecy and cunning, coupled with fugitive sensibilities, are critical to the success of an art form's craft. For art protects its own sense of order, under cover, and ambushes society from under that cover of secrecy. Cunning, as well as physical distancing, is exploited in order to awaken that society and help guide it under its new dispensation. Thus the artist may confront society amicably or fight it in a hostile encounter—but always from what the South African writer Nadine Gordimer in another context describes as the "jealous hoarding of private experience for transmutation into fiction."[5] This is particularly true of the fiction of song, theater, and dance. Nothing that the creators of art works could say or think would be truer than the fictions they offer in the forms themselves: literary symbols; shapes frozen in wood, stone, and clay; sound structured into song; or isolated movement assembled into dances. The eternal paradox of fiction as the purveyor of truth is but one of the many paradoxes that nourish and challenge the creative artist, just as the use of the mask as persona, itself a form of fiction, has nourished a people's strategy of cultural resistance throughout their creative existence.

Another paradox of painful urgency in developing societies such as those in the Caribbean is the contradiction of the artist's unrepentant self-containment and autonomy without the chance of ever escaping his having to define that self-containment and autonomy in terms of a wider social reality. The tension is revealed most clearly in the region's significant cultural products.

One must avoid the arrogance of interpreting one's society exclusively through one's private life. Through such self-indulgence an otherwise creative life "drags on only as an appendage of the social process"[6] and does not become an integral part of that process. The torment of this contradiction is part of the presumption of being a creative artist.

With the fullest appreciation of the mediation of the creative process by social reality, the creative artist in developing countries must break the privilege of privacy without surrendering totally to public prying. The artist must be involved and yet detached, concerned and caring but also aloof and skeptical. Jamaican society—true as well of the wider Caribbean area—is a beleaguered victim of underdevelopment, endemic poverty, and a threatening spiritual debility manifest in chronic self-doubt, cultural ambivalence, and almost pathological preoccupations with recognition and status. Thus the society challenges the artist with intense contradictions.

Caribbean society still manages to educate and socialize much of its population to self-negation. This distorted vision of self and society compels certain creative artists to respond. It is their "third eye" that has prompted the judgments and perceptions that are necessary correctives to the facile assumptions of unimaginative public leaders making important decisions about the society's material and spiritual destiny. Promoting confidence in the values manifested in fiction, poetry, music, dance, drama, and the plastic arts is what cultural development has been about in Jamaica. The work of writers during the 1930s, and of painters and sculptors later, mirrored this to a fine degree. The story of the dance as it is reflected through the prism of the National Dance Theatre Company (NDTC) of Jamaica must be understood in the context of a tradition of dedication and vision. It is this sense of order and respect for its creative potential that has helped keep the society afloat.

I implicitly believe in the organic connection between the arts of a people and both their everyday living and their historical experience. For the rooting of the products of the imagination—of which the dance may be the foremost elemental expression—in the reality of specific human existence is the surest guarantee of a living art form. It is this connection between the creative imagination and social reality that the National Dance Theatre Company is committed to projecting and promoting. This position does not refer to social realism, which I do not believe in, but rather it supports the answer implied in the question, "What is poetry which does not save nations or people?"[7] The question is equally valid in terms of the dance. For those who want to retain their individuality, or to protect that part of the spirit which must remain alive and inviolable for one to exercise the creative imagination, the fear has long proved unfounded. By its very nature the creative imagination lies beyond the reach of the vilest oppressor—whether it be person or system and no matter how great the advantage of armaments, instruments of torture, or devices that affect psychological disorientation. Yet the artist working in a society of struggle, which postcolonial Jamaica and the wider Caribbean area undoubtedly are, cannot escape the imperatives of the social context within which he or she must work. An artist soon discovers that he cannot have it both ways. Yet no special plea is being made for engaged dance theater or music. Rather one speaks in the spirit of what Mervyn Morris, the editor of a

1983 anthology of Jamaican writing, claims for his volume: in projecting the myriad variations of form and theme, we contribute "to the unending process of our self-definition."[8]

Such self-definition quite rightly seeks to address every aspect of life that would make Caribbean people less than whole. Those deeply involved realize that it is not always easy to be conscious of being a society that struggles toward self-definition and yet certifies values that go beyond that struggle. But that is the challenge of any artist. It has been often repeated that the creative artist cannot escape from the schizophrenia of the dualities inherent in existence: part reality and part dream; inner landscape vying with outward reach; even the dialectical thrust of androgynous sensibilities challenging both men and women to more complex modes of artistic expression. Artists must not make exaggerated claims for themselves. A bad artist is of no more use to society than an inept mechanic, but a good artist—writer, performer, or plastic artist—must make society understand that the practice of craft requires keen observation and a special perspicacity, which results only from being able to move "under the surface of human lives," as it has been again aptly put by Gordimer.[9] It is this capacity that will continue to give the Jamaican dancer, as well as other artists, not only a sense of place and purpose but also a permanent dynamic influence on society's thoughts and feelings. If it is true that art lies at the heart of all events, then the investment by the artist in textured living and in a sense of history can only pay dividends of the highest order. A society of struggle needs this intuitive grasp of reality on the part of its artists, who must in turn be convinced that, even before the leaders are aware, the people usually know what to do.

It is the collective wisdom of the Jamaican people that signifies the richness of their collective experience. For it is in the crucible of that experience that much of what became known as Jamaican and Caribbean has been forged over four or five centuries. Survival on the village plots, and later in free villages, through practical frameworks of their own making; suffering on the plantation and now in the cities of "Babylon"; and severance from homelands—these processes together constitute a serviceable historical–cultural reference and a vibrant source of energy, not only for the creative impulse but also for the working plans of social mobilization and economic development.

Placed against the historical and existential realities of survival, suffering, and severance, the dance in Jamaica assumes special meaning beyond that traditionally given it by the ruling classes, who may have seen it as yet another atavistic indulgence of a semiliterate, uninitiated people. Early accounts of the nature and function of dance, as designs for social living, among the slaves—and later among the freed black masses—leave no doubt about the majority's view of the status of this most elemental of creative acts.

NEGRO FIGURANTI.

Negro Figuranti, by Richard Bridgens. Not only European travelers to Jamaica but also local missionaries and colonial planters felt that the natural dance movements of the native population were indecent, describing them variously as "lewd," "lascivious," and "violent." Such extreme attitudes persisted even after emancipation. (*National Library of Jamaica*)

Early Responses to Jamaican Dance

In the eighteenth and nineteenth centuries there is no shortage of evidence of missionary and planter disapproval of the "severe exercise [the slaves] undergo in their violent and athletic dances"[10] or of the dances and playing which were "so far from being Acts of Adoration of a God, that they are for the most part mixt with a great deal of Bawdry and Lewdness."[11] Such perceptions persisted even after emancipation. The body movements carried "strange and indecent attitudes."[12] When not construed as vulgar and ungodly, the dances of the blacks were considered ludicrous. An eighteenth-century writer noted that the slaves "dance minuets with the mulattoe and other brown women, imitating the motion and steps of the English, but with a degree of affection that renders the whole truly laughable and ridiculous."[13] These movements might well have been intended as a mockery of betters by their inferiors, but, according to the same writer, the slaves' "own way of dancing is droll indeed; they put themselves into strange postures and shake their hips and great breasts to such a degree that it is impossible to refrain from laughing though they go through the whole performance with profound gravity, their feet beating time remarkably quick; two of them generally dance together, and sometimes do not move six inches from the same place."[14] Two other commentators, both writing in the nineteenth century but one before emancipation and the other after, found the dances of the slaves a "display of unseemly gestures"[15] and those of their descendants an exhibition of "lascivious attitudes with which the greatest favourites were characterised."[16]

There is no need to romanticize the slave as a paragon of virtue. Like their masters, whom they sometimes emulated as much as they resisted, slaves no doubt were also capable of coarse behavior, drunkenness, and sexual adventurism, but to deny them any capacity for noble actions, intellectual ability, or moral integrity is to deprive them their humanity—a somewhat unrealistic approach as events during slavery and afterward clearly demonstrated.

The response to music was the same. Most Europeans found the music of the Negroes cacophonous, although some observers did make concessions to the black man's natural sense of rhythm. Such critiques of the indigenous dances and rituals would hardly foreshadow the invention of a classic Jamaican or Caribbean dance theater, since, according to most European commentators, the native dances lacked aesthetic weight, moral purpose, kinetic logic, discipline, or noble intent.[17]

As the poet and historian Edward Kamau Brathwaite quite rightly concludes in his study of the history of Jamaican Creole society, there was no way that a post-Renaissance European could understand the lack of distinction between religious and secular cultural expressions of the slave who "danced and sang at work, at play, at worship, from fear, from sorrow, from joy. . . . And because this music and dance was so misunderstood, and since the music was based on tonal scales and the dancing on choreographic traditions entirely outside the white observers' experience—not forgetting the necessary assumption that slaves, since they were brutes could produce no philosophy that 'reach[ed] above the navel'—their music was dismissed as 'noise,' their dancing as a way of (or to) sexual misconduct and debauchery."[18]

The facts of history—and therefore of the culture created by the people themselves—have served to reaffirm the staying power of the dance as part of a society's ancestral and existential reality. As the American cultural anthropologist Judith Lynne Hanna asserts, to dance is human.[19] From the activities of those who, like the Jamaicans, have always expressed themselves in dance, Hanna discovers that "dance interweaves with other aspects of human life such as communication and learning, belief systems, social relations and political dynamics, loving and fighting, and urbanization and change."[20] Everything in Jamaica's history confirms the dance—whether in rural clearings, on ghetto streets, or on the theater stage—as elemental human behavior in its various dimensions—physical, cultural, social, psychological, economic, and political.

While the physical aspect of dance is instantly represented in the explosive energy released during ritual worship and recreational play, the cultural dimension of these two forms of dance expression has always reflected the profound value systems of the Jamaican people. But dance also embodies social behavior, historically proven by the complex of the jonkonnu ceremonies,[21] which allowed Jamaicans to master their social environment through the irony of masked comedy as an expression of serious social commentary. The physical environment itself provided the Maroons the camouflage for dances celebrating the invincibility of the human spirit in armed conflict. The psychological dimensions of dance find expression not only in the spirit-possession responses to the tensions of everyday existence but also in the therapy dancers are offered in formal studio training or actual performance. Although the economic aspect of dance, in terms of paid professionals, has limited application in the Jamaican experience—since the Company dancers are all unsalaried—there has been a long tradition of full-time variety show artists and cabaret dancers, as well as Christmas mummers, who literally take to the streets for money. Audiences have always paid to see dance presentations, both amateur and professional, and many dancers—from the eighteenth century, when Haitian set-girls[22] provided entertainments for the great plantation homes (the Great Houses), to the present day—has had literally to dance for their supper. Dance can also be a political tool, and in the Jamaican experience it has cloaked defiance of the power structure through mimicry and has concealed the planning of slave rebellions. In contemporary times dance has reasserted itself in determining Jamaican self-definition, itself a political concern.

Above all the dance in Jamaica continues to be one of the most effective means of communication, revealing many profound truths about complex social forces operative in a society groping toward both material and spiritual betterment. These social forces are ignored at the peril of economic planning, political decisions governing developmental strategies, and ethical refinement. The perspectives of these various dimensions of dance must be kept in mind as we take a closer look at the features of survival, suffering, and severance that have shaped both the historical profile and the contemporary realities of Jamaica.

Dance and Survival

As a foremost creative activity serving Jamaican cultural resistance—not only throughout the periods of slavery and colonialism but also following independence—dance was a primary instrument of survival. First, it is a skill that depends on the physical and mental capacities of the survivor. One's body belongs only to oneself, despite the laws governing chattel slavery in the English-speaking Caribbean, which until 1834 allowed a person to be the "property" of another.[23] Second, the language by which the body expresses itself does not have to be anyone else's language, least of all the master's; even when there are borrowings, which are inescapable in a multicultural environment, they can be given shape and form on the borrower's own terms. These strategies are crucial in a situation of pervasive dependency, where all influences are dictated by the overlord. It is the exercise of the imagination—manifest in all forms of creative activities, from a dance or a few bars of music to the invention of various forms of worship—that has proved the best guarantee of survival, from the period of chattel slavery and colonial domination to the conditions of postcolonial geopolitical and economic encirclement. To function in the modern world, Caribbean citizens, despite the presence of expressive Creole tongues, may indeed have to write and speak in the master's language (French, English, Spanish, or Dutch); yet they can survive, dancing their own movements and singing their own music. Because of such modes of existence, this civilization may be unique. Such a claim to cultural uniqueness was conceded by the West Indian Nobel laureate and political economist Arthur Lewis, who stated that the creative products of the Caribbean imagination constitute the one contribution "above all others we know we can make to the common human heritage."[24]

This ability to contribute is both the cause and result of survival, and the jealous preservation of the means to do so becomes part of the common heritage. Consequently the majority of Jamaicans discover a flexibility in coping with a society that is yet to be organized in the interests of that majority. A hold on any activity beyond the control of a cynical power structure is a valuable weapon of cultural self-defense. The art of dance, comprising the dancer's own body movements informed by his own spiritual and emotional states, is such a weapon. Allied with music—which utilizes various African-derived drums and idiophones as well as European instruments such as piano and strings—the dance takes on compounded energy as a source for survival.

Reaching beyond mere survival, the dance in Jamaica long ago refused to get stuck in genres of light-hearted entertainment, despite the ring games, lancers, schottische, and quadrille suitably adapted from the court and country dances of Europe. Instead the dance preserved its force through integrated links with religion in the worship of forbidden but persistent gods, divination rituals, and the configurations of a nether world beyond the master's laws. It has given to the cultural heritage of Jamaica such enduring life sources as kumina, pukkumina (popularly known as pocomania), etu, tambu, gerreh, dinkimini, Zion revivalism, and Rastafarianism.[25] Many of these rituals have their counterparts in other parts of the fragmented Caribbean, carrying names such as voodoo (Haiti and Santo Domingo), santeria (Cuba), shango (Trinidad), and cumfah (Guyana).[26] The cunning survival strategies may be well-concealed in religious rites reserved for the initiated, but they are no less effective when exercised openly in dance-filled jonkonnu masquerades, burru, dinkimini, bruckin party, or pre-Lenten Carnival. Such seemingly harmless merrymaking activities offer appropriate vehicles for the oppressed masses to comment freely, often in the form of wicked wit and ribald punning, on a society that gives them short shrift socially, politically, and economically. Such activities involve energies that are released through otherwise forbidden behavior, especially in what may appear to be uninhibited and suggestive movements. Mimicry, artistic license, understatement, and ironic metaphors certainly were not lost on the originators of formal Caribbean dance theater, as the repertoire of the National Dance Theatre Company clearly illustrates.

In an effort to escape the negative effects of persistent poverty and psychological and cultural isolation, Jamaicans historically found refuge in collective endeavors. Circles of protection—whether provided through community cooperation, configurations of the extended family, or ritual dances performed in the round to exorcize evil or celebrate communal achievements—offered the African-in-exile some kind of solace. Dance, which took the form of recreational ring games played under the full moon or the ceremonial worship of votaries moving around a table (pukkumina and Zion revival) or around drummers invoking ancestral spirits (kumina), reinforced the protective aspects of group activities. Dance was the organic link with Africa, helping to alleviate the isolation that threatened the cultural heritage of the individuals who ended up in the Caribbean. Life itself continued to be viewed in cyclical terms, involving the dead, the living, and those unborn. Ancestors close the circle when libations are poured.

The dance is not only a performing art, it is also an art of community effort that proclaims the virtue of cooperation over unrestrained individualism. It is self-evident how this relates to self-government, nation building, and social organization. Traditionally government leaders have dismissed the sensitive intellectual gifts of peasant experiences, precisely because they have been regarded as too mundane or folkloric to guide affairs of state. Yet it is the peasant who realizes that the individual dancer usually has little to offer outside of community ritual. Even when he performs alone, the ritual dancer must have either a responsive audience or acceptance by the community spirits. Votaries, whose religious functions are clear-cut, must operate within a larger framework, which invests such functions with purpose and meaning. Rivermaid, Cooing Dove, Engine

Spirit, Bell Ringer, Indian Spirit—all such ritual participants relate not only to one another but also to the overall pukkumina rite. The characters of a masquerade band are always members of a team. What the violated individual is deprived of by the wider society is provided in ancestral riturals or contemporary ceremonies organized by the people themselves. Opportunity is given for social interaction which invests each actor with the dignity of a persona, even if it is as a "king" or a "queen" for only a short period of time. The slave, the denigrated African, the exploited proletarian, or the powerless worker in a factory—all with the lowest status during most of the year—can be shepherd, captain, king, queen, or courtier for a night or two in pukkumina, kumina, or bruckin party.

An inevitable interdependence is found in all social activity. Such activity draws on the mobilized energies of a wide range of participants in creative interaction, which is not only the essence of nation building and other forms of communal organization but also the essence of the efforts of a performing group, whether dancers, actors, singers, or musicians. The choreographer, for example, is nothing without the dancer, who participates in the creation of the final product. A writer can discard material that doesn't work. But a choreographer cannot ignore the dancer, who is an instrument of his expression. A dance company—employing, besides dancers, the varied skills of singers, musicians, creative technicians, and stagehands—by definition offers a valuable example of the creative molding of energies and skills into an organic whole. Joan Mc-Culloch, an Englishwoman residing in Jamaica, wrote in 1946 from her experiences as a ballet dancer and teacher in England: "The ballet brings together so much artistic talent—apart from the dancers and choreographers there are the composers, musicians, writers and artists. It is this artistic cooperation all working together, not for themselves, but for the whole, which gives us something for enjoyment that few other arts can equal."[27] McCulloch's claim may be a trifle exaggerated. But the dance as a multidisciplinary art does offer opportunities for the development of talent through participation in a larger community. A sense of individuality is formed in the crucible of social interaction.

It is the collective experiences of the common people that are usually ignored by economic and political strategists of postcolonial Third World countries like Jamaica. These new power brokers in the Third World continue to look for solutions within the context of metropolitan centers, where they may have gained their formal education. Thus cultural activities are still afflicted by the externalization of consciousness; metropolitan dance culture continues to dazzle Third World devotees into uncritical imitation or artistic paralysis. Such aping cannot be the basis of participatory democracy, which is the battle hymn of every republic seeking political stability as well as the judicious balance between social and economic justice for the individual and the responsibilities of collective action. Nor can it be the basis of any serious Caribbean effort at self-definition through artistic achievement.

As a traditional survival technique in the ordinary Jamaican's self-made design for social living, the dance offers an excellent tool for human development as part of the nation's strategies to shape a new society. Contemporary dance expression, rooted in a traditional—ancestral dance culture, encourages patriotic commitment, therefore avoiding the alienation and anomie that result from colonial dependency. Sustained structured training in preparing the body for performance—as well as the obvious rewards derived from the expenditure of energies—fosters productive work attitudes, self-discipline, and physical stamina. The by-products—not only increased health, body awareness, and physical and mental coordination but also a better appreciation of the nation's cultural history through music and folklore studies—will add to the quality of life by transporting society beyond a preoccupation with mere survival to social concerns, such as the creative ordering of contemporary life. The dance as a force in the overall cultural development of Jamaica during the first two decades of independence has served to enrich the infrastructures of cultural life, taking the country from colonial outpost for commercial profit to an aspiringly self-reliant and self-respecting social organism.

Dance and the History of Suffering

The whole discussion of survival is involved with the potentials of existence through the exercise of the creative imagination, which is at the root of culture. But just as important to Caribbean life is the crucial fact of suffering, which has forced the individual to a quicker understanding of the dialectical imperative of the unending struggle to define self and society.

The nature of suffering in our discussion is centered less on the historical facts of physical maiming, legal curtailment of civil liberties, sexual exploitation, or even the dehumanizing mechanisms of social control and psychological conditioning that set off plantation slavery throughout the Americas from anything that preceded it. The suffering we are concerned with, which is of great importance to creative artists and cultural representatives, focuses on the enduring consequences of that historical experience. The negative consequences of contemporary experience in areas like the Caribbean describe the profile of suffering: the persistent powerlessness of the majority nurtured on self-negation and a false consciousness that leads to identity crises; the institutionalized debasement of the creative products of those of African ancestry; the psychic and intellectual dependency of the entire Caribbean region on metropolitan standards sustained by the use of culture as a weapon of ideological penetration; and the threat of spiritual paralysis. The malaise that results from cultural domination by imperial mores parallels the dire consequences of economic domination manifested in the operation of the International Monetary Fund and World Bank loans, the debt trap, protectionist trade, and tariffs favoring the developed world.

The suffering of societies like Jamaica and other Caribbean nations is exacerbated when the new ruling classes become the most uncritical perpetrators of the old values and simply make the new regime nothing more than the old imperial order with a darker skin. Notions of elegance and manners are at the heart of the metropolitan cultural ethos. Some of these notions are harmless enough. But a perennial problem for the new nations revolves around the question of transforming the empty power of manipulated symbols into power with substance. What is the power that must be mastered? Is it not the capacity of a people to make their own definitions about themselves and to be able to act on the basis of those definitions? No development strategy is likely to succeed without pinning its objectives to such definitions. The transfer of technology and developmental assistance makes more sense when self-definition is fostered. The world of culture in general has always claimed a capacity for self-definition and has demonstrated its mettle under the imperial regime, when the colonial child was expected to copy the image of the imperial parent. Hence those rebellions have been most successful that address the suffering that results from self-doubt and self-negation. It was easy for the native successors to imperial rule to utilize the creative arts to develop the national consciousness and encourage pride in self. Energies expended on popular expressions of culture were acceptable so long as the authority of the new power structure was not threatened. Sometimes it was: indigenous cultural activities such as Rastafarianism (religion) and reggae (music) provoked displeasure and an ultimate ban by the Jamaican government.[28] But in general cultural expressions that seek to define a new order received support from Jamaican political leaders, who committed themselves to the free expression and liberal promotion of the creative arts. The dance, without losing its independence, has been a direct beneficiary of this governmental goodwill. If the dance as well as other art forms can be transformed from a passive position to an adversary one that attempts to relieve suffering and promote self-confidence, they will gain a special place in the development of a modern Caribbean society.

But the arts will not succeed in the Caribbean unless the people themselves show respect for their intrinsic characteristics and view them as having a central position in society. The dance is particularly vulnerable in this regard: the legacy of Anglo-Saxon cultural attitudes undermines its acceptance, particularly among those who are ambivalent about the creative products of their own society. Among the grassroots population of the Caribbean, dance appeals in several ways to the ordinary experiences of the individual. Stripped of its reference to traditional life, however, dance is threatened by the indulgence of art for its own sake, without an organic center and with all the usual hang-ups of Western culture. Thus the view of dance as a divertissement or a minor art form suited the racial conceit of European masters, who normally considered the intellectual and artistic achievements of their African subjects inferior in all respects. The Puritan ethic—which condemned the expressive use of the body, the very instrument of dance—had an especially negative influence on the acceptance of the art by even the educated Caribbean population. This was particularly true of the educated male population, who confused eloquent body movement with Anglo-Saxon fears about effeminacy and homosexuality, a fear of great import to a male population reared on concerns about sexual prowess and the emasculation of their manhood under slavery. Nor was dance regarded as a suitable subject for the serious study of human behavior. The American scholar Judith Lynne Hanna places the blame for this on a combination of Puritan ethics, social stratification, concepts of masculinity, and detachment from nonverbal behavior. She points out that, after the collapse of the effete French monarchy, the "emergent bourgeoisie, anxious to protect its power, transformed the body from an instrument of pleasure into one of production. Furthermore, the body became a victim of social snobbery—a brute linking the bourgeoisie to the lower classes."[29] Such attitudes were adopted by the educated classes in colonial outposts like the Caribbean. As soon as European classical ballet was accepted by the wielders of social power in the mother country, Caribbean cultural leaders immediately followed in their footsteps. The Sadler's Wells Ballet (later Royal Ballet) became the model of serious art dance. The Jamaican white upper classes and aspiring light-skinned middle classes took a natural fancy to the developments spearheaded by Ninette de Valois in England.[30]

In the Caribbean the art of dance was connected to class status and racial considerations because of a historical race–class correlation. The dances of the black majority remained African-inspired and Creole in content and stylistic orientation. The dance forms of the establishment population were naturally Eurocentric. The European classical ballet, despite its firm roots in the national folk dances and court dances of Europe, became the hallmark of refinement and culture to the uncritical colonial. Therefore the society's psychic suffering also mainfested itself in the field of dance. Contemporary European historians and travelers of the eighteenth and nineteenth centuries had found the native people's dancing quaint, barbaric, exotic, and lascivious. Such perceptions, which persisted even in the twentieth century, are evident in an article by H. V. Ormsby Marshall published in 1939 in *The Dancing Times* of London: "Notwithstanding all that the European landowners and the upper classes have done for the blacks by methods of education and gradual civilisation, there remains yet much to be desired to alienate them from the natural savage instincts which they inherit from their forefathers."[31] With patronizing resignation the writer conceded that these people "show a natural symmetry in all their movements; their walk has a swinging grace about it that few could acquire from the most excessive desire or practice, and there is a distinct rhythm in all their folk dances." She felt, however, that it was "in their mode of dress, and *in their dances*, that they revert most frequently to their instinctive barbarism."[32]

Such have been the prevailing attitudes to the customs of people of African ancestry. In fact, anyone of African heritage was subject to crude but subtle forms of racial and class discrimination under the British crown colony system established in Jamaica in 1866, giving the official representatives of the crown complete jurisdiction over public administration of the colony. Although the British imperial leaders never officially pursued an assimilationist policy—as the French did in their empire—all institutions of growth, particularly educational and cultural ones, were determined in their indoctrination, preparing the native population to approximate as much as possible Englishmen or at least Western "civilized" habits. Thus the colonials were taught a cultural sensibility that defined good art in terms of the dominant culture, extolling operas, symphonies, and sonatas; Shakespearean drama and the poetry of Tennyson, Wordsworth, and Kipling; the paintings of Gainsborough and Constable; and the kind of dance that the fledgling Sadler's Wells company developed following examples of Diaghilev and the Russian émigrés. The brown middle classes imitated well enough but never totally escaped the ignominy of their African heritage. In due time these middle classes rebelled. It was they who spearheaded a nationalist movement seeking recognition for an autonomous existence. Thus, in effect, they caught up with the black peasant and artisan classes, who had created their own language (Jamaican patois), mating patterns (matriarchal and extended families), religious expressions (pukkumina and Zion revival), economic institutions of mutual aid (partner and cooperative day labor), music (mento and religious spirituals), and their own forms of dance (jonkonnu, kumina, bruckin party, burru). These expressive strategies of survival constituted the so-called subculture, in the view of those few who governed on behalf of the imperial power. This cultural domination was assisted by many native Jamaicans, who identified intellectually and aesthetically with the expatriate overlords.

When the brown middle classes, from whom the viceregal aides were drawn, became frustrated with their lack of power, they allied with the black laboring classes—as they had during the final days of slavery—to fight against the alien ruler. Although they provided the leadership for organizations struggling against colonialism—such as political parties, trade unions, and demonstration groups—they surrendered, as if by barter, to the indigenous creative impulses of the black majority. Some even blackened their faces to lend greater authenticity in performing Jamaican folksongs. The alliance provided black endeavors in theater, publishing ventures, and, later, music recordings with administrative and promotional expertise drawn from the privileged, educated Jamaican middle classes. At least partial victory over suffering was gained, particularly in terms of a society's self-identification and sense of place in the world.

The dance benefited immensely from this new development. Despite a con-

Hazel Johnston, choreographer and dance instructor, inspired theater dancing (classical ballet) in Jamaica in the 1940s and 1950s. (*National Library of Jamaica*)

Ivy Baxter, a pioneer of Jamaican creative dance, was a major influence on the movement that sought to instill cultural self-definition in Jamaica and the Caribbean in general. This picture was taken in the 1950s. (*National Library of Jamaica*)

tinuing preference for the refined dance forms of the mother country, emerging ideas about indigenous dances as being the source of any true expression of Jamaican dance theater began to take shape. Such ideas prompted from Hazel Johnston, a London-trained pioneer of dance theater in the European classical mold, comments that reveal an interest in a Jamaican dance theater based on the native culture. Johnston also underlined the effects of psychological and cultural distancing of the privileged middle classes from the genuine artistic achievements of the Jamaican people. She felt that it was impossible to attempt anything in the direction of an indigenous style of Jamaican dance theater until an "intensive study has been made of the habits and gestures of the people. If there were in existence any recognised folk dances, the task would be very much simplified, but Jamaican native dances consist of improvisations which, however, bear similarity to each other. This is in itself proof of the spontaneity and natural aptitude of our people, but it presents almost insurmountable difficulties to the choreographer."[33] The truth is that spontaneity and improvisations had always found purpose and distinctive form in everyday life—in formal reli-

Beryl McBurnie, the dance theater innovator from Trinidad,and a strong advocate of Caribbean cultural integrity, with (left to right) Norman Rae, theater director and former critic; Hugh Morrison, educator, former dancer, and member of the National Dance Theatre Company's first Management Committee; Rex Nettleford, then a young lecturer at the University of the West Indies; and Jeff Henry, McBurnie's assistant at the university's summer dance session in 1957.

gious worship and in the recreational play of the people. Doing fieldwork a decade before Hazel Johnston, Martha Beckwith had discussed the existence of this tradition in her book *Black Roadways*.[34] About fifteen years later the choreographer and anthropologist Katherine Dunham in a journey to Accompong, the village of the ancestral Maroons, was inspired to a vision of a dance theater style that admirably exposed the experiences of plantation America.[35]

The difficulties for the choreographer, which Hazel Johnston mentioned, were insurmountable for the Jamaicans supposedly because of the lack of a ready-made technique and vocabulary and an acceptable aesthetic framework, as the imported European classical ballet readily offered. Ivy Baxter, a former pupil of Hazel Johnston, was not daunted by such difficulties, and even before she made an intensive study of the gestures and habits of the people, she surveyed the immediate environment and began to create dances in the spirit of Jamaican realities, drawing on stories and folksongs as well as street gestures and the life of the marketplace.[36] In her search for a Jamaican way of expressing reality through dance, Baxter even took liberties with the technique she had learned at the Johnston studio. She gained further confidence in her contacts with the Trinidad dance theater innovator Beryl McBurnie, the "mother of Caribbean dance," who entertained no doubt that in Trinidad there were the makings of a Caribbean form of dance out of the rituals, gestures, improvisations, and rich history of three centuries of struggle.[37] Both Beryl McBurnie and Ivy Baxter are real pioneers who took the first creative steps in attempting to alleviate the suffering of the Caribbean people, particularly their sense of psychic inferiority and cultural deprivation.

In all fairness Hazel Johnston did sterling work in the dance as she perceived it, giving Jamaica a notion of excellence and integrity in dance theater.[38] Johnston died young, before the full impact of the self-government movement goaded Jamaicans like Ivy Baxter to the belief that they could be the creators of their own destiny not only through their skill at political adminstration—with the vote, universal suffrage, and a native parliament and ministries—but also through their creative imagination. A university was established in 1948, and cultural ferment in literature, painting, sculpture, and musical theater was perceived as part of the process of Jamaicans becoming themselves. Baxter was one of the beneficiaries of this activity: her group, the Ivy Baxter Creative Dance Group formed in 1950, was supported by native nationalist-oriented political leaders, one of whom, Norman Manley, placed cultural development at the center of his program for political change. Some of the early members of Baxter's group would have been the proud bearers of the new cultural orientation. When *Creations in Dance*, the first major expression of Jamaican dance theater, was mounted at Kingston's Ward Theatre in 1954, the pièce de résistance was *Rat Passage*, Baxter's tale of a Jamaican stowaway on a banana boat to the mother country which was danced to locally composed music rather than to excerpts from traditional European classic fare.[39]

Dance and the Phenomenon of Severance

These early efforts to achieve through dance a unification of the historical experiences merely underlined the persistently fragmented nature of Caribbean society. The notion that classical ballet traditions were superior to the barefoot dancing of the Baxterites—who were drawn from less privileged socioeconomic groups (unmistakably black and colored)—was still being claimed, despite the demands of a burgeoning nationalism. In 1956 the newly formed Ballet Guild of Jamaica sponsored a joint concert featuring the Ivy Baxter Creative Dance Group, the Rowe School of Dancing, and the Fonseca School of Ballet. The titles

A performance of Jamaican dance theater in the 1940s. These students of Hazel Johnston are (left to right) Jennifer Bourke, Penny Soltau (reclining), Dorothy Fraser, Graham McCormack, Barbara Fonseca (standing), and Punky Rowe. Fonseca and Rowe later taught movement to dancers who became members of the National Dance Theatre Company; Fraser became a Company performer. (*National Library of Jamaica*)

of the dances themselves were illuminating: *Les Sylphides, La Boutique Fantasque,* and, from the Baxter company, *Danse Élémentale*. The severance of the Jamaican from himself was manifested by the frenchified titles, which in the minds of some seemed to guarantee the legitimacy of dance expression (the following year even the more earthy modern-style dance show inspired by Eyrick Darby was presented under the title *Danse Moderne*).[40] The music for the 1956 Ballet Guild concert, which was distinctively different from that for *Rat Passage*, reflected the orientation of the dances. Baxter's choreography was hailed by the critic Orford St. John, who stressed that it was a welcome departure from folk dances because Baxter had "produced a ballet of ideas having some kinship with Massine's symphonic ballets."[41] Real challenges were apparently admitted only when the ideas were not rooted in Jamaican folk tradition or when the dances were modeled on European choreography. The Ballet Guild did not last, but the phenomenon of a society of severance, which the Guild sought to address, persisted.

The West Indian writers George Lamming and Edward Kamau Brathwaite have addressed the problem of fragmentation in the Caribbean, which in the beginning entailed the geographical and cultural isolation of the Caribbean islands from the cultural destinies of mainland territories, continued with a history of fragmented expectations in respect to liberation from slavery and colonialism, and now embraces contemporary experiences of cultural, ideological, and economic disintegration.[42] Fragmentation is an integral part of severance: a striking example is the brutal effects on human beings forced to leave their homelands. But severance further involves the subtle effects on individuals cut off from each other or separated within themselves. The conscious denial of continuity and tradition, of consistency and a unified existence, is a result of that severance. The phenomenon once placed Kingston culturally and politically nearer to London (today New York) than to Havana, and Havana closer to Madrid (today Moscow) than to Kingston. Curaçao is oriented more to Holland than to Trinidad, and Port-au-Prince still retains stronger ties with Paris than with nearby Santo Domingo. The separation was reinforced by a loss of contact with the native language. Entire populations had imposed on them the language of the imperial

Madame May Soohih with four of her pupils. Two of them, Melanie Graham (far right) and Monica McGowan (next to her), later became principals of the National Dance Theatre Company. (*National Library of Jamaica*)

Eddy Thomas (seated at piano), Ivy Baxter, and Rex Nettleford, discussing the score for *Once upon a Seaweed*, a musical with book by Alma Mock Yen and music by Thomas. Noel Vaz directed and Baxter and Nettleford choreographed. The picture was taken in 1960, two years before the Company's founding. (*Daily Gleaner*)

powers. Consequently there is not one Caribbean but many—English, French, Spanish, and Dutch—each existing in its separate linguistic universe, a significant example of the cultural severance that resulted when imperialism staked out its spheres of influence.

Within Caribbean communities linguistic segmentation—standard dialect versus Creole—reflects the prevailing ambivalence toward self-definition throughout the region. Despite this, there was the common experience of the struggle between confrontation and collaboration, between resistance and assimilation—in short, the process of creolization from which there was no escape. As a result greater communication between communities in the region, as well as between different classes and ethnic groups within the communities, was facilitated. Some cultural forms lend themselves more easily than others to this kind of communication: for example, religion, from early syncretized religious expressions to contemporary Rastafari; politics, from the liberal support of self-government to the Third World ideas about postcolonial transformations; and music and dance, nonverbal communication that freely crosses linguistic, racial, and class barriers. Reggae and calypso and merengue and mambo belong to all the Caribbean people, whatever their place of origin. Such are the antidotes to severance.

Another aspect of cultural severance was the historical uprooting—both voluntarily and by force—of people from their ancestral homelands. For some, transplantation to the Americas drastically impinged on cultural memory. Yet there can never be a total uprooting: some notions of heritage would always be retained. Although there was a continuous influx of Africans to the Caribbean, by a strange paradox direct contact with Africans—and thus with vital cultural consciousness—was curtailed and in some places totally cut off after the abolition of the British slave trade in 1807. Thus in the British-controlled colonies in the Caribbean the creolization process among inhabitants of African ancestry occurred much earlier than among the non-African arrivals. The Europeans, who exercised political and social power, traveled freely to their countries of origin, and consequently the political, cultural, and religious institutions were continually replenished from Europe, preventing a sense of alienation from the homeland. Later the immigrant Indians and Chinese were allowed contact between their adopted country and ancestral homes, and even the Lebanese merchants, fleeing the anti-Christian Turks, were eventually able to make contact with their country of origin. The indentured Indians and Chinese could return at the end of their contract. If they remained, they retained their cultural identity: they were allowed to buy land, worship their own gods, speak their own languages, run their own schools, sing their own songs, and dance their own dances. In practice this was not always observed to the letter, but there was an ethical and a legal commitment to indentured laborers. This cultural pluralism in its negative—and exploited—sense tends to encourage severance and fragmentation among the African majority. In its positive sense pluralism offers diversity, which becomes a springboard for the unifying forms that would inevitably emerge out of the process of creolization.

The search for unity in diversity is the traditional concern of nation building—that is, in a strictly political sense, creating a nation out of a single geographical entity or forming from several entities a larger federation. Unity is also a concern of Caribbean culturalists, who view the area, with its common history of colonialism, slavery, and the plantation, as a cultural entity. This unifying concept of a definitive civilization forms the basis of the wider concept of an American civilization. For all of modern America was the result of the meeting of ancient civilizations—European, African, Asiatic, Levantine, and Amerindian—in circumstances historically perceived as expatriate settlers confronting the indigenous population, as imperial powers commanding subject colonials, or as economic masters exploiting slave and indentured labor.

Such a repertory of conflict would inevitably produce psychic severance of self from self, saddling entire communities with an identity crisis. The Caribbean, entirely a product of colonialism, was particularly vulnerable. It was not until the 1930s that there was a general acceptance of Jamaica as a place the individual would freely choose to live in. It was the self-government movement that at-

Negro Dances in Jamaica to a Creole Air, c. 1820s. During the period of slavery and later under colonialism, imitation of the dominant culture and the persistence of African forms produced two distinct Caribbean forms of cultural expression. (*National Library of Jamaica*)

tempted to change the historical perspective, proclaiming that all Jamaicans, whatever their race or class, who were committed to living in and working for the country not only had a right to the land but should have the privilege of determining the future of the terrritory. Thus the problem of psychic disunity was being addressed for the first time. Belief in self was critical, not only in fostering universal education but also in guiding the creative efforts that would inform progressive social action. Cultural activity was understood as a critical aspect of the search for the underlying unities of Caribbean life that would forge the social cohesion necessary to a society torn within and from itself.[43]

Dance, as well as music, can indeed help restore to the Caribbean its existential unity, which was fractured by the continual struggle with the profoundly negative effects of the common experience of transplantation. The proposal being put forward here must not be misconstrued as the advocacy of using dance, through the rigor of its training, to support a society administered by command with little opportunity for participation from below. The correlation be-

The attitudes, dress, and ancestral rites of the Jamaican countryside became important models for the dance theater work that developed in Jamaica beginning in the late 1940s, challenging the assumptions of an earlier perception of Caribbean dance. This photograph, taken in the nineteenth century by Adolphe Duperly and Sons, depicts women carrying bananas for export. It was this type of employment which inspired the first segment of Ivy Baxter's *Rat Passage*, and the costumes for Rex Nettleford's *Myal* were based on the women's style of dress. (*National Library of Jamaica*)

tween the excellence achieved in classical ballet and the efficient state apparatus of the Maryinsky Ballet and the Bolshoi Ballet in czarist Russia, and the Bolshoi in the Soviet Union, may be an overstatement. But Nazi Germany did make a fetish of youths marching in well-choreographed formations, placing great emphasis on the precision and symmetry of gesture, from the extended arm hailing Hitler to the outstretched foot goose-stepping Germany's path to conquest. Caribbean society—in its groping pluralist, albeit rebellious, state—is not likely to utilize its dance for such political effects. Yet it may help to forge a sense of order—made necessary not only by modern technological realities but also by the chaos of a fragmented history—which will force the region to develop its own discrete political, economic, social, and cultural configurations.

As a result of historical severance, Caribbean dance has many diverse forms. But increased study of these forms points to the existence of underlying unities. Dance, then, is subject to the challenge of preserving its texture without giving in to the myth that Caribbean creative experience has no structure or order and, worse, does not even exist. The dilemma is central to the cultural dynamics of Caribbean life. Fortunately there are those, making unequivocal cultural choices, who are committed to the search for underlying unities, who will not settle for a status quo of disparate expressions and also reject the dominant metropolitan modes as the norm.

The dilemma is not restricted to the dance. The teaching of language, whether standard English or standard Creole and its variants, involves the same conflict. Despite a global ecumenism, Caribbean religious experiences reveal a traditional struggle between Christian orthodoxy—the religious counterpart to European classical ballet in colonial Jamaica—and its populist model manifested in evangelical fundamentalism and syncretized revivalism; in turn Rastafarianism is in conflict with both the orthodox and populist expressions of Christianity. Although other world religions such as Hinduism, Islam, and the Baha'i faith are tolerated, Jamaica is considered a Christian nation with its ethos firmly entrenched in that religion. Significantly there is no parallel to the ethnic realities. Ninety-six percent of the island's population is of African ancestry; yet Jamaica is never officially described as a black nation.

Ambivalence in cultural certitude continually forces the dance to discover what will in the end be the fusion of thought, feeling, and form out of the real experiences of Jamaican and Caribbean life. The involvement is no different from that of political leaders, as nation builders, economic planners, and social engineers. Many creative artists, however, tend to accept the attitudes borrowed from Europe, which they perceive as creative activity set apart from everyday life. This approach is alien to ancestral traditions, not only in Africa or India, where the mass of the Caribbean population originally came from, but also in the Caribbean itself, where the task of coming to terms with their physical and psychic environment compelled Jamaicans to find new designs for social living. The notion that the gifts of refined perception and sensitive observation do not relate to social reality points to other sophisticated attitudes inherited from Europe, which are committed to the excesses of art for art's sake and encourage the risky pose of the impoverished artist as an indication of real artistic talent.

Artists are encouraged to indulge in certain poses by a society that should at times leave them alone rather than try to analyze the impulses that goad them to creative work. To explain unfamiliar behavior, mental disorder is not infrequently the diagnosis. Charges of sexual oddity and inefficiency—particularly by a society whose values are measured by conventional notions of sexual prowess and by the gross national product—are other stereotypes. Such perceptions run counter to the practical experiences of those at the core of Caribbean creative energy. For they are the ones who sing and dance, recite their poems, and tell their stories as part of an existential reality. Men dance vigorously and with mock fayness (the female characters in the jonkonnu ritual are all men) without fear of being labeled sexual deviants, and the dances and rituals of spirit possession are appreciated by votaries and onlookers alike without fear that the participants are ready for the madhouse. Obviously one's upward mobility to the middle class may encourage some doubt in the minds of potential participants. Yet it is incumbent on these very people—who have the necessary skills developed through formal education—to offer some rational organization, not only in building the economy and administering public affairs but also in effectively utilizing the creative gifts of the imagination in order to give a sense of purpose to a developing society like Jamaica.

2 · The National Dance Theatre Company: History and Development

For three hundred years in Jamaica both the integrity of the arts created out of the Caribbean imagination and the humanity of the people who produced them were denigrated. Yet during all that time many Jamaicans resisted the suffering that resulted from such cultural severance and deprivation.

On August 6, 1962, Jamaica pulled down the red, white, and blue flag of imperial Britain and replaced it with the gold, green, and black flag of an independent Jamaica. A national anthem and other new emblems also marked a break with the past. In the wake of these symbols of a new political order the National Dance Theatre Company asserted itself with restrained enthusiasm and guarded confidence. The Company's purpose was to secure for the Jamaican people one way of articulating their cultural identity and to build faith in a historical reality that was virtually denied by the three centuries of British subjugation. There was a sense of cultural fragmentation that had been imposed upon the majority of the people for as long as anyone living in 1962 could remember. The National Dance Theatre Company was a cultural institution created not out of hubris but out of the genuine belief that, in order to survive as a political entity, a nation must nurture the ambience within which the creative spirit of the people can enrich the polity.

Against the background of cultural ambivalence wrought by severance and suffering, the dance—as well as related religious and recreational forms that eventually influenced contemporary dance theater—historically was perceived as an instrument of survival. But by 1962 dance was also perceived as more than an expressive means of coping with the exigencies of daily existence. It could secure for the new nation not only a sense of place and purpose but also that self-confidence that would enable the society to make decisions in its own interest and establish sound principles for its internal transformation without psychic or material disintegration.

In a 1962 memorandum to the founding members of the National Dance Theatre Company the objectives were stated as follows:

Rex Nettleford and Eddy Thomas, founding directors
of the National Dance Theatre Company, in 1962.

(1) to provide a vehicle for well-trained and talented dancers who wish to perform and create works of excellence, that is, works of standards comparable to those found in any other part of the world; (2) to help widen an informed and critical Jamaican audience that will be responsive to works of excellence in the theatre arts, particularly theatre-dance; (3) to experiment with dance forms and techniques of all kinds with a view to helping to develop a style and form that faithfully reflect the movement patterns of Jamaica and the Caribbean area; (4) to encourage and, where possible, conduct research into indigenous dance forms in Jamaica and the Caribbean area.[1]

A note of exhortation was added: "For the above objectives to be achieved, it is necessary that work in the dance be done under laboratory conditions with the application of hard work and dedication to the dance and the arts in general by the best material available, working together over a period of time in a sustained programme of training and presentation." The objectives have remained a general guide throughout the Company's existence.

In setting itself these goals, the National Dance Theatre Company would have to prove that the dance itself was not only an instrument for social change but also an art form in its own right, capable of utilizing its intrinsic strengths to effect that change. This was fully appreciated even before the Company was formed by the dancers and their associates, all of whom brought to the project their invaluable experiences of coping with the social problems of preindependent Jamaica. All of the founding members were the beneficiaries not only of a long tradition of everyday expressions of dance and music describing Jamaica's ancestral underpinnings but also of the recent efforts at establishing dance as an art form rooted in contemporary cultural realities of Jamaica and the Caribbean. Those realities were complex in their contradictions and in their pluralist implications. Besides the significant pioneering work of Ivy Baxter, who drew directly on the culture of the masses to suggest a national expression, was the work in the European classical ballet idiom. Although the European classical tradition perpetuated indefensible notions of the superiority of imperialist cultural modes over indigenous creativity, it nonetheless helped keep alive the concept of dance as a culturally acceptable expression in the life of a people.

The formation of the National Dance Theatre Company in 1962, shortly after the independence celebrations, was not only the culmination of long years of intensive work but also the outgrowth of the recent developments of Jamaican dance theater. The moving spirits behind the formation of the Company were Rex Nettleford, staff tutor in political education at the University of the West Indies, and Eddy Thomas, who had recently returned from studying and dancing in New York as a result of an arts travel grant from the Jamaican government. Both of them had trained formally with Ivy Baxter, whose group, the Ivy Baxter Creative Dance Group, was the first to bring Caribbean creative dance to the stages of Jamaica and other countries in the West Indies. Under Baxter's lead-

Greta and Henry Fowler, founders of the Little Theatre Movement, consult about the pantomime *Banana Boy*, choreographed and directed in 1962 by Rex Nettleford, which featured many of the dancers who later that year became founding members of the National Dance Theatre Company. (*LaMonte*)

ership, and with the assistance of the musician Mapletoft Poulle, Eyrick Darby—the Jamaican dancer then based in Nassau—and Eddy Thomas himself, the dance group raised national consciousness to the possibilities of a native dance based on Jamaican folk idioms.

Instructors in the rudiments of classical ballet also made important contributions at the time to the development of Jamaican dance; there were Hazel Johnston, Fay Simpson, whose biyearly school performances produced some fine female dancers, and the Russian dancer Anatole Soohih, whose influence was continued through the work of his widow, Madame May Soohih. The burden of experimental work, however, fell on the creative dance approach concentrated in the early days in the Baxter dance group and later in the Eddy Thomas Dance Workshop. But this did not satisfy the demands being made by fairly sophisticated audiences as well as by a group of dancers who were receiving advanced training at the summer schools organized by the university's Department of Extra-Mural Studies. Through these summer schools Jamaican dancers were being exposed to dance techniques developed elsewhere. In 1955 Lew Smith, the first American modern dance instructor to teach in Jamaica, had come from New York, and later Lavinia Williams, the modern dance exponent who developed techniques based on traditional dances of Haiti, also taught at the summer sessions. Jamaican dancer Neville Black, who was working in Chicago, contributed a technically strong but free and lyrical style through his training in the techniques of Doris Humphrey and Charles Weidman and through his studies with the modern dance pioneer Sybil Shearer working in Chicago. In 1961 Black introduced Maggie Kast, whose incisive mind and knowledge of dance composition served as a catalyst to Jamaican dancers. By this time the government's Social Welfare Commission had added dance to its activities.

Lavinia Williams (second from right), who was a dancer, choreographer, and exponent of Haitian dance forms, had a strong influence on Jamaican dance theater. She is shown in 1960 teaching a summer school class at the University of the West Indies. On the left is Haitian drummer Edner Cherisme. (*Daily Gleaner*)

The National Festival, an annual competition devoted to all categories of the arts, first took place in November 1961, and offerings in dance, mime, and song proved the most productive. The annual musical pantomimes of the Little Theatre Movement had by now integrated a good deal of dance movement, and that company's Henry and Greta Fowler all but dedicated the last three pantomimes to dance itself.[2] The most successful of these pantomimes was *Banana Boy*, which had a record run and was selected for a short season during the independence celebrations. A December 1962 article in *Spotlight* magazine placed these developments in perspective: "There was no doubt that dance was the most dynamic thing in the theatre then. This could be seen in the roadside concerts, in the village celebrations, at the Denbigh Agricultural Show, in the musical *Banana Boy,* and in the Independence dance show *Roots and Rhythms*."[3]

What the article in *Spotlight* did not emphasize, probably because it was taken for granted, was the fount of public goodwill that greeted the formation of the National Dance Theatre Company following *Roots and Rhythms*, mounted by Thomas and Nettleford for the independence celebrations. The main participants were members of the Dance Theatre Group, an ensemble of dancers who had been working together for three years prior to the celebrations, mainly in musicals performed locally but even on a tour to Washington, D.C., and Baltimore in 1961 with a show bearing the predictably exotic title *Sun over the West Indies*.[4] Unlike the 1956 Ballet Guild concerts, the *Roots and Rhythms* show was more integrated, since it brought together both ballet-trained dancers and dancers trained in a more indigenous mode into a disciplined unit to perform works expressing a specific Jamaican style. The Ivy Baxter Creative Dance Group had been the pioneer of this style, and the tradition was continued in the Little Theatre Movement's annual pantomimes, in which by 1960 the dance portion of the programs had progressed from only a pleasant interlude to an integrated concept that helped advance the plot. The dancers' experiences with the pantomines between 1959 and 1962 gave them an opportunity to test their stamina in four or five consecutive performances a week over a three-month run, in addition to two months of grueling rehearsals. During this period the group of dancers worked together five or six months every year. They also spent four weeks together in the university summer school sessions.

The sculptor Edna Manley, who became a founding patron of the National Dance Theatre Company, delivers an address in 1960 at the opening of a dance summer school session at the University of the West Indies, which was attended by many future Company members. Around the table (left to right) are Ivan Harban, from the Trinidad Little Carib Dancers; Lavinia Williams; Rawle Farley, head of the university's Department of Extra-Mural Studies; Rex Nettleford, at the time resident tutor in charge of summer school programs; Mrs. Rawle Farley; Ivy Baxter, founder of the Ivy Baxter Creative Dance Group; Neville Black, dance instructor from Chicago; and Isobel Seaton, from the Jamaica Social Welfare Commission. (*Daily Gleaner*)

Hugh Lawson Shearer, at the time prime minister of Jamaica, joins Eddy Thomas, ballet mistress Yvonne daCosta, and Rex Nettleford backstage at the Théâtre Port-Royale during performances at Montreal's international exposition Expo '67.

The Company as a National Institution

By the time of the National Dance Theatre Company's formation, collaboration among the members had finally overcome the conflicting factions, and through teamwork effort the Company could withstand the occasional assaults from their detractors. For instance, the year following the formation of the Company a correspondent for Kingston's daily newspaper *The Daily Gleaner* questioned the right of the National Dance Theatre Company to use the word "national" in its name because she felt that a national organization should belong to the people.[5] In light of the Company's achievements over the next two decades, this correspondent's objections should have been dissipated. A special point to be made is that along with other national artistic enterprises—such as the training schools, the Little Theatre Movement, and the National Chorale—the National Dance Theatre Company exists solely through the voluntary work of a large number of Jamaicans in order to define a culturally acceptable expression of an art form that suffers no government interference. The Company has also avoided becoming a scratch group deployed at the whim of a bureaucratic tourist ministry eager to entertain and amuse vacationers lured to the exotic delights of the

Caribbean. Yet as recently as 1983, in the twenty-first year of the Company's existence, these developments have escaped the sensibility of a Jamaican critic who in the same newspaper dismissed the Company as "national in name only."[6] In fact the National Dance Theatre Company is *national* in a deeper and more organic sense than either the 1963 native correspondent or her 1983 expatriate successor seemed able to comprehend.

As I have reasoned elsewhere, in a comment on its twentieth anniversary, the Company is a "national" organization precisely because of the scope of its artistic vision as well as the thematic range of its repertoire. It is national because of the organic nature of its indigenous sources serving as fountainhead for creative action: the Company is committed to distilling the essences of traditional Jamaican cultural forms manifested in the nation's music, movement patterns, and language. The Company has provided its country with crucial dance instruction as well as an awareness of the significance of this work by presenting its work at home and abroad not only through live performances but also on film and video recordings. Above all, "it is national because of the unprecedented catalytic effect it has had on dance, theatre, and the related arts throughout Jamaica."[7] There is still no other dance ensemble in Jamaica of comparable scope and breadth.

Thus national cultural institutions are legitimized more through their intentions and actual accomplishments than through the mere acquiescence of government decree, especially when they reflect the existential realities of the wider population. The democratic assumptions of the self-government movement had traditionally depended on the formation of voluntary national institutions— whether they were political parties, trade unions, community development organizations, or the myriad grassroot mutual aid societies that have sustained an

Joseph Cools-Lartigue (right), the first chairman of the Company's Management Committee, greets Sir Clifford Campbell, the first native governor-general of independent Jamaica, on the governor-general's arrival at a performance in 1965 at Kingston's Little Theatre. (*Daily Gleaner*)

existence plagued by continuing marginalization. From the beginning of the twentieth century Jamaican cultural institutions, in particular, accepted this challenge, and the governments following recent independence have all depended on voluntary efforts for cultural development. In the creative arts self-determination has meant self-discipline, commitment, self-confidence, artistic integrity, unbounded intellectual and spiritual energy, humility underpinning a vigorous self-assertion, hard work, and mastery of technical skills. These are the very values that have continually guided the National Dance Theatre Company.

Fortunately the Jamaican government also appreciated these values at the time the Company was established. Thus, when Edward Seaga, the minister in charge of culture, learned about the formation of the National Dance Theatre Company, it was natural for him to endorse the idea enthusiastically. In keeping with the spirit of Jamaican independence—which fostered increased participation by the citizens in the exercise of their newly acquired power, transferred from Britain not to one special-interest group but to all the people of Jamaica—Seaga sent the following letter of endorsement.

Dear Mr. Nettleford:

One of the greatest obstacles to artistic development in Jamaica is the fragmentation of art groups into small performing bodies, too small to make any outstanding contribution.

It is my policy to weld together wherever possible such performing bodies in the hope that they will constitute national performing companies.

The Arts Celebrations Choir, which performed outstandingly under the direction of Mr. James Verity during the Independence Celebrations, showed what results could be obtained where independent groups were successfully merged. In that instance, every major choral singing group, save one, merged themselves to form the Arts Celebrations Choir with excellent results, and I sincerely hope they will continue to perform frequently as a single body.

I was, therefore, more than pleased to see that a National Dance Theatre Company had been formed. . . .

You know of my deep interest in dance forms and particularly those expressing indigenous art. It was no secret that I was very pleased at the way in which some of the material was handled in the Independence Celebrations performance of *Roots and Rhythms* under your leadership, and I sincerely believe that a body of performers have been assembled who are now capable of handling indigenous material with a sensitivity for its heritage and its traditions, and that we now stand a chance of accomplishing what I have dreamed of seeing in Jamaica for nine years, performances which can dig deeply and freely into the treasure chest of our folk heritage.

You are aware that I have collected over the years a quantity of folk music taken by me in live performance in rural Jamaica. These include Maroon, Kumina, Pocomania, Zion, Ring Play, Digging Sport, Burru, and so on. With the expectation that such material can now be properly handled I am more than willing to help the National Dance Theatre

Edward Seaga, Jamaica's minister in charge of culture between 1962 and 1972, encouraged the early development of the National Dance Theatre Company as part of his vigorous program of cultural development. A social anthropologist by training, Seaga became a founding patron of the Company in 1962. (*Jamaica Information Service*)

Company . . . by exposing this material to the body as well as by arranging for members to see and learn from live performances of the various groups mentioned wherever possible. I hope that by Independence Day 1963, your theatre will be able to give us the first true performance deeply based on indigenous material.

I am grateful to you for doing me the honour of asking me to be the patron of the Company and I am more than pleased to accept. My ministry will extend its patronage and give the Company its blessing.

Norman Manley—Jamaica's national hero who was premier from 1955 to 1962, the period just prior to the country's independence—spearheaded efforts to make cultural awareness an important part of national development; he laid the foundations for the cultural achievements of both Seaga and the younger Manley. Here Norman Manley addresses an audience at the Brixton Town Hall in 1965, after a performance by the Company on its first tour of Great Britain.

When the Arts Advisory Council next convenes I will ask the council to recommend a suitable member to sit on your interim Management Committee as requested.

Yours sincerely,
Edward Seaga
Minister of Development and Welfare[8]

Seaga's personal and professional interest in the dance as a means of social formation should not be underestimated. As minister in charge of culture between 1962 and 1972, he showed a deep appreciation for the arts in general. The succeeding administration, led by Michael Manley from 1972 to 1980, was also deeply committed to culture as central to national development.[9] Manley's family background helped prepare him for this enlightened approach: his mother, Edna Manley, was Jamaica's leading sculptor and moving force on the cultural scene, and his father, Norman Manley, spearheaded a self-government movement whose political vision placed the creative arts at its center. On Edward Seaga's return to power in 1980 as prime minister, the government's good-will toward cultural continuity was an important part of his program.[10]

The National Dance Theatre Company, along with other Jamaican cultural institutions, was the beneficiary of the cultural vision of the two major political parties. Postcolonial Jamaica may indeed be a model for the developing world, where economic pressures and the necessity of defusing class or tribal warfare often tempt the new leaders to try to control all aspects of political and social endeavors. Expressions of the creative imagination, which thrive underground despite repressive imperialist regimes, are wisely encouraged to flourish above-ground following independence. Thus civilized social interaction, which determines the ethos of society, will temper the excesses of power within a new government.

In often unsuspecting ways, the arts have exacted governmental restraint in Jamaica; yet the power structure has been criticized in some quarters. The country has not been short of protest songs, musical revues satirizing politics, or Rastafarian-inspired art and music defiant of received notions of mores. As a self-directed voluntary organization, the National Dance Theatre Company itself has made uneasy those who would prefer more central control. Thus the power

Michael Manley (right), prime minister of Jamaica from 1972 to 1980, inaugurates an exhibition at Devon House in 1972 which featured photographs of the Company taken by Maria LaYacona (middle). As minister of culture throughout the period, Manley actively supported the development of cultural institutions like the National Dance Theatre Company. Rex Nettleford is at the left. (*Errol Harvey, Jamaica Information Service*)

Sir Florizel Glasspole, the governor-general of Jamaica, delivering a message at the National Dance Theatre Company's twentieth anniversary commemoration service in March 1982 at the Saint Andrew Scots Kirk in Kingston. Also in attendance (on his left) are Rev. Ernie Gordon, an Anglican, and Rev. Ken Mock Yen, a Roman Catholic, who had been a dancer with a group that was forerunner of the Company. (*Arthur Smith, Jamaica Information Service*)

structure has had to come to terms with varied expressions of social criticism. At times self-serving supporters of a particular party in power wanted to ban reggae music and replace it with "serious music," meaning the music of Europe; they encouraged the critics to savage the political satires and the dancers to dress in elegant chiffon tutus and toe shoes rather than perform barefooted in cotton, too much a reminder of former slavery. There are even those who would have liked to see the dance disappear altogether. Despite the existence of these negative attitudes, the political leaders since 1955 have been fairly decent about supporting the creative arts, offering Jamaica a tolerable existence in the face of such hardships as increasing unemployment, rising crime rates, soaring inflation, foreign exchange imbalances, and internal doubts about the viability of a lopsided society inherited from slavery and colonialism.

Thus the National Dance Theatre Company operates within the larger social context, with all of its members affected by political and social concerns. But since the Company also operates within the framework of its own needs, questions about its organization and its development alongside Jamaican·independence need to be addressed. Despite the controversy that surrounded its formation, its early legitimation as a cultural force provided fertile soil for its subsequent growth and nurturing.

The imprimatur of the Ministry of Development and Welfare in 1962 was undoubtedly a great help. The Company's founders had clearly anticipated the minister's plan "to weld together wherever possible such performing bodies in the hope that they will constitute *national* performing companies."[11] But ministerial planning is one thing, whereas actual implementation by a neocolonial bureaucracy quite another. The fact exists that a group of Jamaican citizens from various backgrounds willing to form a dance company, and also sustain it themselves, wisely received governmental sanction. Thus the new nation was able to enjoy an outstanding cultural contribution without a financial burden on the public.

The Arts Celebrations Choir, mentioned in the minister's letter, did not endure, although there was a nostalgic reminder when the choir was reassembled in 1983 for the country's twenty-first anniversary celebrations. It was ten years after independence before the National Chorale was formed, with membership on a voluntary basis. In the 1960s a ministerial initiative to create a national drama company came to nothing, but the annual Little Theatre Movement pantomime, long perceived as tantamount to a national theater, competed successfully with the cinema. Jamaican dance must also face this competitive reality. The presence of the National Dance Theatre Company inspired the proliferation of dance groups throughout Jamaica. Some of these groups performed in cabarets, the annual festivals, and studio shows, while others, through more ambitious efforts, wanted to experiment outside the philosophic orientation of the National Dance Theatre Company. Some of these efforts were organized in a spirit of emulation, others in a spirit of challenge, but none of these groups was oblivious to the achievements of the Company.

Besides emulating the Company's high standards of performance, these aspiring dance groups had to take stock of the difficult lessons learned by the National Dance Theatre Company. Significant achievements in the dance can be won only through hard and dedicated work, and not through capriciousness or self-indulgence. The guiding vision must entail a philosophy that places the gift of human creativity in relation to the needs of an emergent society. These goals may at times seem unattainable, but they are worth the try. Much of the early endurance of the Company was based on such a resolve on the part of the founding members. With relatively little turnover of members during the seminal years, the Company benefited from the founding members' continuity of self-discipline, devotion to hard work, and a consensus about the Company's direction—at times in the face of personal inconvenience and financial hardships. Their experiences encompassed a variety of skills, perceptions, and social backgrounds that tested the mettle of the artistic leadership but also contributed to the enrichment of the artistic output. If eclecticism marked the early style of the Company, the spirit of adventure in the struggle for coherence and aesthetic logic gave the effort tremendous verve and vitality in those fledgling years, from 1962 to 1967.

In the early postindependence years the deceptive peacefulness within society was merely the gathering of the storm that preceded the turbulence that erupted in the late 1960s. The period began to witness social upheavals: the black power movement, discontent among unemployed youth, the demand for jobs as well as cultural expression among the indigenous population, and the insistence by the poor on material betterment. None of these tumultuous developments escaped the notice of the National Dance Theatre Company. The mask of stability covering the nation's wrinkled brows during the early years of independence was mirrored by the Company's early repertoire. The deceptively celebratory *Plantation Revelry* articulated deeper problems of identity than the pantomimic story suggested. Social conflict, explored in *Games of Arms*, and the challenge of an assertive underclass against privilege, put forward in *Two Drums for Babylon*, were just two of the social issues that were investigated by the Company. There were ironic presentations of the tragicomedy inherent in Jamaican life; self-assertion without overt rage was a paradoxical response at a time when the social power among a newly prosperous urban middle class was ostentatiously allied with the old oligarchy perched precariously above a restive class traditionally deprived and marginalized. Such contradictions of a society groping to define itself demanded of all artists, not least the members of the National Dance Theatre Company, sensitivity, intelligence, understanding, and cultural integrity. The founding members offered these qualities and therefore made possible the survival of the Company and its varied and expansive repertoire.

The Founders

In terms of technical range and performing skill the founding dancers' versatility figured prominently in the early responses to the Company. Quite properly the Company was judged primarily on its dances and dancing rather than on its philosophy. The richness of the offerings was undoubtedly augmented by the diverse backgrounds of the dancers themselves. They had proven their technical capabilities as well as their powers of concentration and physical stamina. At the time the Company was formed many of the members were teaching dance and had already created their own dances. All of them had a separate profession: graphic artist, school teacher, university lecturer, laboratory technician, stenotypist, clerk, telephone operator, or civil servant. But they were all linked by the challenge of the dance in more than one of its many dimensions.

Rex Nettleford   Eddy Thomas

Not all of them grasped the full import of the historical and philosophical implications of the effort, but none of them would have missed the excitement of the challenge, or the sense of occasion, that Jamaican independence offered that branch of the arts to which they had devoted so much of their time and energy for much of their young lives.

When the National Dance Theatre Company was formed in 1962, the two dancers who accepted responsibility as codirectors were Rex Nettleford and Eddy Thomas. At the time, they also became the major choreographers for the Company.

Rex Nettleford had danced and acted from an early age in rural Jamaica and in the tourist resort Montego Bay, where he produced biennial variety shows. While an undergraduate studying history at the University of the West Indies, he trained formally as a dancer with Ivy Baxter and led the University Dancing and Gymnastics Society (later University Dance Society). He also worked with visiting American and Caribbean dance instructors at the university's summer schools, which he organized for many years. While at Oxford as a Rhodes Scholar, he developed his choreographic skills by extensive work with the Oxford University Dramatic Society and the Experimental Theatre Company as well as with the Oxford Opera Group.[12] In 1959 Nettleford was choreographer to the

Sheila Barnett

Maureen Casserly

Oxford Theatre Group, which appeared at the Edinburgh International Festival of Music and Drama.[13] He returned to Jamaica that year to take up an academic post at the University of the West Indies. Prior to the 1962 Jamaican independence celebrations he choreographed three pantomimes, also directing one of them, and staged several dance shows. With Eddy Thomas he conceived the dance program *Roots and Rhythms* for the 1962 celebrations. He had traveled widely, working with dance groups in Trinidad and British Honduras (Belize), as well as in Nigeria and Ghana, where he studied African dance forms. For two years he directed the Ivy Baxter and Eddy Thomas studios during their absence from Jamaica. Essentially a dance educator and choreographer, Nettleford perceived his art form as an important means of enriching Jamaican life.

Eddy Thomas was not only a dancer and choreographer with the Company, he was also a musician, costume and set designer, and commercial artist. He directed the Eddy Thomas Dance Workshop, with branches in Kingston and Mandeville. His four years with Ivy Baxter developed into a partnership in which he acted as dancer, costume designer, or composer and Baxter as choreographer. Works that grew out of this cooperative effort, such as *Rat Passage*, *Seven Stages*, *Once upon a Seaweed*, were all artistic successes in Jamaica. He played the lead in two Jamaican pantomimes and choreographed several musicals, including *Finian's Rainbow*. In 1959 Thomas won the Jamaican gov-

Ronan Critchlow

Bridget Casserly

ernment Arts Council Award and studied in New York and at the Connecticut College Dance Festival in New London with Martha Graham and other modern dance exponents such as Merce Cunningham and José Limón. He joined the Graham company for a season on Broadway and later returned to Broadway with *Kwamina*, choreographed by Agnes De Mille. He returned to Jamaica to coproduce *Roots and Rhythms* and to help establish the National Dance Theatre Company. He had toured Trinidad and Cuba and joined the goodwill tour to Washington, D.C., and Baltimore in 1961. As a costume designer, Thomas had a sensitive grasp of the colors of tropical Jamaica and was responsible for most of the costume designs for the Company's repertoire. His main role at the time, however, was that of teacher and choreographer.

Sheila Barnett, like Thomas, doubled as dancer and choreographer. She brought to the Company the value of her training in the Laban technique [14] at the Chelsea School of Physical Education in England. In 1962 she was teaching dance and drama at the Saint Josephs Teacher Training College in Kingston. A dancer with graceful lines and noble carriage, Barnett possesses the gifts of intelligence, characterization, dramatic power, and performing strength. She danced the lead role in *Once upon a Seaweed*, mounted in 1960 by the Baxter group, and in 1963 she made her choreographic debut with the Company with Carl Sandburg's poem *Jazz Fantasia*.

Ronan Critchlow, the brother of Sheila Barnett, was for some years a leading dancer with the Ivy Baxter Creative Dance Group. He was the first highly acclaimed male dancer in the creative, or modern, dance idiom in Jamaica. He was a civil servant but taught dance as well, not only in Jamaica but also in Antigua and Grenada, and in 1961 he had revived his historic role of the stowaway in *Rat Passage* on tour to Washington, D.C., and Baltimore. Critchlow studied the technique of hand drumming with Haiti's master drummer Tiroro during Jamaica's 1955 tercentenary celebrations. Thus it was natural that he became the Company's principal drummer when he gave up dancing soon after the Company's formation.

Maureen Casserly and *Bridget Casserly* were sisters who came out of the Soohih School of Dance. One of the most acclaimed dancers at the time, Maureen Casserly (later Maureen Holder) joined the Company as a performer with a wide range of technique and stage experience. Her versatility and physical endurance were principal assets for the new ensemble. She had taught at the Soohih school and had also been a leading dancer in many Little Theatre Movement pantomimes. She had the lead role of Susan in *Finian's Rainbow.* Bridget Casserly was less well known, but besides the valuable performing experience from her years of apprenticeship with the Soohih School of Dance, she also brought to the Company a lively intelligence and an analytical mind for both dance and economics, which she had studied at the University of the West Indies as an undergraduate.

Audley Butler had his training in creative dance in both the Baxter and the Thomas studios. By 1962 he had gained much performing experience in six of

Audley Butler

Shirley Campbell

Joyce Campbell

Yvonne daCosta

the Little Theatre Movement pantomimes, and he brought to the Company an innate musicality, a sense of the street, and great dedication.

Joyce Campbell and *Shirley Campbell* were virtually household names to the audiences of the Baxter group during the 1950s. Joyce Campbell had recently begun work in rural Jamaica, teaching and researching dance under the auspices of the Jamaica Social Welfare Commission. Because of this work, she was responsible for the dance, mime, and song presentation at the 1961 National Festival. In 1963 she established her own studio, the Jayteens Dance Workshop, which still flourishes. She brought to the Company a profound understanding of Jamaican traditional dance. Shirley Campbell, who shared her sister's flair for traditional-dance style, taught dance for the University Dancing and Gymnastics Society at the University of the West Indies. She doubled as wardrobe mistress when the Company was established.

Yvonne daCosta came to the Company from the Fay Simpson School of Ballet, where she had studied classical ballet. Later she received training in modern dance at the Eddy Thomas Dance Workshop and at the university's summer schools. Her graceful lines, technical range, dramatic power, musicality, and phenomenal memory established her almost immediately as a major dancer. Her appearances in Little Theatre Movement pantomimes apprenticed her for the vital work she contributed during the Company's first decade, both as lead dancer and as ballet mistress.

Barbara Requa

Mavis Stoppi

Barbara Grant (later Barbara Requa) studied with the Baxter group. She trained in England toward a diploma in physical education, gaining at the time knowledge of the Laban technique, and studied at the University of the West Indies summer school sessions. She entered the Company while teaching at a Jamaican high school. She benefited from theater exposure with pantomimes and other musicals, bringing to the Company technical versatility, performing style, and sound knowledge of movement.

Pansy Silvera (later Pansy Hassan) was another Simpson-trained dancer who, like daCosta, combined classical technique with the creative dance idiom gained from her work in the Eddy Thomas Dance Workshop and the university's summer schools as well as in the Little Theatre Movement pantomimes. She took an early leave of absence to continue her training in New York before returning to the Company in the late 1960s.

Mavis Lai (later Mavis Stoppi), from a Jamaican Chinese family, was also classically trained in the Soohih School of Dance and brought to the Company a sense of lyricism and comedy as well as a dedication that lasted until her untimely death in 1975.

Monica McGowan, a kindergarten teacher who preferred teaching, was nevertheless an excellent performer with great technical competence. She had studied and performed with the Baxter group and at the Soohih school as well as at the university's summer schools. She had also staged dance shows for the Institute of Jamaica's Junior Centre, which she ran at the time.

Bert Rose brought youthful energy and enthusiasm as well as a powerful stage presence and performing talent. He received his basic training with Eddy Thomas and in the university's summer schools. As a result of his studies at the Jamaica School of Art, he added an aesthetic sensibility to his sense of style in the major roles he danced in the repertoire. He developed further through his dance experiences in New York with Martha Graham.

Rosalie Markes, a natural science graduate from the University of the West Indies, brought dance intelligence and a special feel for Caribbean-style movement to the Company. She had studied with Baxter and the University Dancing and Gymnastics Society in the 1950s as well as in the university's summer schools.

Gertrude Sherwood was another of the newer generation of dancers who emerged from the Baxter studio, Little Theatre Movement pantomimes, and the university's summer schools. She had a natural gift as a dancer and a powerful stage projection. She was studying the cello at the time of the Company's formation and brought to the group musicality, self-discipline, and the kind of enthusiasm that stimulated her to further study abroad, with Eileen Crofton in London and Eleo Pomare in New York.

There were three nondancing founding members, who acted respectively as the Company vocal soloist, secretary–treasurer, and lighting director.

Joyce Lalor, a graduate of the London College of Music, taught for many

Pansy Hassan (*Amador Packer*)

Monica McGowan

Bert Rose

Rosalie Markes

years at the Kingston Technical High School. At the time she was a well-known singer on the Jamaican stage and radio. She had sung solo with the leading choirs in the nation's capital and for many years had been a featured singer in Little Theatre Movement pantomimes. Her wide-ranging repertoire encompassed both Jamaican folksongs and European classics. When she joined the Company, Lalor made the challenging decision to concentrate on Caribbean traditional music, and at the time she also embarked on a new career in educational television.

Verona Ashman, who had worked in the theater with the Repertory Players, was a cultural administrator as registrar of the Jamaica School of Art. Intelligence and administrative experience underpinning her total commitment made her a great asset to the Company.

George Carter was the pioneer lighting designer in Jamaica. Beginning in the 1940s, he had lit every major Jamaican theater event—musical, pageant, play, dance. In 1961 he was awarded the Jamaican government Arts Council Award to study lighting in Great Britain and North America. He gained valuable experience with the Sadler's Wells Ballet, the Shakespeare Memorial Theatre at Stratford-upon-Avon, and the Welsh National Opera Company in Cardiff. In the United States he worked with the Western Spring Theater in Chicago and the Loeb Theater Center at Harvard.

Gertrude Sherwood

Joyce Lalor, vocal soloist.

Barry Moncrieffe, although not strictly a founding member, should be mentioned here since he has had an unbroken record of service with the Company during its twenty-one years, starting out as a supporting dancer and continuing today as a lead male dancer and an artistic coordinator. Moncrieffe became a full member within a year of the Company's formation and brought dedication and devotion to hard work as well as naturally expressive movement and technical competence.

Verona Ashman, secretary of the Company.

George Carter, lighting director.

Barry Moncrieffe

Maria LaYacona, Company photographer.
(*J. J. Wood*)

Such was the core of this new dance company, all of the members with separate careers but with a sense of collective purpose and dedication to the Company without expecting remuneration. They were confident that the psychic satisfaction that comes from performing valuable work would be its own reward.

The young Company was greeted in Jamaica with some hostility, which because of the nature of theater in general may have been predictable. Perhaps that resentment was prompted in part by Rex Nettleford's strong peasant sensibility and social consciousness, by Eddy Thomas's commitment to the American modern dance idiom, and by the classlessness—in terms of Jamaican dance traditions—of performers like Sheila Barnett and Barbara Grant. There was further provocation because the Casserly sisters, Yvonne daCosta, Pansy Silvera, and Mavis Lai seemed to turn away from what they had been taught, in their classical training, as the proper form for the dance. Because the Company seemed to usurp the tradition nurtured by the classical ballet instructors and by Ivy Baxter, it was greeted with some suspicion, especially by Baxter supporters.

Even if a spirit of rebellion was prevalent within the new group, a much more important motive was the desire expressed by the complete membership, especially by the leadership, to affirm the past experience of Jamaican dance theater and at the same time to celebrate the richness of the ancestral heritage. From the beginning the dangers inherent in rebellion were tempered by a sense of order. Not a rigid military order or the will to power of an elite corps of rulers, rather it was the order of the pukkumina rituals or the jonkonnu ceremonies, all

Above: Felix Barnett and Frederick Hickling, stage managers.
Right: Frederick Hickling; Baldwin Lennon, sound director;
and Barbara Kaufmann, wardrobe mistress.

with shape and form rooted in the substance of their being. It was not the order of the European classical ballet in its strict and proud formalism or of the American modern dance with its technically ordered asymmetries. It was the order underscored by the organic nature of Caribbean village life—church, school, and family—with its sense of purpose.

The inculcation of that sense of order which is the basis of what is considered civilized life was also evident among the educated middle classes and had its

Marjorie Whylie, pianist, drummer, and composer, became the Company's musical director in 1967. (*Bryan Studio*)

Mapletoft Poulle, a lawyer and an accomplished musician, was the Company's first musical director, from 1962 to 1966.

effect on the pioneering artists. Edna Manley and her husband, Norman Manley, one of the architects of Jamaican independence, invested their design for social living with that sense of order, and without denying spontaneity and organic vitality they offered culture and the arts a legacy of discipline. Ivy Baxter brought the same spirit to the creative dance movement, which sought form through indigenous sources. No doubt her conscious mission was to dance proud beside the formalized European ballet, which she had studied but which remained outside her reach and very much the province of the privileged. By the time the Nettlefords and the Thomases appeared on the scene, the habit of systematic study and exploration had taken root. Nettleford's own academic training at both the University of the West Indies and Oxford and his rural and religious background prepared him for that kind of discipline. Because of their backgrounds, as well as their training and job experiences, the other founding members were also prepared for disciplined work with the Company.

Perhaps this demand for order had a sense of urgency about it. After all, Jamaican life had traditionally been marked by severance; it was a life in which pattern was the exception rather than the rule. Yet the Company founders refused to yield to the monotony of repetitive routine, indulged in at the expense of instinctive creativity and experimentation. In fact the tension between form and spontaneity continues to inform the Company's creative dynamic. In their desire to preserve the spontaneous and organic flow of dance movement, some groups have stressed the dancer over the dance. The National Dance Theatre Company's approach has always been an insistence on complete integration of the dancer and the dance itself.

Strategic Support: The Early Years

The clarity of its objectives, the seriousness of its purpose, and the national orientation of its image did attract crucial support from strategic quarters. Institutional support came immediately from the Little Theatre Movement, which had actually nurtured the Company's founding. Although the Company's request to have Noel Vaz, the University of the West Indies's instructor in drama, sit in an official capacity on the Management Committee was refused by the head of the department on the grounds that the Company was a private endeavor, Vaz was allowed to join the committee as a private individual. As a brilliant theater director, he had helped transform the Little Theatre Movement's annual pantomimes from their English amateur-theatricals roots to innovative professional musicals drawing on Jamaican indigenous sources and talents. He brought to the management of the Company his experiences not only as a director of the classics but also as an inspirer of native West Indian theater throughout the eastern Caribbean. His sense of propriety and his knowledge of theatrical presentation informed his generous guidance of the Company. He also offered advice in stage managing and accompanied the Company on overseas tours. The University of the West Indies had of course given its institutional support by organizing the summer school sessions, which was important for the technical training of the Company's early dancers. Subsequently the university was a base from which the artistic director could not only build the Company directly but also shape national cultural policy in Jamaica.

Another university member who joined the Management Committee was Hugh Morrison. Besides being an educational broadcaster, he was one of the first male dancers who worked outside the strictly classical tradition or the cabaret idiom. After training with Herma Diaz[15] and La Ciba Sonami (Ione Williamson), who is credited with having introduced modern dance to Jamaica, Morrison appeared in early revues and musicals under the pseudonym of Gabriel. He worked for a short time with Ivy Baxter and continued to be a firm supporter of creative dance movement. Wycliffe Bennett, a cultural administrator, also lent support. More than anyone else he had promoted drama and the other performing arts throughout rural Jamaica. As the cultural coordinator of the independence celebrations, he brought a national outlook, which corresponded with the Company's aims. After study in the United States at Yale University and work in Jamaican theater and broadcasting, Bennett later became a serious dance critic and a scholar of the history of Jamaican theater. The actress Carmen Manley, the painter Barry Watson, and the Little Theatre Movement's founder and president Greta Fowler augmented the management team from outside the Company. The lawyer Joseph Cools-Lartigue was the Company's chairman till his death in 1969.

There was also support from the dance world. Madame May Soohih, Barbara Fonseca, and Punky and Betty Rowe, all instructors of classical ballet, offered their services as teachers. Young civil servants attached to the ministry in charge of culture were caught up in the enthusiasm to give traditional cultural activity new form and meaning for the young nation. The Company benefited from the sensitivity of these civil servants, such as Jean Smith, who developed, over the following two decades, a unique expertise in cultural administration.

The encouragement of the Company's founding patrons was also of psychological importance. The sincere endorsement of the Company's aims by Edna Manley[16] as well as by Louise Bennett,[17] the great folklorist and poet who wrote in the language of the people, was a great benefit. Robert Verity, the tireless advocate of cultural education of the young manifested in his work as deputy director of the Institute of Jamaica, also lent his name as patron, as did Edward Seaga, a social anthropologist turned politician who had done fieldwork on Ja-

Company dancers in the late 1960s included (standing, left to right) Frank Ashley, Noelle Chutkan, Bert Rose, Patsy Ricketts, Derek Williams, Joyce Campbell, Sheila Barnett, Barbara Requa, Audley Butler, Pansy Hassan, Cheryl Ryman, Milton Dawes; (sitting on boxes) Monica McGowan, Eddy Thomas, Neville Black, Barry Moncrieffe; (sitting on stage) Dennis Scott, Gertrude Sherwood, Jean Summers, Yvonne daCosta, Rex Nettleford, Bridget Casserly, Shirley Campbell, Tommy Pinnock, Carol Miller.

maican folklore and cult music. Martha Graham, the genius of American dance, also became a founding patron.[18] Symbolically she provided an important link to the modern dance traditions of North America. Her vigor and the assertiveness of her original technique served as inspiration for the Company. More directly she had been an influential teacher of Eddy Thomas. Graham had in fact taken a personal interest in the National Dance Theatre Company as exponent of Jamaican dance, as the numerous scholarships offered the Jamaican dancers in her school testified, at first with Bert Rose, Barry Moncrieffe, Audley Butler, and Derek Williams and later with dancers such as Tommy Pinnock, Noel Hall, Patsy Ricketts, and Frank Ashley, as well as those who attended classes for shorter durations, including Pansy Hassan, Monica McGowan, and Gertrude Sherwood.

The vigor of the young Company also attracted talented musicians and stage technicians. The musical personnel included the budding composer Oswald Russell, a graduate of London's Royal School of Music and the Juilliard School in New York; Mapletoft Poulle, the Company's first musical director, who previously had been musical director for both creative dance and ballet performances as well as for many of the pantomimes; and the young Marjorie Whylie, who later succeeded Poulle as musical director. Baldwin Lennon served as sound director; Felix Barnett as stage manager; and Barbara Kaufmann and Judy Wedderburn as supporting dancers who are still with the Company, with Kaufmann later becoming wardrobe mistress. The most popular folksinging group at the time, the Frats Quintet, complemented the Company's vocal soloist in the early performances. Individual singers—such as Vin James and Paula Johnson,[19] practiced choristers who are still with the Company—frequently appeared in various choral combinations.

Such were the valuable resources available to the new Company. These resources were mobilized over the next twenty-one years into a cultural force of national as well as Caribbean significance. Between 1964 and the beginning of the 1970s the Company attracted many new talents critical to its growth and development. In 1964 a highly skilled American-born professional photographer, Maria LaYacona, volunteered her services to the Company. Her inspired photographs of the dancers and dances, all taken in performance, were utilized extensively for publicity purposes. These dramatic representations were printed in the annual program brochures and later in the book *Roots and Rhythms*, published in 1969.[20] Neville Black teamed up with the Company as a choreographer on his permanent return to Jamaica, bringing to the repertoire wit and the modern dance style he had developed in his work in Chicago. Frederick Hickling, a young medical student who had coordinated the shows for the independence celebrations, brought energy and enthusiasm to the chores of stage manager. New dancers of excellence emerged, foremost among them, Noelle Chutkan, Dorothy Fraser, and Patsy Ricketts. Chutkan had been trained in Jamaica. Fraser, first training with the early generation of Jamaican classical ballet dancers, later studied and performed with the London Festival Ballet. Ricketts gained technical strength and a distinctive performing style from her study in New York with the Graham company and from work with Arthur Mitchell at the Dance Theater of Harlem, which she and Derek Williams joined as founding members. Among the men were Dennis Scott, an expressive dancer who was also a gifted poet and playwright; Tommy Pinnock, who had an uncanny sensibility about urban street style and an eloquent dance expression; and Noel Hall, whose versatility and dance intelligence served him well in his later dance career in the United States. Other dancers, who had not left Jamaica, helped in the experiments toward discovery. Madge Broderick, Andrea Nash, Jean Binns, Yvonne Ffrench, Melanie Cook (Melanie Graham), Judith Pennant, and Cheryl Ryman, who rejoined the Company in the early 1970s following her training in methods of dance research in West Africa and Canada, added texture to the continuing work of the Company.

None of the Company members received remuneration, which is true even today. Full membership in the Company carries the odd status of unpaid public servant. The early musicians worked for a fee, but on taking over the musical direction of the Company in 1967, Marjorie Whylie broke this tradition and offered her services without pay. The Company singers (NDTC Singers) were also established on this basis in the same year, with Joyce Lalor, as leader, accompanied by Vin James, Paula Johnson, Hope Foreman, Noel Heron, and Stanley Irons. Other musicians followed in this spirit, starting with the bass player Lloyd Mason, then a noncommissioned officer of the Jamaica Military Band. At the invitation of the artistic director in 1976 the entire orchestra, comprising Minky Jefferson, Barbara Boland, Leighton Johnson, and Steve Golding, was integrated into the rest of the Company as unpaid members. For a full discussion of the musicians, technicians, administrators, and other personnel, see Chapter 6.

The Watershed Period: 1967 to 1968

The period 1967 to 1968 was indeed a crucial time for the Company, as it was in general for the society. Eddy Thomas left the Company to concentrate fully on his own school, the Eddy Thomas Dance Workshop, leaving Rex Nettleford as the sole director. His departure was also critical in the area of costume designing, to which he had added his own distinctive style. The choreography for his major works, such as *Legend of Lovers' Leap, Games of Arms, And It Came to Pass*, and *Footnotes in Jazz*, revealed his sense of elegance, sophisticated wit, visual and theatrical effects, and technical proficiency in the modern dance idiom. It was clear that his contribution to dance theater was invaluable to the Company's early development. Beginning in 1968, the Company placed greater emphasis on a specific Caribbean style of dance theater. Thus the Company was forced to sharpen its focus in those terms and to establish its own training program since the facilities of the Eddy Thomas Dance Workshop, where many Company members had taught and which had served as a primary source of new recruits, were no longer available to the Company.

By the end of the 1960s the National Dance Theatre Company had already developed a truly distinctive dance theater style, a style that by 1971 manifested itself in such a signature piece as *Kumina*, which Derek Walcott described as "older than revolution."[21] Although at the time the Company's expressive work was central to contemporary dance theater, a wider network of dance activities was also developing. Sheila Barnett was responsible for including dance in the physical education curriculum of Jamaican schools and teacher colleges, thus strategically extending the influence of the Company's ideals into the educational system. As the dance officer for the Jamaica Festival Commission (later Jamaica Cultural Development Commission), Joyce Campbell organized annual dance competitions with entrants from all over the island. Rex Nettleford chaired the commission's voluntary committee that directed dance policy, while other Company members helped design the syllabus and establish criteria for judging the competitions. The organic relationship between the Company and the educational system offered the dance world in general an ever-expanding reserve of talented young performers.

If the Company was expected to be a showcase of dance works of excellence and influence the society, its continuing strength depended on the support of an actively engaged educational system and responsive community programs. By the early 1970s it became increasingly clear that the Company had to fulfill its original aims more explicitly and move to the pulse of Caribbean cultural traditions rather than those of Europe and urban America. Moreover, it was important that the Jamaican people develop an appreciation of their own cultural achievements. A willingness to contribute within the scope of these objectives would ultimately dictate membership within the Company. Inevitably some people found the objectives limiting, due to natural philosophical differences. Both within the Company and among the public crucial questions about the artistic aims of the Company were being posed. Some of the questions were misguided, but the concern over whether the group was serious about articulating an art form that dealt with the realities of Caribbean life was a legitimate one.

Would the Company be a replica of an American dance company, which is what exposure to the influential modern dance idiom might have led some members and audiences to expect? Would it be a Jamaican version of the European classical ballet, which seemed unlikely considering the Company's beginnings? Would it be a variety-type ensemble without aesthetic focus or organic vocabulary, which all art forms must have? The denial of the possibility of the integration of form and feeling in the dance, despite the disparate elements that constitute the Jamaican cultural universe, corresponds to the age-old denial that the Caribbean masses are capable of making sense of their historical experience and creative potential. It was mandatory that the Company members reach an agreement on their commitment to explode that myth through their work. That commitment also sought to exact from its audiences and the critics a serious appreciation of the historical, social, and cultural context in which the development of the dance and other expressions of the Jamaican imagination was taking place.

It was when the dance was perceived as art that the Company was most accountable. The Jamaican critic Winnifred Risden, herself a former dancer, gently warned that a sound technical foundation was the final test.[22] Norman Rae, a critic who was also involved directly in theater work, was worried in the early days about the Company's lack of stylistic focus.[23] Foreign critics mentioned the eclecticism in both approving and disapproving terms, and the Cuban critic Alejandro Alonso, writing in Havana's daily *Juventud Rebelde*, bluntly stated that the Company made sense only when it came nearest to expressing a Caribbean attitude.[24] Deborah Jowitt, writing in 1973 in the influential New York weekly *The Village Voice*, hoped that the Company for all its enthusiasm and charm made it "either back to their roots or into today." "I think," she continued, "that, for them, Graham tradition is a cul-de-sac."[25] Two years later William Littler of *The Toronto Star* took a similar line about the Company's development: "Can its dance adapt to societal change without becoming a pale imitation of North American models?"[26] By 1981 Littler's response was somewhat reversed, with an enthusiastic review of the Company's season at Toronto's Ryerson Polytechnic Theatre.[27]

Yet at home some Jamaicans, including some of the dance critics, did yearn for North American models. After 1968 the National Dance Theatre Company held firm to its vision. The technical and stylistic inheritance of the Company was indeed varied and wide-ranging. Eddy Thomas had discovered form in the Graham technique, but Nettleford resolutely rooted his work in Afro-Caribbean patterns, insisting that the inspiration must be derived primarily from Caribbean traditions rather than from the studios of New York. Among other founding members there were also notions about style and form, whether based on European classical ballet, which many had studied; German modern expressionism, as transmitted by Ivy Baxter through her brief exposure to Sigurd Leeder in London; or more direct expressions of movement patterns introduced by certain dancer-choreographers, such as Sheila Barnett, who had studied the Laban technique and other methods of educational dance. How could these disparate sources be melded into a serviceable technical foundation for original creation?

No doubt the early days were confusing to many. The eclecticism offered something for everyone in the audience, thereby satisfying Caribbean pluralist prejudices—an arabesque for the balletomanes, contractions derived from Graham technique and turned-in legs for those who had heard of modern, a sculpted earth-centered African stance for those committed to national heritage, and the light coquettish reels and turns for those oriented toward Creole cultural traditions. The elements of Caribbean dance could not be discovered simply through judicious samplings from the various cultural traditions throughout history. Direct research into traditional dance and music rituals had to be pursued seriously. Literacy in the world of dance became mandatory, and dance as an educational tool was getting its full attention. There was greater demand on the dancers, who accepted the decisions of the Company's artistic director, but most of all, as the Jamaican actress Maud Fuller later averred, they shared the "vision of what gives the Company its qualitative tenor and are willing to submit themselves to the rigorous discipline that transposes effort into achievement."[28] The approach to choreography based on a profound study of Jamaican and Caribbean traditions, especially movement patterns and music, produced in the 1970s such works as *Kumina*, *Mountain Women*, *Celebrations*, *Ni—Woman of Destiny*, *Drumscore*, *Myal*, *Backlash*, and *I Not I*, all imbued with the stylistic icons and aesthetic intent of a classic indigenous dance theater.

The roots of the National Dance Theatre Company are to be found in the indigenous rituals and dances extant in rural Jamaica. Company members here participate in a 1968 bruckin party ritual in eastern Jamaica.

Many works not directly related to Caribbean concerns were also created at the same time, but they were now being performed with a distinctive aesthetic. Thus an American commentator could write in 1970: "The Company may perform to music that ranges from Bach to Brubeck, from drumbeat to symphony, but the interpretation is the mood and movement of Jamaica."[29] In the following year Derek Walcott spoke of an integrated Company and noted that "whatever their color, when they dance black, are black."[30] The Puerto Rican composer Hector Campos-Parsi compared the Company's work to an expression of the "Antillean soul."[31] It was becoming more difficult for anyone to function within the Company who did not believe in the capacity of Jamaicans to create something out of their own experience. For example, it would be difficult for a Company member who regarded the vibrant innovation of reggae with contempt. A society in search of a definition of itself would naturally have to look to the dominant modes of cultural expression for clues. The dances and music of the majority certainly must figure in the quest for a definitive artistic expression. If the very presence of the masses was useful in helping to transform the society from a political fief of the mother country into a self-governing polity, why shouldn't the creative imagination of those people also be a source for transforming the cultural echo of Britain into a self-directed civilization with its own logic and consistency? It is this type of process that the National Dance Theatre Company accepted for itself in order to make dance expression capable of bringing about some changes in the society's self-perception. In a society in which the culture is becoming increasingly Americanized, and, for instance, in which the disco genre of music threatens to assimilate both the contemporary Jamaican popular music and the rich ancestral inventions of the Caribbean, the Company's aesthetic stance may pose a problem for some audiences, as well as for some of the younger generation of dancers who, despite exposure to the ancestral sources, perceive the dance vocabulary of America's modernism and Europe's classicism as the acceptable norms.

From the very beginning critics of the Company challenged the group to find its path not merely in terms of the techniques dictated by an international dance vocabulary but also in terms of the substantive dance traditions of the Caribbean. The debate on the philosophical commitment of the Company reached its climax in 1967, when George Beckford, an agricultural economist lecturing at the University of the West Indies, confronted the Company about its responsibilities in addressing existing values, taking a primary role in raising the consciousness of its audiences, and offering alternative models for economic and political as well as artistic progress. Technique without content, he concluded, would soon become sterile.[32] In its defense, it was only natural for the Company to appeal to the artist's freedom to explore and make mistakes, thus being spared the constraints of ideological cant, but Beckford and allied critics could not be faulted in their claim that unless Jamaicans first and foremost were themselves no one would take them seriously. A decade later Keith Calhoun, a young American graduate student at Stanford University summarized the Beckford–Nettleford dialogue: "Nettleford, as a concerned Jamaican intellectual, recognizes the national significance of creating a strong cultural identity as quickly as possible, yet as an artist he reacts to what could develop into political manipulation of the arts for whatever good reasons."[33] If Beckford advocated the progressive view, there were others who took the opposite approach, evaluating the Company in terms of conventional European dance theater and European aesthetics in general. The debate continues to the present day and is not likely to dissipate until the society at large comes to terms with itself as part of the process of decolonization and self-definition.

More important for the development of the Company was the appreciation on the part of the members themselves of the problems involved in discovering form through the spiritual energies of the Jamaican people and re-creating it with technical authority and aesthetic logic. Such a task demanded of the Company dancers, choreographers, and other creative personnel not only technical facility but also insight and a genuine curiosity about their own cultural history and social dynamics. Not all of the members were responsive, but those who were found it possible to fulfill their specific artistic needs within the framework of the Company's commitments. One dancer who understood the challenge was Dennis Scott, whose insight as a poet and playwright may have lent him an advantage. In 1970 Scott made the crucial observation that in order to create at all in the Caribbean society one must deny the verdict that the past deprived the artist of everything. He felt that when a former slave society like Jamaica "imposes discipline on itself from within, it begins to wipe out a tradition of submission. . . . It is the beginning of freedom to choose."[34] Rank imitation is never discipline from within, and indiscriminate use of other artists' creativity passed off as one's own never reveals the freedom to choose. Scott's vision was shared by Sheila Barnett, whose choreographic skills matured at the beginning of the 1970s. Marjorie Whylie, as the musical director, also shared the vision of a group that would work toward its own definitions of life and art. Other strategically placed Company members were guided by that commitment over the years, for example, Yvonne daCosta (ballet mistress), Verona Ashman (secretary), Maurice Stoppi (chairman), Joyce Lalor and Vin James (singers), and Frederick Hickling (stage manager).

Criticism was sometimes voiced against too much intellectualizing as well as what was considered the Company's overweening concerns with psychodrama and social commentary. But the Company held to its vision, fighting on many fronts and setting the record straight whenever facts were distorted. It held out against the domination of foreign influences and petty dance politics. The public could always be relied upon. Increasingly over the years, the audiences were able to judge the most important test—that is, the dance works themselves, which demonstrated in action the quality of the Company's achievements. The Company's impact on society was given wider scope by means of lecture demonstrations throughout Jamaica and the dance systems that were developed by Company members for training the nation's young people. The electronic media were crucial in disseminating the Company's work to a wider audience. In 1964 the Jamaica Information Service, instructed by the ministry in charge of culture, recorded the early dances on film. The television wing of the Jamaica Broadcasting Corporation, soon realizing the value of the work, also filmed the dances and broadcast them nationally.

Company members in Moscow's Red Square, in September 1979. (*Ted Cunningham, API*)

The Company Abroad: Overseas Tours

Beginning in 1963, the overseas tours brought international recognition to the National Dance Theatre Company.[35] In a culturally insecure, postcolonial country, nothing pleases the population more than approval of their endeavors by foreign nations, especially approval from the most powerful cultural centers. By the same token nothing satisfies the local detractors better than the bad reception of overseas audiences or critics, who, it is often assumed, are more knowledgeable in cultural matters.

During its first twenty-one years the Company has toured sixteen countries, including those in North and South America, Europe, the Pacific, and the Caribbean itself. It has performed in forty-three cities, more than once in many cities. It has played to capacity crowds in such houses as the Brooklyn Academy of

Alicia Alonso, the celebrated Cuban ballerina, shares a point with Rex Nettleford during the visit of the Ballet Alonso de Cuba to Jamaica. (*Errol Harvey, API*)

Movie star Dudley Moore visited the Company backstage at London's Sadler's Wells in 1972 to meet his former Oxford colleague Rex Nettleford, whom he had worked with in theater at Oxford during the 1950s. Moore is talking with master drummer Ronan Critchlow. (*Syd Burke*)

Music and the City Center Theater in New York, the O'Keefe Centre in Toronto, the Opera House of the National Arts Centre in Ottawa, the Teatro Lorca in Havana, the Theatre Royal in Sydney, the Beethovenhalle in Bonn, the Georgetown Cultural Centre in Guyana, the Tchaikovsky Concert Hall in Moscow, and the gigantic Palace of Culture in Kiev.

Gough Whitlam, the controversial former prime minister of Australia, who had invited the National Dance Theatre Company to Australia in 1976, met with Company members backstage at the Canberra Theatre. Also in the picture are (left to right) baritone Vin James, Rex Nettleford in costume as a kumina king, Frederick Hickling, and Verona Ashman.

The Company's second visit to London was in 1972, when the group appeared at Sadler's Wells to enthusiastic audiences. (*Gray Studios*)

Outdoor performances in front of mass audiences were special challenges, posing difficult problems of projection and energy. In 1967 there were tens of thousands in the audience at the United Nations Plaza for Montreal's international exposition Expo '67. The following year an audience of 15,000 filled the Nutmeg Theatre, an improvised outdoor facility, in Saint George's in Grenada. The most exhausting outdoor performance was the December 1982 appearance at halftime during the football game at the Orange Bowl in Miami—the Miami Dolphins against the Minnesota Vikings—which was solemnly "dedicated to the people of the Caribbean and the dignitaries attending the 1982 Miami Conference on the Caribbean."[36] This dedication was significant, since it came in the middle of discussions about the Caribbean Basin Initiative, President Ronald Reagan's plan to develop the region within the American sphere of influence.[37] Outside of Caribbean capitals, the cities of New York and Moscow—two great cultural centers with enviable records of achievement in dance—have been perhaps the most sympathetic in their critical responses to the Company's varied offerings. But it has been the young audiences everywhere who proved the most spontaneous in their direct responses to the work.

The unofficial ambassadorial status of the National Dance Theatre Company was increased with each overseas tour, thus encouraging goodwill and substantial assistance from both the Jamaican government and the private sector as a matter of national pride. The national airline, the bauxite multinationals operating in the country, a number of banks, an international cigarette company with a local branch, and many other business firms have cosponsored overseas tours. The Company members employed in the private and public sectors are given leave of absence by their employers, usually with pay, to represent their country in these cultural exchange ventures.

The first overseas tour by the Company took place in 1963 at the Stratford Festival in Ontario, Canada. It was under the joint auspices of the Jamaican government and the Stratford Festival Foundation. Tom Patterson, the foundation's founder, had come to Jamaica searching for a group like the Trinidadian Little Carib Dancers, which the previous year had performed at the festival, that would add variety and a new dimension to the festival. The Company opened at the Avon Theatre on August 23, 1963, before a capacity audience headed by Lester Pearson, Canada's prime minister at the time. The Company garnered good critical notices, which allayed some of Patterson's original fears about failure.

This first Canadian tour brought the Company to the attention of the organizers of England's first Commonwealth Arts Festival, which took place in 1965.

Eddy Thomas and Rex Nettleford in an exuberant moment with Lady Molly Huggins, wife of a former governor of Jamaica. Critic Peter Williams, editor of England's prestigious dance magazine *Dance and Dancers*, is in the background. (*Syd Burke*)

A marriage on tour. Dorothy McFarlane, a dancer with the National Dance Theatre Company, congratulates colleague Andrea Nash on her marriage to Jamaican swimming star Paul Nash at the time the Company was engaged at Sadler's Wells in London.

The Company of over fifty dancers, singers, musicians, and technicians arrived in London on September 9 of that year. After the Kathakali classical Indian dance company was grounded in India because of the outbreak of a border war between India and Pakistan, the National Dance Theatre Company of Jamaica filled in, besides their regularly scheduled performances, appearing in front of capacity audiences in Cardiff, Liverpool, Coventry, Bournemouth, and London. The favorable notices and the broad audience appeal brought the Company further invitations to perform overseas. In 1967 at Montreal's Expo '67 the Company inaugurated the new Théâtre Port-Royale, playing to enthusiastic audiences. Theodore Sealy, the editor of Kingston's *Daily Gleaner*, who perceived the Company as an institution of growth in the newly independent nation, arranged for full coverage of the early tours abroad. He even sent Barbara Gloudon, one of his youngest and brightest reporters, to tour with the Company,

Louise Bennett, the great folklorist, entertainer, and poet, appeared with the Company on their 1963 tour to Stratford, Ontario. Supporting her is the Frats Quintet, a choral ensemble led by Winston White (far right). This well-known singing group, active at the time, performed with the National Dance Theatre Company from 1963 to 1966. (*Peter Smith*)

In 1965, Prince Philip, the duke of Edinburgh, visited the Company backstage after the opening performance in Cardiff, Wales, inaugurating the Commonwealth Arts Festival. (*Western Mail and Echo, Cardiff*)

and she sent back reassuring reports about the Company's foreign successes.

The National Dance Theatre Company's Caribbean tours—outside of Jamaica itself—were rewarding. The impact was instantaneous, promising a Caribbean future for the Company. Perhaps something in the dances implied an underlying unity within the entire Caribbean region. The first exposure was in 1965, when a small contingent of the Company went to Nassau as guests of the Nassau Civic Ballet at the invitation of Alex Zybine, one of the ballet company's codirectors, who had worked with the Ballet Russe de Monte Carlo and the Metropolitan Opera Ballet before taking up residence in Nassau. In April 1968 the Company went to Nassau again, this time with a full contingent of dancers. In 1969 Grenada hosted the Carifta Expo,[38] and at the last minute the Jamaican government decided to have the Company represent Jamaica. They performed to a record crowd in Saint George's at the Nutmeg Theatre, a temporarily erected outdoor facility.

The reception in Trinidad and Puerto Rico in 1971 confirmed the existence of shared aesthetic sensibilities throughout the region, although it was inevitable that a few of the urban middle-class intellectuals would accuse the Company of not being sociologically aggressive, which prompted from Derek Walcott one of the most insightful critiques ever made of the Company's work.[39] The political disturbances in Trinidad during February 1970 had attracted many converts to the black power movement and a nationalism rooted in African traditions. The National Dance Theatre Company apparently did not satisfy the ideological aims of these converts, although during the tour in August 1971 many critics did praise the Company's artistry in glowing terms. At the end of August the performances at the University of Puerto Rico were wildly received by the student

Lester Pearson, former prime minister of Canada, and Mrs. Pearson greet the Company backstage at the Avon Theatre after the opening performance of the Stratford tour in 1963.
(Peter Smith)

audiences, and the underlying Antillean identification became evident. In July 1972 the tour to Bermuda, at the invitation of the Bermuda Arts Council, was a success, despite the strained relations between the Jamaican working-class migrants and native Bermudians.

By the 1970s Cuba was projecting a Caribbean self-image, emphasizing its African as well as its Latin heritage. During the decade the National Dance Theatre Company made two tours to the island, with performances in Havana and Santiago on the first visit and solely in Havana on the second. Alicia Alonso, a legendary figure in Cuban ballet theater and a heroic image in terms of the country's revolution, visited the Company backstage at Havana's Teatro Lorca on opening night of the first visit. The reception was emotional, no doubt influenced by the strong bonds of friendship that had developed officially between Jamaica and Cuba. The Company also recognized a kindred spirit in the artists of the Danza Nacional de Cuba, which was promoting the same principles as the Jamaican Company, and of the Conjunto Folklórico.

It was during the first Caribbean Festival of Arts (Carifesta) in Georgetown, Guyana, in August 1972 that the Company seemed to have realized a genuine Caribbean aesthetic. Significantly the festival coincided almost exactly with the tenth anniversary of Jamaican independence and the formation of the National Dance Theatre Company. The Guyana experience was a liberating one, which prepared the Company psychologically for the difficulties encountered during its three-week season in London at the Sadler's Wells in September.

The Sadler's Wells run marked the second visit made by the Company to Great Britain. During the earlier visit, in 1965, the emphasis had been on showing off their abilities to their former colonizers; whereas the intention in 1972 was to attract the large West Indian immigrant population in London to the theater. The Sadler's Wells promotional machinery was slow in realizing that special approaches to publicity were needed to get the West Indians into this august hall. Hope Sealy, the Jamaica Tourist Board representative for Great Britain and Europe, brought a determination to the task which finally convinced the theater managers to release for sale in black neighborhoods a hundred tickets, a somewhat token number at that. It was the most challenging overseas undertaking by the Company up to that time. At stake was not only the impact the dance works had on British audiences generally but also the significance they held for the young black Britons of West Indian parentage, who were becoming a social problem for Britain. Their crises of identity might find some small relief in their brief contact with Caribbean cultural expressions which reflected their ancestral traditions. After the performances they flocked backstage to meet the dancers. Reggae and the blue beat were yet to fill the gap. Newspaper criticism ranged from strong praise to dismissal of the Company's artistic aspirations. The audiences themselves were uniform in their enthusiastic reaction. The hallowed por-

Edward Seaga, minister in charge of culture, poses with the Company in his Kingston office prior to the Company's first overseas tour, to Ontario's Stratford Festival in 1963. (*Daily Gleaner*)

The National Dance Theatre Company opens its 1983 New York dance season at the City Center Theater. It was the Company's fourth visit to New York City; previously they had appeared three times at the Brooklyn Academy of Music, twice at the invitation of Harvey Lichtenstein and once in collaboration with Marta Vega's Caribbean Cultural Center.

tals of the Sadler's Wells were challenged by the irreverent exuberance of the West Indian theatergoers, many of whom had rushed at the last minute to buy their tickets at the door.

Further overseas tours during the 1970s were undertaken with a bit more assurance. The 1975 appearance in the Palacio de Bellas Artes in Mexico City was the Company's second visit to that theater. In 1969 the Company had given seven performances there as well as three in the Teatro Degollado in Guadalajara. The 1975 tour was in conjunction with the state visit by the Jamaican prime minister, an example of new cultural agreements dictated by a policy of Third World collaboration. In 1969, just before the final performance, the Company was forced into a virtual strike action because of the Guadalajara impresario's refusal at first to pay contracted fees. In a dramatic turnabout during the 1975 run Luis Echeverría Álvarez, the president of Mexico, tried to convince the Company to remain three months to tour the whole country with all expenses paid. Unfortunately Company members could not stay away from their jobs for that length of time.

In 1976 an offer by the amiable Australian prime minister, Gough Whitlam, who had seen a performance of the Company in Kingston the year before, was accepted. The Company traveled halfway around the world to Sydney, Canberra, and Melbourne, playing to great notices. The Australian Elizabethan Theatre Trust was appointed by the government to manage the tour. Jeffrey Kovel, executive director of the trust and a former dancer with the London Festival Ballet, appreciated the technical and aesthetic requirements of the Company. This was of great help to the tour. Extremely good gate receipts offset the original generous outlay by the Australian government.

In the following year the Company toured the Federal Republic of Germany (West Germany) at the invitation of its government. The tour covered a period of two weeks with performances in West Berlin, Bonn, Aachen, Hamburg, Munich, and Frankfurt. But the problem of transportation resulted in a great learning experience for the entire Company, particularly the encounter with the East Germans at the entrance to the corridor leading from West Berlin through East Germany to the west. A busload of Company members, as guests of the West Berlin government, was kept waiting over two hours, to be processed by East German immigration officers, while other travelers, who had arrived later, were attended to first. An irate impresario and his two helpless assistants,[40] all West Germans, could do nothing about this humiliation. The Company sweated it out, finally being allowed to drive through to Bonn, where Keith Johnson, the Jamaican ambassador, was on hand to greet them. No less memorable was the German impresario's insatiable appetite for food and the fine restaurants he engaged for the Company's postperformance meals. His interest in the Company's personal needs was at times in inverse proportion to his ability to find a suitable theater for performance. The members were not amused when they ended up in Munich in the Zircus Krone with a stage that not only was unprepared but also reeked of odors of the elephants used in a recent circus performance there. Despite such trying circumstances, which may afflict any touring group, all members of the Company, convinced of their role as cultural

Company members listen attentively to Ian Hunter, director of Great Britain's Commonwealth Arts Festival, on his visit to Jamaica early in 1965 to scout for talent to participate in the first festival.

ambassadors, settled down and gave what was probably the most inspired performance of the entire German tour. Artists sometimes will alleviate their frustrations and anger through the best performance.

It was natural that the German Democratic Republic (East Germany) should also invite the National Dance Theatre Company on tour: Jamaica's diversification of its cultural contacts was a reflection of its diversified markets and loan sources. But the Company was never able to visit East Germany—or Hungary, which also expressed interest. In 1979, however, the Company did make a tour of a Communist nation, the Soviet Union, appearing in Moscow, Leningrad, and Kiev. Due to the well-organized machinery of the Soviet cultural ministry's sponsorship, many rewarding experiences awaited the Jamaicans. In the hotels they stayed in as well as the shops they entered, the Company members were struck by the deference paid them as artists. Many Russians seemed intrigued by the Jamaicans' description of themselves as "workers who dance" rather than "dancers who work." Marius Liepa, former star of the Bolshoi Ballet in Moscow, was fascinated by the Company's training exercises and warm-up classes, and members of the Moiseyev Dance Company flocked from their own classes in the

In front of London's Scala Theatre in 1965. Company principals (left to right) Barbara Requa, Eddy Thomas, Sheila Barnett (seated), and Yvonne daCosta pose for a mug shot of the dance *Dialogue for Three.* (*Syd Burke*)

The National Dance Theatre Company leaves Jamaica on one of its many overseas tours since 1962. Air Jamaica, the national airline, is a frequent cosponsor of these tours.

Tchaikovsky Concert Hall to watch Company rehearsals. Photographs in front of the Winter Palace in Leningrad, breathless leaps across the enormous stage of the Palace of Culture in Kiev, as well as the guarded references in Moscow to the news about the first defection by a Bolshoi Ballet star to the United States were just a few of the poignant memories of what was a historic tour for the Jamaicans.

The Company tours in North America have been among the most significant and highly rewarding. Because of the hundreds of thousands of West Indians residing in the United States, the Company members have often found a home away from home. The Company's North American debut in Ontario in 1963 followed by performances in Montreal four years later placed Canada in a special category. By the 1970s West Indian immigration to Toronto had greatly increased, and in May 1975 the Jamaican National League, led by Hugh Evelyn and Geof Brown, decided that perhaps the Company's appearance would help defuse some of the hostility developing among the conservative citizens of Toronto, who felt that their tranquil city life was being disturbed by the presence of hot-blooded black youths from the Caribbean. The league felt that the dance troupe would bring some understanding of Caribbean cultural traditions. The Company appeared at Toronto's O'Keefe Centre and in the Opera House of the National Arts Centre in Ottawa. In 1981 the Company returned to Canada, performing in Toronto at the Ryerson Theatre and in Kitchener-Waterloo at the Centre in the Square Theatre under the auspices of the Organisation for Caribbean Canadian Initiatives, directed by George Eaton of York University, a prominent Jamaican-born academic and public servant. As with the previous appearances in Toronto and Ottawa, the 1981 tour benefited immensely from the advice of Maud Fuller, a Jamaican teacher in Toronto who had earlier connections with the dance world in Jamaica. This visit to Canada included a number of workshops in Toronto as well as a lecture demonstration in the city of Hamilton for an audience mainly made up of young Canadians of West Indian background.

In the United States the National Dance Theatre Company had by this time established something of a reputation. The Company's American debut had been in May 1970, when it performed in the Miami Herald Travel Show at Dade County Auditorium under the auspices of *The Miami Herald*. Later that year the *Herald* invited the Company's artistic director and a group of dancers, accompanied by the musical director and the master drummer, back to Florida for a series of lecture demonstrations at the Dade County high schools. Two years later, at the end of April 1972, the Company returned to Miami, performing at Dade County Auditorium a second time, again under the auspices of *The Miami Herald*. The Company did not return to Miami until ten years later, at that time performing in the formal gardens of the Villa Vizcaya Museum and Gardens under the auspices of the Caribbean Central Action Committee for delegates attending the sixth annual Conference on Trade, Investment, and Development in the Caribbean.

A few of the tours to the United States were sponsored by American universities. In 1969 the Company was invited to Atlanta through the artist-in-residence program organized by Spelman College.[41] During this run the Company joined with the Spelman Glee Club in the December 3, 1969, commemoration ceremony honoring the memory of Martin Luther King, Jr., in the Sisters Chapel of the college. In 1976 the Company was the guest of another American university— Howard University in Washington, D.C. The visit was made possible by a grant from the Inter-American Foundation, which showed a keen interest in the cultural dynamics of Latin America and the Caribbean. Howard University's Center for Ethnic Music formally presented the National Dance Theatre Company in performances as well as the artistic director in a series of lectures on the history, politics, and cultural imperatives of the Caribbean region. Other cities, such as Philadelphia in 1974 and New Orleans in 1975, were visited by the Company under university or civic sponsorship.

The New York appearances between 1973 and 1980 offered both artistic and organizational success. In 1973 the Jamaican dance troupe made its New York debut in the Opera House of the Brooklyn Academy of Music, playing seven performances to capacity audiences. Harvey Lichtenstein, the energetic revitalizer of Brooklyn's major theater, knew about the Jamaican ensemble from its London appearances. Through Lichtenstein's faith and Air Jamaica's generosity the Company performed not only in 1973 but also in 1974, when a season of ten performances, along with a lecture demonstration at John Jay College of Criminal Justice, brought the Jamaicans spirited audience responses and critical acclaim. It was six years before a return visit to Brooklyn Academy materialized—this time under the auspices of the Visual Arts Research and Resource Center Relating to the Caribbean, directed by Marta Vega.[42] She was assisted by a strategic contribution from the Jamaica Progressive League, chaired at the time by Carl Rodney. The three sold-out performances at the Academy, which were given over the 1980 Thanksgiving holiday weekend, were preceded by a stint in Macy's Thanksgiving Day parade, with a dance selection emphasizing the most meaningful expressions of life in the Caribbean. The selection—an excerpt from *The Crossing*—had actually been made by the American director of the parade's show, who felt the American public needed an image of Jamaica different from the stereotype of an exotic tourist island.

In September 1983 there were five performances at the City Center Theater, the Company's first experience in a Manhattan theater. The audience response was no less than that at the Brooklyn Academy, and the critical reception by the prestigious *New York Times* was rewarding. It was a definite artistic success.

The sponsoring organization, the Caribbean Educational and Cultural Institute, suffered from their inexperience in dealing with New York's theater labor codes. The institute also did not fully appreciate the financial implications of a Caribbean audience that traditionally does not book in advance, preferring to buy tickets at the door. Regrettably the final Sunday performance had to be canceled. With less than the anticipated assistance from certain Jamaican government agencies operating out of New York,[43] the institute experienced what many dance companies in New York have—artistic success but financial loss. Yet the Jamaican dance troupe had some advantage because of the sense of celebration on the occasion of the twenty-first anniversary of Jamaican independence. The presence in New York of over a half million Jamaicans and other West Indians was also a promotional asset. The run was actually received with great exuberance, and a return visit was offered at the time.

The NDTC Singers had made independent tours to the United States. They received critical acclaim and great audience response wherever they performed. Missouri and Chicago saw them as part of the Jamaica Tourist Board's promotional efforts, and they appeared in 1979 in New York at Carnegie Hall as part of Marta Vega's Caribbean Festival. The singers also visited Mexico in early 1980 as participants in a conference on Afro-American and Caribbean traditional music sponsored by the Organization of American States.

In January 1983 the full Company traveled to Venezuela at the invitation of the Venezuelan government, which since the early 1970s had grown closer to Jamaica and the anglophone Caribbean in general. As early as June 1971 the director of the National Institute of Culture and Fine Arts in Caracas had written the Company's artistic director expressing interest in having the National Dance Theatre Company visit Caracas. At that time, before OPEC gained its financial power, the letter from Venezuela predictably stated that the institute's budgetary situation was unfavorable and they would have to know the specific conditions before they could risk a definite decision. By 1982 circumstances had indeed changed. The Venezuelan government invited the Company to perform in Caracas at the government's expense. The Company gave five enthusiastically received performances in Caracas, including those on television and at the Central University, as well as in the Teatro Municipal in front of Venezuela's president. The event marked the inauguration of Venezuela's bicentennial celebrations of the birth of Simón Bolívar, the Latin American liberator. During his revolutionary struggle against Spanish rule, Bolívar had taken refuge in Jamaica and Haiti and had written his famous liberation letter from Kingston.[44] Venezuelans have never forgotten this debt, just as Cubans still remember that Jamaica once offered a haven to their revolutionary hero José Martí. The Company was well received in Venezuela, the tour confirming the view that a deeper understanding would help promote the developing relations between Hispanic America and the Black Crescent, which is how some Latins refer to the archipelago of English-speaking islands with their different political and cultural orientation from the rest of Latin America.

The international exposure of the National Dance Theatre Company had far-reaching implications for both the dance troupe itself and Jamaica as a nation. Official support by Jamaica's diplomatic representatives abroad was vital to these tours. Many Jamaican officials should be cited for their profound understanding of how the foreign tours by a group like the National Dance Theatre Company was in the best interest of the country's image, among them, Keith Johnson (ambassador to the United Nations, later to Germany and to the United States), Ivo DeSouza (deputy high commissioner in Canada and later high commissioner in Trinidad), Reg Phillips (deputy high commissioner in London and later ambassador to Venezuela), Lloyd Wright and Heather Royes (chargé d'affaires and cultural attaché, respectively, in Mexico City), Gerald Groves (consul general in New York), Martin Mordecai (deputy high commissioner in Port-of-Spain), Evadne Coye (consular in Caracas), Peter Bartlett (deputy head of the Mission to the United Nations), Lorrel Bruce (consul general in New York), and Lance Evans (veteran information officer for the United States).

Their personal understanding and sympathy stood in sharp contrast to a diplomatic colleague who on hearing of the Company's plan to include the work *Pocomania* in the 1965 program for the Commonwealth Arts Festival in England objected vociferously because he felt that the piece would offer the English a distorted impression about the newly independent nation. He died before the Company reached London, averting what might have been a serious problem. Edward Seaga, the minister in charge of culture, viewed the repertoire of the touring Company from a slightly different angle. In 1963 he had expressed concern that the dance works being taken to the Stratford Festival in Ontario included too little of native Jamaican material and too much of other West Indian elements. But the Company's objectives had to be seen in perspective, not only in historical terms but also in terms of the new nation's social texture and its organic connections with the wider Caribbean region. Overseas tours continued to test whether the Company had something unique to say about the Caribbean experience or anything special to add to the world of dance through its own technical achievements. Paradoxically the local Jamaican audiences had to be educated about their own dance, not only the content but also the vocabulary underlying the art as well as the aesthetics of style and technique.

The Company at Home

Twenty-one seasons of dance at the Little Theatre in Kingston began with only nine performances in 1962 and had increased to thirty-two in 1982. The audiences ranged from 50 faithfuls on many nights in the early 1960s to capacity houses of 600 at the Little Theatre and 5,000 in the National Arena during the 1970s.

A comparison of statistics for two periods—one in the 1960s and the other in the 1970s—shows encouraging figures for increased audiences, both nationally and internationally, viewing the Company's work. For the year 1969 the figures recorded by the Company[45] show that in Kingston during the limited season at the Little Theatre the audiences totaled 5,000 with an additional 4,000 viewing a special performance in the National Arena during National Heritage Week. During this year tours to Mexico City, Guadalajara, Atlanta, and Miami meant that 19,500 people outside the country were able to view the Company's work. There was an obvious discrepancy in the ratio of overseas audiences to local ones; the task facing the Company was to find a way of offering all Jamaicans the opportunity of experiencing the Company's work with some regularity between seasons.

The figures for the period covering August 1974 to July 1975 showed some improvement. Besides the 11,000 viewers for the regular 1974 season in Kingston, the Company also put on a miniseason in the city, which brought out 1,500, as well as a special performance for Julius Kambarage Nyerere, president of Tanzania, which was performed in front of an audience of 2,600. There were 4,900 viewers during this period in rural performances (Montego Bay, Falmouth, and Seaforth). On foreign tours—both in the Caribbean region and in North America, including Havana and Santiago in Cuba, New Orleans, Ottawa, Toronto, and Mexico City—the audiences totaled about 25,400. The Company's appearance on television on the "Bill Moyers Journal," viewed by millions in the United States and Canada, makes the year even more impressive in terms of audience exposure.[46]

The Jamaican audiences expanded not merely in numbers but in terms of class origin, social background, and age range. By the end of the 1970s a new generation of young people was attending not only dance theater but other theatrical performances as well. Besides the regular season in Kingston, a dozen or more miniseasons and isolated performances in the capital in addition to appearances in rural Jamaica brought the Company within wider reach of audiences on the island.

Special occasions have sometimes exposed the Company to audiences that might never had made it to the Little Theatre. Both the Company dancers and the NDTC Singers, for example, have been pressed into service by church congregations. There was a history-making appearance in 1968 at the Saint Andrew Scots Kirk in Kingston, which was commemorated later during the Company's twentieth anniversary celebrations in 1982. Beginning in 1980, an annual Easter Sunday morning concert of movement and music attracted capacity audiences to the Little Theatre, even at the early hour of six. During Easter 1975 the Company offered works such as *The Rope and the Cross*, *Homage*, *Alleluia*, and *Glory Road* as part of church services around the nation's capital; *Alleluia*, created specifically for the church services, was not part of the standard repertoire.

President Samora Machel of Mozambique greets Rex Nettleford after a 1977 performance in Machel's honor at Jamaica House in Kingston. Right of the president is Michael Manley, Jamaica's prime minister at the time; Arnold Bertram, minister of state for culture, is behind Nettleford.

During a historic state visit in October 1977, President Fidel Castro of Cuba meets with the Company dancers after a performance at Jamaica House in Kingston. Dancer Fitzroy Hunt shakes hands with Castro; also pictured (on Hunt's left) are Patsy Ricketts, Barbara Requa, and Melanie Graham.

The 1968 appearance in Saint Andrew Scots Kirk, featuring *Ave Verum* and *Misa Criolla*, was the first time in Jamaican history that dance was allowed in church as an integral part of the worship. The Anglican bishop, who came with a team of clergymen to the Company studio to view *Misa Criolla* in rehearsal, thought the dance work was a "trifle vigorous." So the Presbyterians took it instead.

Frequently in recent decades newly independent nations have been chosen as the site for state visits and international conferences, and Jamaica is no exception. State visits by various members of the British royal family and by foreign dignitaries offered yet other opportunities for the Company to gain recognition. There were particularly memorable official occasions in which the National Dance Theatre Company participated. The Commonwealth Parliamentary Association Conference held in Jamaica in 1964 had an influence on the government's decision to have the Company represent the nation in the Commonwealth Arts Festival in Great Britain the following year. In 1975 the appearance before thirty government leaders in Kingston attending the biennial Commonwealth Heads of Government Meeting resulted in an invitation from the Australian prime minister. Performances in 1977 in connection with the visits of Third World leaders Samora Machel of Mozambique and Fidel Castro of Cuba meant a second visit by the Company to Cuba, for the eleventh World Youth Festival held in Havana in 1978.

Because of the nation's strong position as representative of Third World demands for social justice and a new international economic order, many special events, which the Company participated in, were scheduled in Jamaica. In 1976 the Company performed in front of the historic Rose Hall Great House in Montego Bay for an audience of over 2,000, comprising the delegates and their Jamaican hosts to the meeting of the Inter-American Development Bank. On December 10, 1968, the Company appeared before an audience of 4,000 in the National Arena on the occasion of Human Rights Day, when the Jamaican government presented the specially created Marcus Garvey Prize posthumously to Martin Luther King, Jr., who had been assassinated earlier that year. His wife, Coretta King, accepted the prize. Throughout the 1970s the Company performed before many international conferences hosted by Jamaica, for example, the Latin American Energy Organization,[47] the International Education Conference, the Caribbean Ministers of Health Conference, and the Commonwealth Heads of Government Meeting. It was at this 1975 meeting of Commonwealth leaders that gave the Company an opportunity to have as guest artist Clive Thompson, the internationally acclaimed Jamaican dancer who was then a member of the Alvin Ailey American Dance Theater in New York.

Great Britain's Queen Mother receives dancers of the Company after a performance in February 1965 at King's House in Kingston. Standing next to her are Sir Clifford Campbell, the governor-general, and Greta Fowler, cofounder of the Little Theatre Movement.

Queen Elizabeth and Prince Philip are introduced to the Company on one of their many state visits to Jamaica since independence.

On August 5, 1983, the Company performed before an audience of 25,000 in the National Stadium as part of the nation's twenty-first anniversary of independence. It was, of course, the Company's twenty-first birthday as well, and the event was viewed by thousands on television, which helped imprint on the national consciousness the significance of the work created during those years. The piece performed was the 1974 homage to Jimmy Cliff, entitled *Tribute to Cliff*, with the duet at the end danced by Barry Moncrieffe and Melanie Graham to Cliff's popular song "Many Rivers to Cross" from the movie *The Harder They Come*.[48] Earlier in the week the Company had presented *The Crossing* to an audience of 5,000 people in the National Arena as part of the twenty-first anniversary *Mello-Go-Round* presentation directed by Joyce Campbell.[49] At that event Clive Thompson, as guest artist, performed "I Got to Be Ready" from Alvin Ailey's *Revelations*.

Another means of gaining audience exposure for the Company at home was through the lecture demonstration. In the early 1960s these were presented with great frequency throughout Jamaica. Because of the development of other Jamaican dance ensembles by the late 1960s, the Company began to cut back its

The 1968 Company appearance at the Scots Kirk in Kingston pioneered the presentation of dance in church services in Jamaica. Yvonne daCosta and Rex Nettleford perform in *Ave Verum*, choreographed by Neville Black.

work in rural areas. But lecture demonstrations were still offered to visiting groups, schools, and other special groups, ranging from civic organizations to meetings of journalists and historians, including a conference of Caribbean history scholars for whom the Company conducted a lecture demonstration in early 1983 on the historical sources of such Company works as *Back to Bach*, *Ni— Woman of Destiny*, *The Crossing*, and suites of Caribbean songs. The lecture demonstration was also an important complement to performances overseas, where the specific orientation of Company works often needed some clarification.

Films and videotapes were another important means of extending the Company's exposure beyond theaters and concert halls. Since 1965, when a short feature was shot during the Commonwealth Arts Festival for the British Broadcasting Corporation,[50] the Company has been featured in numerous films and television broadcasts at home and abroad, especially in the United States, Canada, Great Britain, Cuba, and the Soviet Union, where a specially televised performance was taped in Moscow for transmission throughout the country. British-made documentaries on Jamaican social development which featured the National Dance Theatre Company also brought the background of the Company into perspective for those who had not seen the group perform. One of the most significant of these documentaries was Vanya Kewly's *Rastaman* in the BBC "Everyman" television series. The dance *Court of Jah*, choreographed to the music of reggae superstar Bob Marley, was used in this film to demonstrate the mood of depression in the urban ghettos of Kingston.

Rastaman was never publicly shown on Jamaican television because of the contractual agreements with the Rastafarian participants, who, having smoked marijuana openly in the film and spoken explicitly against Babylon[51] and the

Dame Peggy van Pragh (right), artistic director of the Australian Ballet who visited Jamaica in May 1967, is welcomed by Eddy Thomas and Yvonne daCosta.

Olatunji (left), the Nigerian drummer, visits the National Dance Theatre Company in April 1975. (*Eric Tello*)

police, were afraid of reprisals. Safer ground, however, had been covered in 1968 by Mike Bukht of the Jamaica Broadcasting Corporation when he produced a film on the creation of *Two Drums for Babylon*, a 1964 dance piece about the defiant Rastafarians, who were battling for recognition at home and had not yet attracted the serious attention they later did, even abroad. This television film, as well as footage of other dance works in the archives of the Jamaica Information Service, is an invaluable record of the Company's early achievements. The radio, through interviews, critiques, and panel discussions on the arts, also informed the public about the Company's work. Archie Lindo's "Lively Arts" radio program for the Jamaica Broadcasting Corporation contributed much to this. Through their three recordings the NDTC Singers have increased the popularity of the Company as well.

For the reading public in Jamaica the National Dance Theatre Company also began to take on special meaning. The newspapers carried not only critical notices on the annual seasons, but regularly during the year there were also feature articles and photographs, which educated the public about the aims and work of the Company and about dance in general. Throughout the 1960s, in the wake of independence, *The Daily Gleaner*'s editorial efforts to assist cultural institutions and their support of the arts in general complemented the encouragement of the Jamaica Broadcasting Corporation and the Jamaica Information Service. In addition, *Roots and Rhythms*, the history of the first six years of the National Dance Theatre Company, was published in 1969, and national and international journals carried articles on the Jamaican experiment in dance.

By the beginning of the 1970s the Company had established an international reputation, which enhanced its legitimacy at home. National respect and recognition were given not only to the group as a whole but also to individual members because of their own achievements. Sheila Barnett, Joyce Campbell, George Carter, Maria LaYacona, Joyce Lalor, Eddy Thomas, and Marjorie Whylie all received the coveted Musgrave Medal as well as the Centenary Medal from the august Institute of Jamaica. Whylie and Barnett also received the Prime Minister's Award, presented during the 1983 ceremonies celebrating the twenty-first anniversary of independence. Other recipients of the Centenary Medal were Bert Rose, Barbara Requa, Monica McGowan, Barbara Kaufmann, Yvonne daCosta, Ronan Critchlow, and Verona Ashman. George Carter received the nation's Order of Distinction for his continuing work in theater arts, while Rex Nettleford received the Order of Merit for work of international distinction in the fields of cultural development, theater arts (especially dance), and adult education. Nettleford was also awarded the 1981 Musgrave Gold Medal for his work in cultural development, particularly in the area of the dance.

In 1972 on the occasion of the National Dance Theatre Company's tenth anniversary, *The Daily Gleaner* in its lead editorial acknowledged the impor-

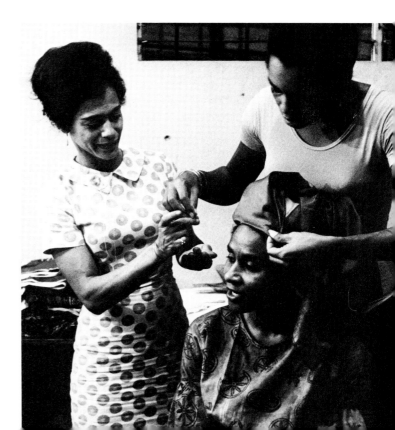

Wardrobe mistress Barbara Kaufmann (left) and Barbara Requa assemble a headtie on Sheila Barnett for the dance work *African Scenario*.

tance of the Company as a reflection of a national cultural expression, at a time when reggae was yet to make its mark internationally as a Jamaican phenomenon: "Along with political and economic progress and advancement, the development of the cultural side of the Jamaican nation has come in for attention, although it cannot truly be said that this has taken any great national form. Jamaican painting and sculpture have taken on a recognizable 'style.' The same, regrettably, cannot be said in entirety for Jamaican music and Jamaican literature. So it is in the dance, really, that perhaps the fullest and finest flowering of the Jamaican artistic talent has been seen. In performances inside and outside of Jamaica, the National Dance Theatre Company has shown that it is something indigenous, something born out of the roots and rhythms of the people."[52] Perhaps the most distinctive tribute to the National Dance Theatre Company, as a national institution mirroring its contribution to the art of the dance and to Jamaican cultural life in general, was the issue in July 1974 of a series of commemorative postal stamps featuring the Company.

For the celebrations of the Company's twentieth anniversary there were not only laudatory messages from political leaders, major artists, and the general public; the Company also gained the first Outstanding Achievement Award presented by the newly established Royal Bank Foundation. The Company used the cash award to form the basis of its Development Fund. The Jamaican private sector, which had a tradition of awarding the Company grants and commissioning new works, continued its support. Even controversy over the Company's future signified the importance of the group in national life. Above all, the continued support from audiences, which have learned to become discriminating without being discouraging and enthusiastic without being indulgent, indicated the extent of public respect and recognition given the National Dance Theatre Company in its native country.

The National Dance Theatre Company and the School of Dance

The development of the Company must also be measured in part by the establishment of a dance school as an instrument of transmitting the aims and commitment of the Company. It is mandatory that a dance company have a natural source for replenishing its membership. The Eddy Thomas Dance Workshop, where many founding members taught, acted as an unofficial source of recruits for the first few years of the Company's existence. After 1968, when Eddy Thomas left the National Dance Theatre Company, the Company decided

jamaica

THE NATIONAL DANCE THEATRE COMPANY OF JAMAICA

The National Dance Theatre Company was formed in 1962 to create an atmosphere in which dancers could create and perform works of high standards ; to encourage the local public to appreciate the idiom of dance ; to research and utilise authentic dance-forms and movement patterns from Jamaica and from the West Indies. During the relatively short period since its foundation it has achieved something of a reputation for artistic excellence taking its repertoire from authentic folk material. The entirely Jamaican cast has performed extensively overseas and has met with unqualified success.

The National Dance Theatre Company is a voluntary group which has managed, not only to stay alive, but also to succeed as a cultural body. Financial support for the Company has come from commercial organisations, from the Government in cases of cultural exchange programmes with other countries, and from individuals. The Company has managed to preserve its amateur status and remain an independent cultural body, but with professional standards.

The government of Jamaica honored the Company on its tenth anniversary with an issue of four commemorative stamps, featuring such works as *Journeys, Promenade,* and *Misa Criolla.* Dancers portrayed on the stamps are Bert Rose, Barry Moncrieffe, Gertrude Sherwood, Rex Nettleford, and Yvonne daCosta.

to set up a school that would not only satisfy its immediate needs but also train choreographers, instructors, and dance educators who would serve the wider society in its cultural needs.

The opportunity of establishing a school presented itself in 1970, when Sheila Barnett and Barbara Requa, Company members who were also codirectors of the Contemporary Dance Centre, along with Bert Rose, who had just opened a small studio of his own, teamed up under the direction of the National Dance Theatre Company to found the Jamaica School of Dance. At first classes were conducted in a shed built by the Company on property donated by the Jamaican government. Sheila Barnett had already been in contact with a group of enthusiastic teachers committed to using dance in the educational system in order to augment physical education courses. Barbara Requa worked with young students, while Bert Rose organized his classes along conventional studio lines for people interested in dance as a performing art. Together they offered high-quality training in technique—such as Caribbean and specifically Jamaican folk dance, modern dance, African and Afro-Caribbean dance movement, classical ballet, and educational dance—as well as study in composition and repertoire and general exercises for muscle control and poise. Other instructors in those early years were the Company's ballet mistress, Yvonne daCosta, and principal dancers Dorothy Fraser and Barry Moncrieffe, along with the Company's artistic director, who also provided overall guidance.

By 1975 the government of Jamaica decided to establish the Cultural Training Centre, under the auspices of the Institute of Jamaica, which would coordinate the national cultural training schools—those devoted to art, drama, dance, and music. At that time the Jamaica School of Dance was formally incorporated into this national training center. Sheila Barnett, former education officer and by now a reputable dance educator, became the director of the Jamaica School of Dance, Barbara Requa the administrator and head of the junior division, and Bert Rose the senior instructor. The Institute of Jamaica provided the infrastructure of physical facilities and administrative staff. The National Dance Theatre

The first graduates of the Jamaica School of Dance include (back row, left to right) Beverly Daley Lewis, Maria Smith, Grace Hamilton, Patsy Ricketts (Company principal), and (front row) Yvette Duncan-Lockhart, Gloria Grandison, Joy Gordon, Jean Summers (Company dancer). (*Rooney Chambers*)

Young students at the Jamaica School of Dance. (*Institute of Jamaica*)

Company—with critical accounting assistance from Edgar Jones, who chaired the school's first Board of Management after 1975—continued to guide the school until 1982 through an exchange of skills and mutual sharing. Most of the present Company members are graduates of the school.

The Company raised funds from the Inter-American Foundation[53] to develop a special project within the School of Dance. The purpose of the project, which lasted from 1977 to 1981, was to provide the country with "cultural agents" who, equipped with a body of discrete knowledge of the dance, would teach children and adolescents, preparing them for daily living. The emphasis was not to create a bunch of barely competent technicians but to foster creativity and invention. Each participant was given individual attention, with the student's own experiences taken into account. The school's full-time staff had already been selected for their general skills, and the plan was to produce instructors who would then offer the Jamaican educational system qualified teachers conceived as motivators of creative talent. In other words the School of Dance was also serving as a teacher-training college. The presence of innovative instructors is still badly needed in Jamaica's primary and secondary school systems as well as in other parts of the Caribbean to which the facilities of the School of Dance and the entire Cultural Training Centre are open.

Another result of the special project has been a codified system of training and a strong curriculum for further development, not only in the School of Dance itself, which offers a four-year diploma course and short certificate courses for teachers and performers, but also in the educational system at the primary and secondary levels. The project offered the pilot group intense training through a new curriculum geared toward preparing dance teachers and choreographers with a more rigorous intellectual grounding in related fields. The curriculum included dance techniques, history of dance, choreography, theory and methods of education, research methods, anatomy and health sciences, studies in Jamaican and Caribbean history and culture, and studies in the related arts. There was a special emphasis on the cultural background of the environment, thus young students were exposed to the richness of their own traditions. It is in this area that the work of the cultural agents had to set the pace for the future work of the School of Dance by building a base for continued experimentation in a movement vocabulary faithful to the realities of Caribbean life without ignoring the rich fund of other dance traditions or the role of dance in the development of all civilizations.

The project produced published instructional material, the result of fieldwork by the pilot group. Publication was naturally done under the auspices of the publication department of the Institute of Jamaica, which is the repository of the nation's folkloric and cultural materials. Sheila Barnett and Cheryl Ryman have been prolific in producing such material.

The leadership of the National Dance Theatre Company is committed to the proposition that in developing countries there is a great need to uncover processes that will more easily release the populace—especially the young generation—from the scourge of dependency, which often stifles an individual in making the necessary decisions that will lead to greater self-reliance and creative daring. The limited experience within Jamaica proves that exposure from an early age to creative responsibilities engenders in young people a spirit of independence, self-assurance, and a sensibility of excellence. This has certainly been the case with the dance. A professional national Company, run on an amateur basis, has been nurtured with dedication, gaining a respected international reputation. The Company has also won great favor with the young, evidenced by the annual festival competitions, which attract thousands of young participants from all over Jamaica.

The work in the primary and secondary school systems has been the responsibility of the Jamaican government through the Ministry of Education and the Festival Office. The National Dance Theatre Company, the Department of Extra-

Mural Studies at the University of the West Indies, and, since 1975, the Jamaica School of Dance have also contributed their efforts at building character and instilling a sense of self-discipline, as well as exposing Jamaican youth to the richness of their heritage. There is often a pattern discernible in developing countries in which each generation starts from scratch without the benefit of the great store of experiences that preceded it. It is therefore important that this valuable work is not lost. Although the activities of the National Dance Theatre Company of Jamaica shall continue, the field of dance needs other dimensions in education to ensure that dance creators, performers, instructors, critics, and audiences are continuously supplied to the nation. The Company will continue to take initiatives to establish stronger foundations in the area of training, in order to assure future generations, during the normal course of education and socialization, a deep knowledge of their cultural heritage and an awareness of the potentials for continuing growth. The Jamaica School of Dance, the Company's gift to the nation, was designed to achieve much of this.

Plantation Revelry (Nettleford, 1963). Nineteenth-century Jamaican women return from finishing school in England and reacclimatize themselves to Jamaican society through creolized dance and music.

3 · The Repertoire

The repertoire of the National Dance Theatre Company developed during two decades into a collection of wide-ranging works drawing upon the myriad sources available to its originators. Artistic congruence and stylistic unity have been sought out without losing the spontaneity and organic texture that are features of the original sources. Variously described, the works are dance dramas, staged rituals based on traditional rites extant in Jamaican and Caribbean society, Creole dances that are based on the pantomimic recreational play of a people greatly influenced by Europe and Africa, and pure dance pieces exploring movement for its own sake. Like the dance dramas, the pure movement pieces also exploit a variety of techniques—dance theater mirroring European classical ballet, American modern dance, which strikes responsive chords in the Caribbean peoples, and Afro-Caribbean modes stemming from ancestral patterns of movement in Jamaica and wherever Africa has met Europe in the Americas.

Underlying the categories of technique are the themes and content of the works; the music, either as an integrated score or as ambient background; and style, which is distinctive enough to defy the impositions of dance theater classifications that pigeonhole companies into classical ballet (Europe's invention), modern dance (America's innovation), and ethnic (everybody else's indulgence). The National Dance Theatre Company is interesting—even exasperating—precisely because all three of these traditions might be integrated into one or another of their dance works.

Over one hundred works have been created for the Company.[1] In a breakdown of the dances choreographed by the original founding members, Rex Nettleford was responsible for over forty pieces, and Eddy Thomas had created eleven works before leaving the Company in 1967; Nettleford and Thomas choreographed two dances jointly. Sheila Barnett has choreographed seventeen dance works, Neville Black ten, Bert Rose eight, and Barbara Requa two. Other members of the Company have over the years produced isolated works: Thomas Pinnock and Patsy Ricketts each choreographed two, Tony Wilson two (plus a short solo), and Jackie Guy one (also a solo) in addition to a short sequence in one of Nettleford's major pieces. As guest choreographers, the American John Jones and the Cuban Eduardo Rivero each created three full-length works, and Clive Thompson produced one. Alvin Ailey, who did not choreograph directly for the Company, allowed excerpts from *Revelations* to be performed by the Company, with Clive Thompson as guest artist. From an earlier era came one short piece by Eyrick Darby, who had worked with Ivy Baxter in the 1950s. Lavinia Williams provided the raw material for a few sequences in the Afro-Caribbean dance suites assembled by Nettleford and Thomas in the early days.

Themes and Content

Thematic classification may not be the most satisfactory way of describing a dance company's repertoire, but such an approach in the case of the National Dance Theatre Company is valuable since the Company has been not only articulating dance as an art but also shaping a new style of dance theater out of a particular people's cultural sensibilities. Besides a few miscellaneous pieces—such as certain interludes and solos—which are not conveniently categorized, the major themes may be broken down as follows: social commentary, matriarchy, African influences, religion and ritual, history and legend, plantation America, dance as movement, and love. The complexity of theme in some works allows them to be discussed in more than one category.

SOCIAL COMMENTARY

Through the Company's consciously intense interaction with Jamaican society, social commentary—itself a traditional mode of artistic expression in

Married Story (Nettleford, 1970). An ambitious mother-in-law rejects a poor country boy as her daughter's suitor.

Games of Arms (Thomas, 1963). The superpowers isolated by a cold war, a commentary on the world situation. (*Daily Gleaner*)

mento, calypso, proverbs, and allegorical stories—is a dominant theme. Foremost are the dance works that were inspired by the native Creole customs and legends. In a celebratory mood, with humor masking the message, these works are immediately pleasurable because of the easily identifiable symbols and pantomimic characterizations. The dances are artfully manipulated in group patterns and solo turns; they are consciously arranged but retain the spontaneity of the traditional folk forms that are their sources.

Plantation Revelry, choreographed in 1963 by Rex Nettleford, was the first example of this genre. The dance, which takes place in the nineteenth century, opens at the pier, where friends and workers from the family plantation gather to greet Miss Amelia, returning from England. Her arrival is awaited with excitement, and her old Nanny sings a folk melody recalling the pleasurable moments they spent together before her charge was sent to England to be educated. The second scene opens on the front lawn of the great plantation mansion. The old butler brings Amelia something to eat, while Amelia's friends greet her in a dance reminiscent of the country jigs of the period. Two working women try to attract her attention, while young men amuse her with a dance in which they imitate the European gentlemen of the period. One of them acts out a mock courtship with her, much to the annoyance of her Nanny. Some of her old

The King Must Die (Nettleford, 1968). The mob turns on the leader and murders him.

friends, dressed up in the costumes of Haitian set-girls, show off their attire. The men return disguised in jonkonnu (John Canoe)[2] costumes, and the revels, heralding her return, end in frolic.[3]

The work was often misunderstood and it is instructive to see how someone other than the choreographer interpreted the narrative. The poet and playwright Dennis Scott, at the time also a dancer in the Company, offered a perceptive analysis:

On the surface the dance is a lighthearted acceptance of the house slave attitude at its worst. A coloured Jamaican girl, thoroughly Europeanized, is the darling of the black society, and the choreographer seems implicitly to accept the rightness of it all. One is not surprised that the first reaction of a black-think audience in Atlanta should have been shock and veiled hostility. But a curious thing happens as we watch the dance. The movements of the girl are at first balletic, European, delicate; in sharp contrast to the more violent, naturalistic gestures of the jealous women, the clumsy, affectionate waiter of whom they make fun. But gradually her movement changes, the dynamics and the very steps of her dances undergo a transformation. She is amused by the mocking parody offered by the young men of white behaviour; she is entranced by the flirtation of the young buck who comes courting; the voice of the drum enters again and again, and quickens her involvement in the folk movement around her. From being the dominant figure in the ballet, she becomes obedient as all the others to the pulse and earthiness of the dances. Haltingly, the *whitened* mulatto attempts to join in with her friends. Finally with the entrance of the mysterious, capering, vaguely menacing John Canoe dancers, she becomes again truly Jamaican, moving as they do, with them, dancing beside the young buck who caught her fancy earlier—he is now masked, significantly enough, as the chief of the dancers, Actor Boy. The ripple-backed rites of the John Canoe proclaim a triumph over Europe. . . . At the end all are frozen flat-backed in a crouch (facing the audience), which is a return to an African movement pattern and an image of watchful protectiveness over the girl in their midst. For those who approach the experience of *Plantation* with their eyes open, it is an assertion of ultimate triumph for our way of movement, our way of life; the tribe reclaims its stray child, and with masked and riotous rite celebrates the permanence of its traditions in the face of Eurocentrism. *Plantation* is a wish fulfillment maybe—it is not always possible to recapture the exile; but it is also an affirmation of faith in the strength, the vitality and the value of the folk tradition and the common community.[4]

Two of the dancers themselves, influenced by the black power movement they were introduced to in New York, felt that the work perpetuated black stereotypes, and a member of the Atlanta audience saw it as a paean to Uncle Tomism.[5] The Jamaican critic Norman Rae dismissed the work as too reminiscent of the American South,[6] forgetting that the Caribbean—with its great mansions, grinning but cunning slaves, gracious plantation mistresses, and revelry masking a serious battle for power in which the slaves finally rule while the masters govern—is definitely a part of plantation America. Yet *Plantation Revelry*

Backlash (Nettleford, 1975). A prisoner's revenge against police brutality.

The Visitor (Nettleford, 1982). A depiction of the new superpower interest, in the guise of a gentleman visitor, in the Caribbean.

revealed something more fundamental: in the final analysis the patterns of life in the Caribbean today directly descend from the slave period.

In the same vein of folk narrative, but with less pointed comment, was Eddy Thomas's *Country Wedding* (1964), which he took with him when he left the Company. It was replaced by *Married Story* (1970), which focuses on a greedy mother-in-law who wants the best—meaning a rich suitor—for her daughter. A good marriage signifies economic security in any class; yet the entire village supports the daughter in her preference for a local boy. The narrative dictates the dance movement as does the turn-of-century setting in rural Jamaica. *Dance Time in Cascade* (1964), another work with a Creole background, used costumes based on Haitian set-girls' outfits designed by the nineteenth-century artist Isaac Mendes Belisario. The quadrille was the source of the movements devised by Joyce Campbell, whose deep knowledge of traditional dance informed the work with authenticity.

There were many other suites of exhibition Creole dances, celebrating folk movement for the sheer joy of motion or for showing off manly vigor, feminine charm and coquetry, or the tension inherent in love encounters and mock quarrels. They bore such titles as *Afro–West Indian Suite* (1962), *French West Indian Suite* (1962), and *Caribbean Suite* (1980). *Character Sketches* (1976) acted out folk songs sung by the singers on stage, as did *Cantos* (1969), Neville Black's witty piece complete with a caricature exit of linked-arm swans. These social commentaries drew on the wit and wisdom of the rural folk people, who often reveal their cogent views on society through songs, stories, and proverbs. The dance suites were assembled in the spirit of this time-honored tradition. The

All God's Children (Nettleford, 1969). The drug culture as social leveler among uptowners and downtowners.

Two Drums for Babylon (Nettleford, 1964, 1980). The defection of middle-class youths into the Rastafari movement.

Rockstone Debate (Nettleford, 1981). A popular government minister, Pearnel Charles, visits backstage to meet Carl Bliss, his look-alike singer protagonist in this political farce by Rex Nettleford (left).

comedic quality of the genre made such dances a favorite with audiences throughout the 1960s and 1970s.

Despite some criticism that Company works in the early years lacked depth, there were a number of dances that addressed profound social problems. Eddy Thomas had in fact dealt with the cold war theme in *Games of Arms* (1963). Set in a children's playground, it was colorfully costumed and featured such antics as American football players in a huddle. *The Times* (London) found in it "wit and sophistication"[7]; Jamaican audiences laughed knowingly at the dangerous folly of the world's superpowers. Dance works like *The King Must Die*, *Backlash*, and *The Visitor* were, on the other hand, more solemn in their approach to the abuses of political power. *The King Must Die* (1968), set to Art Blakey's jazz suite *Africa Beat*, is a good example of this kind of approach. The confluence of separate interests of an ambitious queen mother behind a weak son who becomes the king provided the ingredients for an intense dramatic work, which some people regarded as prophetic of the turbulent circumstances of the 1960s and 1970s. The curtain rises on isolated figures at rest. The music triggers movement; the people, shaking off their lethargy, begin a restless search for a leader. One of them takes up a flag, waving it about. The others initiate their leader, but a troubling note of authority announces the entrance of the queen mother, who enters borne aloft with her legs spread wide by the women. The incipient revolutionaries make their obeisance and leave. The ensuing dialogue between the queen and her women reveal movements expressive of an earth-focused sense of order and ritual within this matriarchal society.

Kas Kas (Nettleford, 1965). A backyard portrayal of criminal encounters with the police.

The queen gives birth to a son, who will be the new leader; soon the man and woman begin their affectionate council of war—at once son and mother, king and consort. The revolutionaries return. In agony they proclaim the need for change, but since a king has already been chosen and groomed for leadership, the autocratic queen mother commands their loyalty. From the moment of the coronation subtle political problems are manifested, for this black king of an emergent nation has chosen as his symbols of power objects associated with imperialist culture: a top hat and cape, images of inflated nationhood. The new state requires stringent policing, and the revolutionaries, now sporting the dark glasses and straw hats of officials of a totalitarian state, have joined the abuses of power.

But the violence of revolution and oppression breeds its own defeat. The revolutionary leader, on the rise at the beginning, is now head of the armed forces; spurred on by his own woman, a young queen mother in the making, he covets the crown. His ambitions are detected by the queen mother, the power behind the throne, who directs the frightened king to confront the rebel leader. The rebel is brutally killed by the army, but the queen mother has dared too

A Question of Balance (Barnett, 1972). Technology encroaches on the human space. (*Cecil Ward*)

Street People (Nettleford, 1973). Characters on the streets of Kingston, representative of all modern urban environments.

Tribute to Cliff (Nettleford, 1974). Comfort for despairing, socially deprived youth.

much. The taste for blood has been acquired, and the power of the royal pair must be curbed. Even while the king revels in his triumph, the queen mother is abused. The rebel woman incites the people to revolt, and they kill the king. Women now with bent backs proceed mournfully across the stage, the listless revolutionaries barely noticing their dead men. The music from the beginning is heard again. One by one the revolutionaries begin to shake off their leaderless apathy. One detaches himself from the group and, followed by the others, moves intently toward the throne. Nothing has changed. The cycle begins again.

In a typically perceptive analysis of *The King Must Die* Dennis Scott has pointed up the significance of the work in terms of current politics. "*King*, it seems to me, is a coldly bitter work about the contemporary situation. The exciting melodies of the music to which it is danced, the inventiveness of the choreography based for the most part on Haitian cult dances—these do not hide its unsentimental statement of the penalties and ironies of Third World leadership, nor the warning it contains for those among us who aspire to power. 'Men need kings, and destroy them, one way or another.'"[8] There is metaphysical meaning underlying this destructive need. In the dance work, after the king is murdered, the women scream their fear and bloodlust in agitated flight across the stage as the body of the king is savaged. This act reflects Frantz Fanon's concept of symbolic killing: a powerless leader is a dead leader, both metaphorically and literally.[9]

Backlash (1975) focused on life in the ghetto, with the reggae music of the popular group Toots Hibbert and the Maytals articulating the consequences of police brutality and state domination. The work is set in prison with brutal policemen, defiant inmates, and concerned women visitors, one of whom passes a weapon to an inmate for his use. It also uses a figure denoting colonial power, the source of Babylon's brutality. The compassionate relationship that develops between the jailers and the jailed is a poignant comment on the nature of domination, whether in prison or under slavery and colonialism. The interdependency of Prospero and Caliban—a recurring theme in Caribbean literary works—is here addressed through dance. Movement expressive of the streets provided a ready vocabulary for the work, which won instant approval among Jamaican audiences in the 1970s.

The Visitor (1982) is a work specifically in tune with the 1980s. There was immediate audience speculation about the meaning of this strange dance set in a high-class bawdy house, which is visited by a customer who turns out to be the Messenger of Death. Could it be the portrayal of the hegemonic ambitions of a superpower bearing gifts to unsuspecting clients such as the welcoming islands

The King Must Die (Nettleford, 1968). The dominating queen mother and her murdered son, the king.

of the Caribbean?[10] The quality of movement eventually switches to the presumed elegance of a kind of neoclassic modern dance approach. There is a definite irony at play here: the music, by the American composer Aaron Copland, is based on the popular Cuban musical form known as *son*, while the dance is performed by the national company of Jamaica, a sometime friend of Cuba, a country which has been ostracized for over two decades by the American superpower.

In 1970 Sheila Barnett turned to the story of Lady Macbeth for her *Shadows*. Nothing is more intriguing for the microcosmic world of the Caribbean than the microcosmic world of a royal court with its passion, greed, rivalry, envy, and familial intrigue. The self-destructive nature of political power came through forcefully in a work that was handsomely served not only by Barnett's striking choreography and the portrayal of the woman alternately played by Dorothy Fraser and Monica McGowan but also by the decor and costume designs of Richard Montgomery and original music by Marjorie Whylie.

The following year heralded a small work entitled *Ballot*, by Thomas Pinnock, which dealt with a timely social issue involving politicians, polls, betrayals, and frustrations. But it was in *Rockstone Debate* (1981) that pantomime and pathos, often the key to actual politics, were combined to poke fun at politicians, while at the same time it challenged them and their electorate to deeper reflections on profound social problems in an emerging society. The work was aided by an actual raucous Jamaican Parliament as model and the prophetic warnings of folk hero reggae superstar Bob Marley. The casting of a singer protagonist (Carl Bliss) who bore a remarkable stage resemblance to a young well-known politician (Pearnel Charles)—who had recommended stone-breaking as a solution to

Court of Jah (Nettleford, 1975). Rastafarian queen and king in dialogue to Bob Marley's "No Woman Nuh Cry."

The Rope and the Cross (Barnett, 1974).

Masques of God (Nettleford, 1966).
The seduced spinster
preys on the brutish bachelor.

Thursday's Child (Rose, 1973). The dominant
mother and her wayward son.

Mary and Judith, two great biblical women,
grieve over the deaths of their sons.

Chainlinks (Barnett, 1979). The grandmother and her female siblings at the center of Afro-Caribbean life.

Ni—Woman of Destiny (Barnett, 1976). Recalling the African heritage through the effigy of a fetish doll.

unemployment—gave the work an immediate appeal for Jamaican audiences in the early 1980s.

Problematic social forces turning on politics and protest have often been selected as themes for theater and art at the risk of being dismissed as vacuous social realism. Choreographers for the National Dance Theatre Company were fortunate in avoiding this charge when exploring such social problems underlying Jamaican society. The power of Rastafarian belief in Jamaican consciousness-raising, for example, found appropriate response in the prophetic *Two Drums for Babylon*, first mounted in 1964 but revived in 1980 to music composed for it by the young Jamaican musician Peter Ashbourne. The updated choreography was based on movement reminiscent of the reggae world, which had not fully emerged until the mid-1970s. The dance work origi-

Resurrection (Jones, 1972). The son is protected by his mother. (*Johnny R. O'Brien*)

Ni—Woman of Destiny (Barnett, 1976). Ode to the great Ashanti war heroine Nanny.

Mountain Women (Barnett, 1972). Ode to the spiritual force of the women of the hill country. (*Johnny R. O'Brien*)

Dialogue for Three (Nettleford, 1963). The man and the other woman, paticipants in the familiar love triangle. (*Owen Minot*)

African Scenario (Nettleford, 1962). African traditions and continuities in the Caribbean.

nally premiered at a time when Jamaica was being threatened by a subculture explicitly challenging the values of a privileged middle class. An underprivileged class, made up primarily of blacks, was searching for social mobility by adopting the mores and manners of the lighter-skinned bourgeoisie. The Rastafarians, disclaiming political, cultural, and religious loyalties to the nation, linked their disaffection with euphoric marijuana smoking, hatred for the establishment (Babylon), and the worship of Haile Selassie as God.[11] The predictable responses of society to this religious group were fear and suspicion, and for the most part the social values being attacked by these outcasts remained unquestioned. It is interesting that even the first version of *Two Drums for Babylon*, choreographed in 1964, was able to predict so convincingly the strong influence this cult would later have over Jamaican youth. In the mid-1960s there were only a few isolated, almost legendary, cases of middle-class youth who rejected their materialistic backgrounds. By the end of the 1960s the Rastafarian movement extended throughout Jamaican society. By the 1970s and later the movement had spread to all parts of the English-speaking Caribbean and to metropolitan centers in the United States, Canada, Great Britain, and France; there was also admiration for it among youths in black Africa.[12]

The scenario for *Two Drums for Babylon* is indeed simple. On the eve of his wedding a young man hesitates because his relationship with the girl seems unsatisfying. He is lured by drums as well as a phantom cultist figure into a Rastafarian camp, where he is initiated. Against the advice of her middle-class friends, the girl follows. Also falling under the spell of the cultists, she becomes possessed, while her terrified friends run away. The boy regrets his allegiance too late; the girl is lost to him.

On the symbolic level, however, the ballet makes a complex statement. All of the representatives of the establishment are women; the Babylonian captivity, into which the boy hesitates to enter wholeheartedly, is a matriarchal society, ruled by sexually alluring females who are yet emotionally unsatisfying. In contrast the confrontations with the community of cultists, led by a male figure, are ritually vital, vigorous, and emotionally fulfilling. The music also emphasizes the differences between the two experiences: the intricate patterns of Aaron Copland's music contrasts markedly with Gene Gutche's *Bongo Divertimento* [13] and drum rhythms based on cult drumming. The delicately self-contained body movements of Babylon is juxtaposed against the writhing unselfconscious passion of the male and female cultists. The stage itself is dominated by the huge skeleton of a drum, symbol of the tribe's heritage and its expressive voice. Again it is worthwhile to cite the valuable insights Dennis Scott has contributed toward an explication of the work:

Sulkari (Rivero, 1980). Motifs derived from African sculpture.

The Brothers (Ricketts, 1978). A mother gives birth to twins and suffers the tragedy of one of them born deformed.

Homage (Nettleford, 1973). African-style attitudes are utilized to shape patterns of movement.

The Crossing (Nettleford, 1978). Depiction of ancestors before the crossing via the middle passage.

The situation of the dance, it seems clear, is that of our society at this very moment. The younger members of the society are rebelling against an often sterile and unfulfilling cultural situation, strongly European, which denies any deep involvement in the instinctive and deeply perceived emotional life of the community. They run away from a situation which demands their alienation from the underprivileged, to a lifestyle whose excitement and ritual sense of community provide a psychic fulfillment and an exaltation connected with being black and poor. The protest provides a sense of identity, a return to recognizable roots. *Two Drums for Babylon* offers a vision of fantastic rites which are deeply hungered after by our people; rites which signify, as in Rastafarianism, the need of the society to "exercise itself, to liberate itself, to explain itself." It is this that Fanon speaks about; both the lovers in this ballet find themselves drawn towards this vision.

Yet there is more to *Drums* than that, I think. The ballet poses a final unanswered question. At the end, the boy finds himself torn between two deeply felt needs: the need

Myal (Nettleford, 1974). The myalmen (herbalists) exorcise the evil
spirit invoked by the Obeahman.

to belong to the cultists with all that means, and his love for the girl, now no longer entirely
his. It is a familiar situation in human life: how far is it possible for an individual to accept a
way of life which seems to threaten his necessary ties and affection? There is a fable of
Sartre's [14] which documents with bitter irony such dilemmas of choice. It is a problem
faced constantly, one suspects, by those of us who strive to balance our societal responsibilities, our political commitments, with an awareness of the more intimate and no less
valid human values. [15]

If *Two Drums for Babylon* confirmed the solemnity and anguish of urban
ghetto life, the tragicomic quality of that life found expression in *Kas Kas* (1965).
The work dealt not only with the betrayals and violence of an urban yard but also
with its protective unity against the police—known throughout the Caribbean as
the Babylonian oppressor—who could, however, be just as easily seduced by
sympathies to the yard from which they originally came. The contradictions of life
found further expression in Thomas Pinnock's *Desperate Silences* (1972) with its
infectious humor and tragic despair portrayed in alternately relaxed and stylized
movements, drawing on Pinnock's strong modern dance technique as much as
on his firsthand knowledge as a child of the Kingston ghettos.

The travails of life continued to inspire Company choreographers throughout
the 1970s. *Street People* (1973) opened to the image of a human scavenger

rummaging among plastic garbage bags—underscored by Desmond Dekker's ballad "Poor Me Israelite"—and ended by laughing at the dalliances of prostitutes, religious fanatics, a dread Rastafarian,[16] and a pimp, all representative of the streets of Kingston and of urban environments everywhere. The piece succeeded in New York, which is understandable, but it fell flat in Havana and was promptly withdrawn from the program. It was obviously a case of culture shock for the Cubans. The Company was also taken by the genius of the songwriter Stevie Wonder, who later embraced Jamaican reggae. The music from his album *Songs in the Key of Life* provided the key to *Wonder Love and Raise* (1977). His mock baroque ballad "Ghettoland" was a paradigm of social comment, relevant to the pseudo-elegant dimensions of Jamaican middle-class life. After Jamaican independence the ghetto was a social challenge for the nation, receiving its finest evocation in innovative musical developments, ranging from ska in the late 1950s to rocksteady[17] in the mid-1960s and reggae in the late 1960s and throughout the 1970s. Music became a source of energy for the poor and oppressed. It challenged all artists—painters, sculptors, potters, fashion designers, and, naturally, choreographers—with the vigor of contemporary life.

All God's Children (1969) explored the continuing class differentiation within Jamaican society by showing that people—whether uptowners or downtowners (sufferers)—were all one humanity even though they could deal with this humanity only under the influence of drugs, specifically marijuana or ganja, on the one hand smoked in a pipe (kutchie) and on the other eaten in cookies on the elegant cocktail circuit. In dance terms the differentiation was significant since the downtowners danced in the idiom of the streets (reggae), whereas the up-

And It Came to Pass (Thomas, 1964). The angel appears to Mary, mother of Jesus.

Lucifer Lucifer (Nettleford, 1970). An encounter between God and Satan.

Pocomania (Nettleford, 1963). Afro-Christian syncretic revival rites of Jamaica.

Kumina (Nettleford, 1971). A libation is poured before the worship begins.

towners utilized American modern dance movements and European ballet techniques to make their statement. Dennis Scott summed up the work as a "portrait of a society that burns to be whole again." [18]

During the 1970s the music of the people provided more than atmospheric support for other important works in the repertoire. Music and movement were organically linked in *Tribute to Cliff* (1974) through the music of Jimmy Cliff, the star of the film *The Harder They Come*. The music inspired a suite of four dances, each with subthemes that celebrate the notion of hope in despair, a frequent theme of reggae. The success it had with Jamaican audiences could not be divorced from the power of Cliff's music, especially his masterful "Many Rivers to Cross," choreographed as a duo with movements that flowed with the plaintive melodic line, ending with the two dancers genuflecting facing the audience in a kind of obeisance to the invincibility of the human spirit and to Cliff's ever-present sense of hope. The costuming in colors reminiscent of liberation— green, red, gold—made a pertinent statement as well: it was a paean to freedom and hope. [19]

Hope is also the dominant mood in *Court of Jah* (1975), a stately work choreographed to the music of the phenomenal Bob Marley, who was gaining interna-

Journeys (Nettleford, 1971). Anguish of the African diaspora in plantation America, inspired by American spirituals.

tional prominence when the work was created. Marley—who was influenced by Jimmy Cliff as well as by the burgeoning Rastafari movement, which gave reggae greater focus—was the epitome of confidence. The children of Jah need not apologize for their dreadlocks or for their claims to divinity. All the world's a court and all its men and women are kings and queens, princes and princesses. The proud and stately mien of the lion on Colin Garland's impressive backdrop is echoed in the noble figure of the Jah, a role played alternately by Barry Moncrieffe and Bert Rose. The mood is maintained throughout, from the assertive peacock progressions in the first sequence and the plastic patterns in the duet danced to the song ''No Woman Nuh Cry'' to the joyous reggae-bouncing and floor-sliding designs of the last section of the dance. An enthusiastic audience applauded the highly visual opening with its bright red, green, and yellow decor set off by the dancers' white costumes with heraldic red, green, and yellow borders. But they felt that the work did not have the robust muscularity appropriate to the native character of their folk hero nor did it offer a direct message of suffering and "downpression" that a piece like *Backlash* did. It is reported that Bob Marley, who attended the season, preferred *Backlash* and its reggae music of Toots Hibbert and the Maytals. In *Backlash*, discussed previously, Toots Hibbert's role as artist linking traditional musical modes, especially revivalism, with contemporary reggae admittedly offered the choreographer a driving tension. The controversy over these works continued among an interested and not uninformed group. Sheila Barnett, with the help of composer Bob Sinicrope, had included a reggae-inspired sequence in her *A Question of Balance* (1972), but this work emphasized the impact of technology on human society rather than the profound problems of ghetto life. Barnett's own training in the techniques of pure movement served her well as was proven by her acrobatic and percussive patterns portraying technology balanced by characteristically soft designs.

MATRIARCHY: THE "SHE" IN DANCE ART

Another theme of major importance in the Company repertoire is the cen-

Misa Criolla (Nettleford, 1967). The credo from the Catholic mass, danced to a Creole musical version of the high mass.

trality of women to Jamaican social life and cultural formation. As an ageless theme for artistic expression, it goes back to ancient Greece. Just as Clytemnestra, Helen, Mary Magdalen, and Joan of Arc have become general archetypes developed from fact and fiction of Western civilization, the Caribbean has had its own heroines, such as Ole Hige derived from ritual myth, Annie Palmer from legend, and Nanny from both history and legend.[20] The choreographers have been able to exploit various aspects of contemporary woman for their symbolic representations: as breadwinner, object of adoration, target of abuse, fount of compassion, victim of chauvinism, survivor, life force, and ancestral icon. Anna Kisselgoff, a critic for *The New York Times*, noticed on the occasion of the National Dance Theatre Company's first appearance in New York that Jamaica is viewed as a matriarchal society by at least one Company choreographer. Kisselgoff perceptively commented that their "refusal to depict this theme in terms of a man-destroying castrating-female image so common to many other choreographers is one of the Company's most refreshing and healthy aspects."[21]

Dialogue for Three (1963), choreographed by Rex Nettleford, involved the eternal triangle: in this case, the women staking claims for the love of the same man. The theme, often considered hackneyed, encouraged facile interpretations. But the perceptive viewer was able to comprehend the choreographer's

Gerrehbenta (Nettleford, 1983). Invoking the spirits of the deceased in deadyard rites, or wakes.

Kumina (Nettleford, 1971). Ancestor worship presided over by the chief celebrants, the king and queen.

intentions. The deeper meaning of the work revealed the total command a woman is capable of in such a situation, despite the usual conventions of a male-dominated society which dictate that the man must be in control. In fact the two women usually understand each other much better than the man understands either one; they are, after all, sisters in emotional knowledge. Thus the other woman eventually returns the man to his wife. The second movement of Joaquín Rodrigo's guitar concerto *Concierto de Aranjuez* provided the backdrop for the terse and highly memorable portrayals by the dancers, Yvonne daCosta or Barbara Requa, as the other woman; Sheila Barnett, Gertrude Sherwood, Bridget Casserly, or Noelle Chutkan, as the wife; and Eddy Thomas or Bert Rose, as the man.

The concept of woman-force explored in *Dialogue for Three* was followed three years later in *Masques of God.* Now it was a frustrated spinster who transformed herself from a brutalized victim into a soul destroyer, with her alter egos mirrored by an accommodating wife and an innocent woman in love. All three

Omegan Procession (Thomas, 1966). A theatrical version of the Garden of Eden, featuring Adam and Eve.

underscore the weaknesses of their various male partners—brute bachelor, irresponsible husband, and naive young lover—all of whom seek refuge of one kind or another, either from self or from spouse. Even the detached commentator—cast as a clown—is unable to escape through detachment. The work had a dramatic logic and explored patterns of movement appropriate to the mélange of recorded music, ranging from Bartók to Dohnányi.

By 1972 there was a certain maturity shown in the portrayal of the woman in *Ballad of a Lady*, a study of a textured life lived just beneath the surface of conventional society. With the retirement from performing of Yvonne daCosta—a major exponent of this type of characterization—a particular conceptualization of woman disappeared, although not before the Company's artistic director cast her as God, with a man playing the Devil, in *Lucifer Lucifer* (1970). [22]

Sheila Barnett has addressed the theme as well. In *Shadows*, also discussed under social commentary, there is an intriguing dynamic that determines the woman's alter egos—witch figures (shadows) that denote passion, greed, and power as in a morality play. In 1972 Barnett choreographed *Mountain Women*, inspired by the vigor, quiet dignity, and independence of Jamaican rural women, whom she observed at close range in her extensive travels throughout Jamaica as dance education officer. This compassionate innovative work utilizes Jamaican folk legends, but more important it transmutes recognizable folk gestures into choreographic delights. The carriage of arms, the percussive beat of bare feet that have walked a thousand miles, the attitudes derived from work postures, the swinging gait of journeys up steep hillsides, and the tenderness of maternal embrace passed from one generation to the next—all were kinetic clues to an emerging indigenous style. This work—difficult even for the dancers, who generally were brought up on urban sensibilities—never received the attention or performances it deserved.

In *The Rope and the Cross* (1974) Barnett shifted to the Bible to study the moods and reactions of two women united in grief over the loss of their sons: Mary, mother of Jesus, and Judith, mother of Judas Iscariot—the one by crucifixion, the other by suicide. Sheila Barnett herself danced the role of Mary and Patsy Ricketts portrayed Judith. *The Rope and the Cross* could only have been created by a woman. All aspects of dramatic interpretation manifested in the work—the technical brilliance in the taut line, the expressive extensions, the

Glory Road (Rose, 1974). Acceptance of suffering through the worship of God.

The Rope and the Cross (Barnett, 1974).
Mary, the mother of Jesus, and
Judith, the mother of Judas Iscariot.

Legend of Lovers' Leap (Thomas, 1962).
During the slavery period, ill-starred
lovers are betrayed by a fellow slave.

deepened and forceful contractions, the sustained stretches of torso unfolding
from a fetal curve on the floor—revealed the fullest anguish of woman's pain.
Barnett persisted in her pursuit of the feminine force that informs and even dominates the Jamaican social reality. In 1976, independent of the Jamaican government's decision to honor the Maroon warrior Nanny, Barnett mounted a tribute to
this heroine under the title *Ni—Woman of Destiny*, for which Marjorie Whylie
composed an original score. Barnett portrayed Nanny as priestess, warrior,

lover, and heroine. She saw Nanny not as a subject of hagiography or of political manipulation but as archetypal woman determining the value of a humane society.

Barnett further explored the theme of woman in a 1979 work entitled *Chainlinks*. It presented a grandmother presiding over a family unit. Collaboration with Cedric "Im" Brooks as composer did not have the organic fusion that her works with Whylie did, and Barnett withdrew the work temporarily from the repertoire until revisions could be made. The choreography did not dehumanize the male characters; in fact Barnett gave them inordinately virile movements, shifting the focus of strength from the grandmother and her female siblings to the men whose lives are intimately determined by the women.

The theme of forceful grandmother also found favor with John Jones, an American guest choreographer, in his 1972 piece *Resurrection* with Joyce Campbell in the lead. Patsy Ricketts's dramatic work *The Brothers* (1978) portrayed the woman as the victim of patriarchal authority in the raising of the family. Bert Rose's *Thursday's Child* (1973) utilized the symbol of the dominant mother raising a son, with the absence of a father an eloquent testimony to the importance of the woman's decision. Rose's less authoritative *Reflections* (1975) analyzed the psychic concerns of three women with various problems. Jackie Guy's solo piece *Solitude* (1981) explored the emotional plight of a woman caught in the anguish of loneliness. In a way it echoed Sheila Barnett's own solo for her-

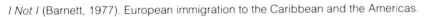

I Not I (Barnett, 1977). European immigration to the Caribbean and the Americas.

The Crossing (Nettleford, 1978). The colonizers (with flags) and the collaborative African (with mask) in the saga of the slave trade.

self, *Homecoming* (1966), mounted many years earlier to a scenario by Dennis Scott. Male creative artists are frequently fascinated by the concept of woman as source of energy.

In traditional Caribbean dance theater women have frequently been portrayed as a sex symbol—the essence of coquetry or an object of the fertility rite. A woman could be the epitome of feminine grace, but frequently she was dressed idealistically in frills and lace or sported the symbol of domestic servitude, the apron. The Company's serious exploration of the female force revealed through matriarchal kinship patterns of the Jamaican people prevented the choreographers from being trapped by these stereotypes. A woman's dignity, as well as her central role in society, has continued to inform the Company's repertoire, augmenting not only its vocabulary but also its technical range.

THE AFRICAN PRESENCE IN THE CARIBBEAN ETHOS

Perhaps it has been taken too much for granted that the African background

Legend of Lovers' Leap (Thomas, 1962). A tale of two slaves whose love is undermined by the plantation owner.

Ni—Woman of Destiny (Barnett, 1976). The story of Nanny, the Maroon heroine of both history and legend, focuses on the power of the woman in Afro-Caribbean society.

The Crossing (Nettleford, 1978). Anguish and apprehension caused by the presence of the Ku Klux Klan.

The Crossing (Nettleford, 1978). The agony of plantation life in the Americas.

Switch (Rose, 1977). The legend of Annie Palmer, the white witch of Rose Hall, a macabre tale recalling a period of planter brutality.

of the Caribbean ethos was an ever-present theme in genuine Caribbean dance theater. It was often assumed that the general dance vocabulary was influenced automatically by traditional continuities, movements, and sensibilities of the people who have forged what is taken to be the quintessence of Caribbean culture. Yet it has always been necessary, and even natural, to force Jamaican audiences into an awareness of the power of the African presence as part of a Caribbean definition of self. For the National Dance Theatre Company the essence of dance aesthetics was directly related to the recognition given the creative expressions of the people of African ancestry. The use of the term "ethnic" to distinguish indigenous cultural developments from European-derived forms was an arrogance the Company, by definition, could not accept. Therefore, the elevation of African influences to their proper place in the classic expressions of the Jamaican people suggested itself in the shaping of the repertoire.

African Scenario, staged at Kingston's Little Theatre in 1962 for the *Roots and Rhythms* show celebrating Jamaican independence, was the first dance work of the National Dance Theatre Company that directly acknowledged this debt to Africa. Without apology or the solemnity of anthropological elaboration the piece played on the senses of both performers and audiences by drawing on the rituals, dress, music, and dances of West Africa and simultaneously focusing on correspondences in traditional Jamaican life. The story seems almost pure in its simplicity. A young girl enters maturity and is betrothed. Losing her loved one to war, she invokes the gods for his return. Finally he returns in safety and rejoicing. This Caribbean portrayal of ancestral rites was set against traditional African scenes of puberty, fertility, war, fetish, and masquerade. Eddy Thomas created brilliant costume designs based on the ceremonial dress of West Africa. Joyce Lalor embarked on a serious study of the songs of the Ga and Akan peoples of Ghana, and the drummers were ecstatic.[23] There was no pretense at reproducing Africa in a literal sense. The piece was presented with a Caribbean vision faithful both to the essence of its ancestral sources and to the realities of the changes that naturally occurred as a result of transplantation to the Americas. Don McDonagh, at the time a critic with *The New York Times*, warmed to the subtle difference when he discussed the Company dancers and musicians: "They never try to overpower the viewer, but persistently and lyrically pour waves of sound and motion out like a net to catch attention. The drums in *African Scenario* don't thunder, they murmur, but insistently. The dancers skitter around endlessly rather than stomp with maximum force, and the effect is made. It doesn't have the biting edge of the original model, but creates its own good-humored one."[24] Nevertheless some members of the Jamaican middle-class audience were disturbed by the work and walked out of the Little Theatre in protest, complaining that the drumming was too loud. In those early days—before black power and reggae had informed a new consciousness—many middle-class Jamaicans could still arrogantly deny the African connection. *Af-*

rican Scenario, which assumed a special place in the repertoire for a decade after its creation, was revived in 1982.

The African quality of Jamaican society was reflected in much of the Company's repertoire. The neo-African society in Haiti was an inspiration, especially after 1955, when Tiroro, the great Haitian drummer, visited Jamaica and taught his art to a few members of the fledgling Jamaican dance movement. Very soon after that Lavinia Williams also visited Jamaica. Williams, an early dancer with Katherine Dunham, was probably the best authority on Haitian dance forms, which she had acquired through a systematic study of the beliefs, music, and dance lore of Haiti.

The sense of Africa is pervasive throughout the repertoire. It informs not only many of the Creole dances already discussed but also some of the dances that fall under other categories—such as history and legend, black spirituals, jazz, and religion—discussed later.

The Gospel According To (Nettleford, 1981). The spirit of plantation America celebrated in Don Shirley's arrangements of American spirituals.

Wonder Love and Raise (Nettleford, 1977). Performed to the soul music of Stevie Wonder.

In 1973 *Homage*, a work that is both religious and secular, was choreographed in tribute to African-derived movements: arched back, arms akimbo, feet planted on the ground on half-bent knees. *Missa Luba*, a contemporary version of the Catholic mass sung in Latin to music in the style of the Bantu people of the Congo, and Neil Diamond's six-part composition *African Trilogy* made up the music. It was an exploratory work that gave joy to the dancers. Some critics were puzzled by the piece; Anna Kisselgoff found its stylizations of African movement confusing and at the same time criticized its modern dance vocabulary.[25] Yet it had an imperceptible influence on some works that followed.

Another important African-based work is Eduardo Rivero's *Sulkari* (1980), which came from the Danza Nacional de Cuba through a Cuban cultural exchange. *Sulkari* not only isolates African forms, it also expands them in a splendid evocation of the vigorous cultural integrity of African life and movement patterns. The theme of the dance involves exaltation of fertility, so that through the male–female relationship human life will continue. The dance forms were inspired not only by the details of carvings, headdresses, masks, and other African sculptural elements of the Yoruba people of Dahomey, the movement of these tribal peoples was also an influence. The critic Wycliffe Bennett asserted that besides *African Scenario* this is the only other explicitly African piece in the repertoire. Drawing on the works of the African scholar John S. Mbiti, Bennett

Footnotes in Jazz (Thomas, 1962). The influence of American jazz, danced to the music of Brubeck and Bernstein.

correctly assumes that *Sulkari* is a powerful invocation of African affirmation of the regenerative principle in society as well as a natural veneration of "the sexual organs as the gates of life."[26] It is also interesting to note that certain American modern dance practitioners have also asserted that dance, as well as life, begins in the pelvis. "The power of the work," to quote Bennett again, "lies as much in the integrated use of myth and imagery as in the relentless buildup of the erotic experience. *The production makes no concession to European notions of line or weight.* There are, for example, a great many lifts, and the stress upon the arms and thighs is always evident. . . . The production proclaims an essential Africanity that expects to be judged on the basis of its own aesthetics, and the results are achieved with economy and impeccable taste."[27]

The African nature of Caribbean life would have naturally served as background to *Ni—Woman of Destiny*, also discussed under the category of matriarchy, if only because of its thematic dictates. But Sheila Barnett made more of it than that. The entire production of *Ni—Woman of Destiny* draws on an African ethos in its deep sense of ritual, its setting of masks and drum figures, its ancestral chorus chanting "Kaya Katumbe" and "Anjooma,"[28] and the use of herbs denoting the restorative power of African healing traditions. The magic nature of herbs is also acknowledged in *Myal*—discussed under religion—and given full explication by Barnett herself in *I Not I*—discussed under history—with the Bush

Spirit (Pitchy-Patchy of jonkonnu) as the central link between ancestral hearth and adopted home in the Americas.

Jamaican choreographers who create with a deep understanding of how the African presence acted as leaven to the creolized Caribbean culture celebrate African influences in the Americas more sincerely than a number of black dance groups in the United States, who attempt faithful reproductions of Senegalese, Nigerian, Ghanaian, and Guinean dances. Thus *Drumscore* (1979)—which is dedicated to the drum, that most ubiquitous of African instruments in the Americas—draws on a Ghanaian proverb for initial inspiration: when a god created the universe, he first created the drummer. But the choreographer relies on the African presence in the Caribbean in order to sustain its momentum. The sounds and rhythms present a panoply of polyrhythms supporting supple movement, alternately flowing and syncopated. The work celebrates the great truth that no people can ever be totally uprooted or deprived of their heritage.

The theme of African permutations in Jamaican cultural reality preceded the black power movement of the late 1960s. The recognition of the African heritage was critical to the identity of Caribbean dance theater and to cultural development in the Caribbean. The dimensions of East Indian culture must also be taken into account, particularly in Trinidad and Guyana, but African-derived elements of Caribbean culture have predominated, despite the evidence of East Indian influences in Jamaican revivalism and masquerade or even in Carnival and the

Soulscape (Nettleford, 1983). Patterns and forms follow the music of Gershwin's *Porgy and Bess*, the classic portrayal of plantation America.

steel band music of Trinidad.[29] That such expressions of confidence should serve as antidote to the Eurocentric arrogance of former rulers is no reason to lead Caribbean artists into constraints of another kind of ethnocentric determinism. The National Dance Theatre Company has avoided this pitfall. Many would share with Dennis Scott, one of its former dancers, the view that "an essential part of our freedom in the West Indies is the freedom to adapt any device from anywhere, and use it to make statements which define our situation."[30] I would like to believe that what is important for the Company are statements that define the Caribbean situation rather than the adaptation of devices from "anywhere." Adapting from anywhere has been at the heart of survival, while the will to define the situation ourselves denotes a life beyond survival, which is the essential aspect of freedom.

CARIBBEAN THEMES OF RELIGION AND RITUAL

Nowhere has adaptation been better achieved than in the area of religion. African belief systems, which were instrumental in the survival of the enslaved population, were quickly forbidden. Substituted in their place were syncretized systems—forms of worship acceptable to the colonizers alongside underground expressions of the original versions, which were forbidden by the overlords.

The Company's repertoire exploring some of the religious belief systems

Dance Andante (Nettleford, 1965). Inspired by Schubert's *Trout* Quintet.

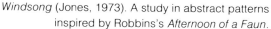

Windsong (Jones, 1973). A study in abstract patterns inspired by Robbins's *Afternoon of a Faun*.

Ring Hunt (Barnett, 1968). Play between dancers with a hoop.

found enthusiastic audiences not only among regular theatergoers but also among church congregations both in Jamaica and in countries abroad. Foremost is the popular ritual trilogy with the individual titles of *Pocomania*, *Kumina*, and *Myal*, all choreographed by Rex Nettleford. The religious impulses underlying these works are older than revolution itself, and through their movement design and structural development they have become hallmarks of Jamaican dance theater iconography.

Pocomania (1963) was the result of actual research by the entire Company in the parish of Saint Mary and in the West Kingston ghetto of Salt Lane. The choreographer also drew on his childhood experiences of the cult as it was practiced in his native village in northern Jamaica. The result was a festival of bands of worshipers, each band led by a shepherd (priest) who had made a three-day

Rites (Black, 1965). Ritual designs are created from abstracted spatial movement.

Images (Barnett, 1969). Exploring dramatic movement designs to conjure up varied images in space.

Drumscore (Nettleford, 1979). Affirmation of traditional Caribbean movement and rhythm.

journey into the spirit world. The shepherds were attended by trumping (or traveling, while producing loud rhythmic breathing, in the spirit world) and cymbaling (or communication with the inhabitants of that world). All this was done to possession dances in response to the Spirit of the River Maid, Engine Spirit, Cooing Dove, and Indian Spirit. In addition there were three whirling shepherds accompanied by worshipers possessed by controlled frenzy and convulsions. The nervous laughter that greeted performances of the work in the 1960s was resolved into reflective silence by the mid-1970s, an indication that the Jamaican populace had become more knowledgeable and confident about the integrity of such aspects of their heritage. Foreign audiences had always responded with solemn respect for the work.

The popularity of *Kumina* (1971), the next work in the trilogy, seemed almost to threaten *Pocomania* with extinction. The kumina rite itself, which involves ancestral spirits, identifies the Congo as its place of origin. The version by the National Dance Theatre Company is based on the rite as it is still observed in Saint Thomas, the easternmost parish of the island. The rite invokes the assistance of the gods on various occasions: mourning, burials, healing, thanksgiving, and even soliciting help in winning a court case or a lover. The use of

Back to Bach, Viva Bach (Nettleford, 1979). Courtly attitudes are reenacted to the music of Bach and Vivaldi.

Trio (Requa, 1983). Olympiad athleticism.

Celebrations (Nettleford, 1972). An exploration of Caribbean folk forms.

traditional drummers—James Walker and Obadiah Lewis—who believe in this religious rite, coupled with the dancers' genuine respect for the rite as a serious aspect of the national heritage, lends the work special qualities of exultation and authority. As a celebration of the African presence in Jamaica, this dance is for many a liberating act that finally offers a sense of epiphany. Audiences usually go wild in their enthusiasm. Edward Kamau Brathwaite felt that from the moment *Kumina* was created, it was as if the Company had been resurrected. He believed that the work produced a special effect not only on each Company member but also on each audience member in communities throughout the Caribbean. As a result of viewing the Carifesta performance in Guyana in 1972, Brathwaite wrote that

Sulkari (Rivero, 1980). African movement patterns danced to a version of traditional Yoruba music from Cuba.

it was as if as audience we were being drawn by a great force . . . nearer and nearer into the movement of the stage no longer stage but lighted ship or island. And as a harsh shiver of voices suddenly breathed agitation of water out of the tide of drums, "I want to know, I want to know," it was as if we had spoken from some deep involuntary something and all this while the body is moving steadily in inexorable progress through song, through sound, through thunder. . . .

Wave upon wave of dancers, diagonal entrances and exits clash. . . . Religious frenzy evoked by rhythmic drum and forceful singing expressed through groups of stamping and gyrating dancers. It was not in the tradition the critics say; it was not of *the* tradition. But where were the structures now? They could not understand; they had been eroded and obscured; and our dancers had revealed the boundaries of form—colonial and capital to boot—as we in Georgetown knew, rising to meet them with the sound of rainfall in our ears applause acknowledging this little victory, so very near our tears.[31]

Myal (1974) inspires no such feelings of redemption. But it is no less rooted in the religious instincts of the Jamaican people. Myalism is also religious ritual. According to the historical records, it once competed openly with Christian orthodoxy, and to this day myal connotes religious mysticism. It goes further back and deeper than pukkumina[32] but not deeper than kumina.

The dance, which is set in the nineteenth century, is about the Obeahman and myalmen (healer herbalists). Jamaicans commonly believe in spirits (known

Waltz Suite (Black, 1965).
An experiment with
the waltz, European style.

Ebb Flow (Rose, 1978).
A love duet.

as shadows or duppies). It is the Obeahman who plants the spirit on someone, while the myalman has the power to exorcise it. The story opens with a burial, pallbearers carrying the body to the grave. The Obeahman follows the mourners in order to catch the "shadow" of the deceased. He is successful and plants the shadow on three young mourners, who then come totally under the spell of the Obeahman. But the mourners' adult mother protectors call up the Spirit of the Herbs from the bush, and the myal, or ritual exorcism, begins. The Obeahman is rendered powerless in the confrontation with the myalmen, who traditionally are omnipotent and immune to even the wiles of the white man.

The success of the myalmen is occasion for rejoicing. Yet the Obeahman refuses to give up. He returns disguised as a peddler of kerchiefs, but the protectors warn the gullible young girls against the deception of the wicked shadowcatcher. He is finally exorcised—but not quite, for he joins the merry-making at the curtain call, describing a circle of confidence over the heads of the rejoicing crowd, an implication that where there is good, evil also exists. Religion and morality would have been impossible otherwise.

Such a profound theological comment had in fact been made in 1970, when *Lucifer Lucifer* was added to the repertoire. This work, which explored the Manichaean myth, presented God and the Devil as interdependent aspects of the human soul. The choreographer organized a ritual marriage between the two forces at the end of the dance, and thus Adam and Eve—mythic primordial humans—were represented as mere evocations of this dialectical argument. The vocabulary of the dance owed much to modern dance traditions. The luminosity of George Carter's lighting and the effectiveness of Colin Garland's simple inventive decor and costumes made it one of the most satisfying pieces at the time.

Right: *Dialogue for Three* (Nettleford, 1963). The eternal triangle, involving the love of two women for the same man.

Far right: *Dialogue for Three* (Nettleford, 1963). In the love triangle the man is in conflict with his wife. (*Syd Burke*)

The Bible has been a ready source of dance creations throughout the Western world, and the National Dance Theatre Company has also seriously explored some of its themes. Barnett's *The Rope and the Cross*, discussed previously in terms of matriarchy, introduced the mothers of Jesus and Judas Iscariot in ways that brought these great biblical figures nearer contemporary understanding. In 1964 Eddy Thomas portrayed the Nativity story in *And It Came to Pass*, a suite of elegantly designed dances to Darius Milhaud's appropriate *Suite Provençale*. The flight into Egypt was portrayed in a strikingly inventive way with Mary undulating on Joseph's shoulders as Joseph, on an upstage ramp, moved in slow motion into the distance, the two of them fading into lowering light. Later Thomas used the recording of Milhaud's *Création du Monde* to accompany his *Omegan Procession* (1966), which offered a highly theatrical Garden of Eden, replete with Adam and Eve and the serpent as well as the multiplying creatures that would replenish the earth.

The Catholic mass was celebrated in dance with the *Misa Criolla* (1967) with great success, especially since the NDTC Singers—with bass Vibart Seaforth and tenor Carl Bliss singing the leads—replaced the recorded music. The music, by the Argentinian composer Ariel Ramírez, was inspired by popular Hispanic folk forms. The dance is a theatrical but reverent commemoration of Christ's sacrifice in moods of joy and penitence. The episodes, using the Spanish liturgical text, follow sections of the high mass: kyrie, gloria, credo, sanctus, and Agnus Dei. The choreography has been described as "simple but strong."[33] The Easter Sunday morning concert, performed by the Company at the Little Theatre, is regarded as an act of worship, and the *Misa Criolla* along with *The Rope and the Cross* are becoming traditional fare at that event.

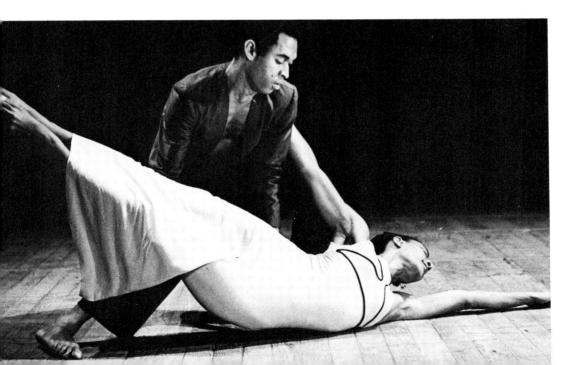

Masques of God (Nettleford, 1966). A reluctant husband is confronted by a pleading wife in a love duet.

Then there are the works choreographed to spirituals, evoking deep religious feelings and communion with a protective higher being that guarantees survival. The solo *I've Been Buk'd* (1973) and the suites of dances to traditional spirituals in such works as *In the Spirit* (1970), *Journeys* (1971), and *Glory Road* (1974) all identify the anguish of the African diaspora in plantation America and promises redemption through spiritual healing. In 1981 *The Gospel According To* was added to the repertoire, as if to restore a healing spirit associated with some of the former works that were no longer regularly performed. The spiritual "Buk'd and Scorned"—the musical basis of *I've Been Buk'd* a decade earlier—turned up as part of the suite and was again isolated for solo performance by Barry Moncrieffe during the Company's twenty-first anniversary season in 1983. Two versions of *Ave Verum*—one created in 1968 by Neville Black, who drew on the pietà as inspiration for his choreographic designs, and the other in 1981 by Bert Rose—were performed by the Company in churches as part of their religious celebrations, but these versions did not become part of the active performing repertoire.

In 1983 *Gerrehbenta*, in the spirit of the ritual trilogy of *Pocomania*, *Kumina*, and *Myal*, was added to the repertoire. The dance derived its name from two of the ancient rites still practiced in Jamaica: the gerreh from Hanover and Westmoreland parishes and the dinkimini, which utilizes the benta, a traditional musi-

Summer Is (Barnett, 1983). A dance theater piece dealing with the various moods of summer.

Recollections (Thompson, 1983). Danced to the music of Ramsay Lewis.

cal instrument, from the parish of Saint Mary. The dance evokes ancestral spirits usually associated with wakes, known as deadyard ceremonies. The dance work also includes the character Horsehead, from jonkonnu, as a symbol of fertility as well as the Yoruba shawling dance known as etu. The work's strong religious bias transfixed audiences, who responded with a revival handclapping applause long after the stage lights had faded on the apocalyptic vision of dancers contorted in a circle around Horsehead. The dance made no compromise to the idioms of modern dance or classical ballet, and thus it entered the select gallery of works that speak directly to traditional Jamaican patterns of movements. Like *Kumina*, it demonstrates the absence of clear distinctions between religious and secular concerns of the Jamaican psyche. The dinkimini and the gerreh are not only honored at deadyard ceremonies, they are also performed for specific secular celebrations.

JAMAICAN HISTORY AND LEGEND

The repertoire has also emphasized the history and legends of Jamaica. *Legend of Lovers' Leap* (1962) by Eddy Thomas was an impressive drama whose visual impact was heightened by the traditional setting. The strength of the muscular technique and the Graham approach to drama and legendary ma-

Married Story (Nettleford, 1970). A love story, country style.

terial informed the choreography of this young Graham graduate. The story-tellers accurately captured the gesticulatory attitudes of Jamaican peasant women in conversation. Based on an account by the Jamaican poet Tom Red-cam, the story recounts the tale of two slaves, Ako and Liza, whose love for each other is thwarted by the lascivious plantation owner, a mischievous pair of housekeepers, and Zeb, a jealous slave. The ill-starred lovers choose death rather than face the heartlessness of the slave system.

Another legend that has stuck in the popular imagination is that of Annie Palmer, the white witch of Rose Hall.[34] Whether Annie Palmer existed or not, she became an historically important symbol of plantation system cruelty, sexual exploitation and jealousy, as well as retributive justice. The work, entitled *Switch* (1977), was choreographed by Bert Rose, who exploited elements of the maca-bre—including a death scream at the end—to create this somber chamber piece. The dancing was more lyrical but no less intense than that in *Legend of Lovers' Leap*, and the dramatic strength of Patsy Ricketts and Melanie Graham, alternating the part of the witch, was an excellent foil to Barry Moncrieffe's noble portrayal of the avenging fieldhand.

Bridging the gap between history and legend is the story of Nanny, discussed previously under the theme of matriarchy in terms of Sheila Barnett's *Ni—Woman of Destiny*.[35] In researching the historical background, choreographer Barnett did not ignore the epic accounts of the supernatural powers of the great Ashanti warrior who flourished during the first Maroon war of 1720–39. *I Not I* (1977) treated Jamaican dance in terms of the historical development of Jamaica—with its main population coming from Europe and Africa—and the ensuing creolization process that gave the society purpose and still describes the cultural dynamic of an entire region.

PLANTATION AMERICA AS CULTURAL SPHERE

The theme of plantation America within a wider cultural framework of which Jamaica is an integral part found expression in *The Crossing* (1978) with a driving musical score by Quincy Jones.[36] The work points up the cultural fact that Jamaicans and all other Caribbean peoples are an integral part of the Americas. The finale, titled "Goodbye, Motherland," speaks not merely to Jamaicans but to all Americans dispersed from their ancestral home. The Americas now constitute the home; yet roots in Europe, the Mediterranean, Africa, or the Orient can never be totally ignored. The outstretched arms of the clustered corps of dancers at the end of the dance point at once to affirmation and doubt—the fate of the

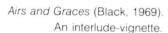
Airs and Graces (Black, 1969).
An interlude-vignette.

uprooted. The plaintive spiritual "Somebody's Calling My Name" is a high point of the piece. *The Crossing* matches other spiritual-inspired Company dances, all of which are evocations of the dynamics of plantation America, where Europe has met Africa on foreign soil and where Europe's melody makes sense only with Africa's rhythm. In this context many Company dance works—such as Sheila Barnett's *In the Spirit*, Bert Rose's *Glory Road,* and Nettleford's *Journeys* and *The Gospel According To*—are tributes to this cultural sensibility, which was brilliantly and unsurpassingly celebrated in Alvin Ailey's monumental *Revelations*. Ailey offered the National Dance Theatre Company this masterpiece, but neither time nor funds were available to bring the work into the repertoire. Yet two brief episodes—the solo "I Want to Be Ready" and the duet "Fix Me, Jesus"—were included in the repertoire, with guest artist Clive Thompson first dancing the former in 1975 and teaming up with Patsy Ricketts for the latter a year later.

Another dimension of plantation America's cultural impact on the Company repertoire can be seen in the jazz works. Jazz is truly the classic music of the United States, one of the most compelling cultural expressions that developed out of plantation America. Eddy Thomas—in *Footnotes in Jazz* (1962), a modern essay on the Dave Brubeck–Leonard Bernstein score *Dialogues for Jazz Combo Orchestra*—was the first Company choreographer to investigate this area. It became an early classic and differed markedly from Neville Black's more conventional, kinetic, syncopated, sharp-turning, fast-moving set pieces such as *Bach, Brubeck, and Company* (1968). Not until 1982 did this kind of driving spatial thrust of Americana return to the repertoire; *Phases,* with obvious quotations from Alvin Ailey, was choreographed by Tony Wilson, fresh out of Chicago and New York. He selected his music from the instrumental version of *West Side Story*. Before that, there were efforts by Nettleford, such as *Peace Offering* (1976), danced to the concert music of Keith Jarrett, and the more upbeat *Wonder Love and Raise* (1977), to Stevie Wonder's music.

Soul music provided inspiration for Bert Rose, who added the love duets *Caro* (1976) and *Ebb Flow* (1978), the mood solo *Moods* (1976), and the group

Murals (Barnett, 1971). A dance mosaic to music by Bach and Villa-Lobos.

The Awakening (Black, 1966). An
exhibition duet celebrates the
dynamics of jazz.

African Scenario (Nettleford, 1962).
First Company work to affirm the direct
debt of Caribbean culture to Africa.

work *Jubilate* (1976), which was a kind of companion piece to Patsy Ricketts's *Someday*, also choreographed in 1976. Neville Black had done a real exhibition duet, entitled *The Awakening* (1966), designed to show off the virtuosity of the dancers as much as to celebrate the dynamics of jazz. George Gershwin's controversial but exquisite *Porgy and Bess* inspired the 1983 dance work *Soulscape*. Although the jazz dimensions were subsumed under a scenario revolving around indecisive love, the work nevertheless was guided by the world of jazz, as was Sheila Barnett's *Jazz Fantasia* (1963) and Eddy Thomas's *Six and a Trumpet* (1965)—no longer in the repertoire—which featured a trumpeter (Billy Cooke) onstage.

DANCE EXPLORATIONS: ABSTRACT FORMS

Another approach to dance form was revealed in works that explored dance for its own sake, the nonnarrative dance. The urge for experimentation, conscious or otherwise, is important to every enterprising creative artist. All of the major choreographers in the Company have been compelled by this urge. Such explorations transcend categories of style and genre—whether dance drama, folk, modern, neoclassic, or ritual. Marked by a high degree of abstraction, they were often devised in suite form. Sometimes there was the barest thread of narrative or there were loosely connected links of a particular pattern. Many were short-lived and others went into a natural decline after having served a purpose as testing ground or prologue to more substantial pieces. Eddy Thomas often worked in pure movement forms in spare, linear pieces such as *A Time to Re-*

Fantasy (Requa, 1982). A young man haunted by his dreams of ideal love.

joice (1962) and *Liza* (1963). In the latter dance he chose the situation of a mournful admirer of the heroine as the focal point of the choreography, also utilizing a chorus of jersey-clad women and a central figure suggesting water, alternately cascading, flowing gently, lying still without being stagnant, or becoming turbulent. Thomas's *Concert Suite* (1964)—a virtuoso set of dances to the music of Lennox Berkely, with the pianist on stage—was suggestive of the European ballet étude form. Neville Black's *Waltz Suite* (1965) and *Night Dances* (1969) went even further with the classical ballet idiom and included decor reminiscent of an earlier romantic mode. These works were diverting, but it became obvious that the classical tradition was a dead end for the Company. Black's *Legendary Landscape* (1968), drawing on the movement of forest creatures and his own facility for inventive shapes and forms, pointed to more challenging dimensions. But the most satisfying and organic of his abstract works was the effectively staged *Rites* (1965), performed to *Sensemaya* by the Mexican composer Silvestre Revueltas.

Sheila Barnett's specific dance training was an important guide in her attempts at making sense out of form, pattern, subtleties of execution, tempo, rhythm, and intensity of movement. *Jazz Fantasia* (1963), a study utilizing the spoken word; *Ring Hunt* (1968), a love duet; *Images* (1969), a design of shapes and forms; *Murals* (1971), a dance mosaic with the stage serving as the wall—all were explorations of movement for its own sake. Each Company dancer was confronted by a challenge, the whole being involved in nothing but motion. Although John Jones's *Windsong* (1973) had a scenario, the main thrust of the choreography was a study in abstract patterns. Admittedly it was based on other important choreographic versions of Claude Debussy's symphonic poem *Prélude à l'Après-Midi d'un Faune*. When it was performed at the Brooklyn Academy of Music in 1974, Anna Kisselgoff was generously discerning about its influences: "*Windsong* . . . is interesting not only because it works on its own terms but because any dance fan will instantly recognize its source. Mr. Jones, who was a member of Jerome Robbins's Ballets: USA company, is giving us a paraphrase of Mr. Robbins's own *Afternoon of a Faun*. But since the Robbins work is

Moods (Rose, 1976). A mood solo to soul music.

also a paraphrase of the Nijinsky original, we have a paraphrase of a paraphrase. Oddly enough, Mr. Jones has gotten away with the impossible."[37]

Rex Nettleford had made his own forays into pure dance explorations. *Gallandar la Pava* (1963), a suite of dances to Colombian folk music, attempted to do with traditional Latin American music what was done the previous year with African forms in *African Scenario*. Modified folk movement can easily lose spontaneity, and as joyful and snazzily costumed as it was by Eddy Thomas, *Gallandar la Pava* deserved no more than the short, though active, life it enjoyed for a few seasons. Although *Night Shelter* (1967) by Neville Black and *Parade Kingston 13* (1965) by Eddy Thomas explored folk material in somewhat modern terms, neither piece was able to overcome the idiomatic stubbornness of traditional Caribbean dance patterns. Success came later, after numerous revisions, with *Celebrations* (1972), which abstracted Caribbean folk forms just enough to achieve a fusion of contemporary sensibilities with ancestral modes. By the time it was ready to travel New York dance critic Clive Barnes felt obliged to describe it as a "delightfully zestful demonstration of the full company's power."[38] Success also attended *Drumscore* (1979)—previously analyzed in terms of the African presence in the Caribbean—which is as much the affirmation of Caribbean movement patterns as it is of the sounds and rhythms that shape those patterns.

More direct affirmations were sought in other Nettleford works such as *Elements* (1978) and *Litany* (1982). Both attempted to share with audiences not only the distillation of the creative process but also the sources of the choreographic movements. *Elements* drew on special interests of Company members: Bert Rose's skill in modern dance, Patsy Ricketts's interest in Rastafari and the reggae culture, Jackie Guy's knowledge of traditional Jamaican dance, and—on second mounting—Eduardo Rivero's familiarity with Yoruba customs and his developed modern dance muscularity, both of which added a new dynamic to the opening section of the work. The patterns for *Litany* were hinged on a scenario involving the birth process and various stages of growth. It included a short sequence by the young Company dancer Duran Hylton, who exploited traditional movement for the male sequence he created.

Another Nettleford work, *Back to Bach, Viva Bach* (1979)—choreographed to the lute and harpsichord music of Bach and Vivaldi—seemed to hark back to earlier explorations like *Dance Andante* (1965), danced to Schubert's *Trout* Quintet. Yet *Back to Bach* not only implied greater integration of movement and form, it also linked Caribbean Creole forms to the antiphonal configurations suggested by the fugue. Eduardo Rivero's quietly assertive *Sulkari*—particularly relevant to the earlier discussion on the Afro-Caribbean ethos—is a different treatment of Caribbean patterns. The arched back, proud carriage, the hold of the back in a spiral twist above a firm pelvis, the flatfooted contact with the ground on bent knees, the acrobatic leaps of the men, the firmly flexed feet, the carriage of the arms set akimbo or held firmly behind the head with shoulder blades touching as in Yoruba agbadza,[39] and the grand processional—all these African-inspired elements are critical to Caribbean dance aesthetics. They resolutely express exploration, celebration, affirmation.

CELEBRATION OF LOVE

Exploration and affirmation are also attributes of the love theme, which is found throughout the repertoire, although this particular theme does not receive the sort of concentration that might be expected. Perhaps the Company has conspired to avoid the hackneyed and predictable treatment the love theme has received in many expressions of modern dance theater. Yet the actual physical nature of the art form is irresistible. Thus the indomitable love duet has often been examined by Company choreographers. Black's *The Awakening*, Barnett's *Ring Hunt*, Jones's *Windsong*, and Rose's *Caro* and *Ebb Flow* are some direct encounters with love, while *African Scenario*, *Dialogue for Three*, *Ni—Woman of Destiny*, *Two Drums for Babylon*, *Masques of God*, *The Crossing*, and *The Brothers* embrace the theme without lingering in passionate embrace. Not even Nettleford's *Soulscape* (1983), which purports to be about the urge to love, tarries on the intimacies of loving. *Fantasy* (1982) by Barbara Requa is likely to be remembered more for the frustration rather than the fulfillment of dreams of a young man's ideal love. Could it be that Jamaicans find demonstrative expressions of private emotional feelings and affairs of the heart embarrassing? This is certainly what is suggested by the lyrics of a suite of love songs in the repertoire of the NDTC Singers.[40] One of the legacies of the Anglo-Saxon heritage in the Caribbean seems to be an entrenched Afro-Saxon reserve in such matters. Yet the 1983 season of dance produced numerous works with love in them. Besides Nettleford's *Soulscape*, these include dances like Sheila Barnett's *Summer Is*, Clive Thompson's *Recollections,* and Tony Wilson's *Progeny*, which, like the earlier *Brothers*, is an essay about family relationships.

INTERLUDES AND DIVERSIONS

The repertoire also includes a group of miscellaneous categories, which in the earliest period were manifested mainly in vignettes exploiting mime and gesture to humorous advantage. They were little more than interludes and diversions, and they were abandoned as choreographic skills developed enough to integrate such elements into larger dance works and as artistic policy turned more toward programs that sought greater unity. Later a series of isolated solos danced to vocal renditions of American popular songs became a favorite with choreographers as well as with audiences. The dances faced the risk, however, of being carried by the vocalist rather than by the choreographer, and their survival was seriously threatened by the constant changes in taste in pop music. Bert Rose's extremely popular *Moods*, mentioned under the category of plantation America, was the most successful in that genre. Roberta Flack's "Let Them Talk" served as the music. Ultimately such efforts could not provide the source of energy for a definitive technique, vocabulary, and style of the National Dance Theatre Company in terms of the Company's stated objectives of forging an art mediated by social reality and possessed of its own logic for inspiring action through creative invention.

Traditional music of the Caribbean forms the basis of many scores arranged for the National Dance Theatre Company. The NDTC Singers, in the background, are being led by Marjorie Whylie, the Company musical director (left on drum), while drummers Billy Lawrence (left) and Leaford McFarlane (right) play the benta, an instrument made of bamboo.

4 · The Music

The National Dance Theatre Company has over the years selected for its rhythmic and musical support a wide range of compositions from many parts of the world—the United States, Latin America, Europe, and Africa, as well as the Caribbean itself, being the primary sources. The choreographers have been inspired by a gamut of musical styles, from Johann Sebastian Bach to Dave Brubeck, from Paul Hindemith to Roberta Flack. They have utilized the popular music of Hispanic America as well as serious music by composers such as Argentina's Ariel Ramírez, Brazil's Heitor Villa-Lobos, and Mexico's Silvestre Revueltas; the Spanish composer Joaquín Rodrigo has also been a favorite. Classical European music forms ranging from ornamental baroque to atonal modern—including the compositions of Georg Philipp Telemann, Antonio Vivaldi, Franz Schubert, Claude Debussy, Maurice Ravel, Darius Milhaud, Sergei Prokofiev, Igor Stravinsky, and Béla Bartók—have been important, and modern American composers for the dance and the musical theater, such as Aaron Copland, George Gershwin, and Leonard Bernstein, were natural choices. But the Company's persistent emphasis has been on the great American jazz classicists such as Duke Ellington, Charlie Mingus, Hubert Laws, Keith Jarrett, Stevie Wonder, Ahmad Jamal, Quincy Jones, Miles Davis, Yusef Lateef, Dave Brubeck, Cannonball Adderley, Art Blakey, Herbie Hancock, and Chick Corea.

Such a range of music may suggest on the one hand a high level of musical sophistication or an eclectic catholicity of taste; on the other it may seem to be nothing so much as a mélange of confusion. Yet a perceptive defense of the use of apparently disparate styles was offered by Pamela O'Gorman, director of the Jamaica School of Music, during the 1982 symposium in Kingston commemorating the collaboration of the National Dance Theatre Company and the School of Dance: "We talk of Jamaica being a multicultural society, but one cannot think of any other theatre or artistic pursuit in Jamaica [besides the National Dance Theatre Company] where we get the different strands of Jamaican culture coming together so naturally. Looking at the repertoire of the NDTC, you have the [European] classical period and also contemporary composers; you have pop music, folk music, composed music, and reggae. These different strands come together naturally. There is never any feeling that they are being forced, and this in itself is an achievement."[1]

Oswald Russell (seated at piano), one of the first Jamaican composers to write music specifically for Company works, discusses a score with Rex Nettleford in 1963.

A page of the score of Oswald Russell's *Games of Arms*, composed for the dance work choreographed by Eddy Thomas in 1963.

The musical selections chosen by the Company are such an integral part of their presentations that the Toronto critic William Littler felt obliged to write about the performances: "If you don't go to watch you can just as profitably go to listen to it. The singing and the drumming by themselves have turned me into a Jamaicaophile."[2] The singing and the drumming Littler refers to is not only the Caribbean music arranged from traditional sounds and rhythms of Jamaica and other Caribbean cultures but also the original compositions themselves. The original compositions are of particular importance because they served the dance works more appropriately than music independently created usually does. Between 1962 and 1980 more than a dozen scores were commissioned especially for Company dances. In 1962 Oswald Russell composed music for Eddy Thomas's *Legend of Lovers' Leap* as well as for Thomas's celebratory *A Time to Rejoice*. The following year Russell again collaborated with Thomas on *Games of Arms,* while Noel Dexter wrote a short jonkonnu sequence for Rex Nettleford's *Plantation Revelry*. Eddy Thomas was also a musician, providing his own music for *Parade Kingston 13* in 1965. There was a hiatus in original scores until 1970, when Marjorie Whylie, the Company's musical director, began her significant collaboration with Sheila Barnett on the dance drama *Shadows,* which was followed by *Mountain Women* (1972), *Ni—Woman of Destiny* (1976), and *I Not I* (1977). Sheila Barnett commissioned other original compositions, such as *A Question of Balance* (1972) from Bob Sinicrope, a visiting American Peace Corps worker, and *Chainlinks* (1979) from the Jamaican jazz musician Cedric "Im" Brooks.

Rex Nettleford's first major commission for original music was in 1980, when the Boston-trained Jamaican musician Peter Ashbourne collaborated on an up-dated version of *Two Drums for Babylon.* The piece is scored for piano syn-thesizer and drums. Ashbourne thought of the drum as the basic element in this work, also re-creating drum rhythms on his synthesizer. Ashbourne's approach to his materials is more lyrical than Whylie's. Yet there is also a great deal of dramatic development, the harmony being pursued for emotional and psycho-logical purposes. Counterpoint is very much in evidence as one of the devices of this composer, who thinks in basic musical terms. On the other hand Whylie, who is steeped in folklore, advances a totally different approach to composition.

The NDTC Orchestra is led by Marjorie Whylie on piano. The other musicians are (left to right) Irvine Jarrett and Steve Golding on conga drums; Lloyd Mason (standing) on guitar; Antonio Henry and Ronan Critchlow on conga drums; and Barbara Boland and Minky Jefferson on flute.

The drummers often provide the rhythms that pulsate in the Company's varied repertoire. Pictured are (left to right) Carl Messado, master drummer Ronan Critchlow, and Marjorie Whylie.

Whylie's *Ni—Woman of Destiny* and Ashbourne's *Two Drums for Babylon* offer an interesting contrast to each other; yet in separate ways they achieve the same end, as Pamela O'Gorman has pointed out.[3]

It was this quiet magic of Marjorie Whylie's music that forged the collaboration with Nettleford for *Litany,* which is like a hymn of praise to the growth of the Company. But earlier there had been many collaborations of a more deeply organic nature in Whylie's arrangements for works rooted in the experiences of Jamaican and other Caribbean peoples with direct references to both their music and their customs. Beginning with the arrangements for the NDTC Singers, audiences have been able to appreciate the beauty and special expressive qualities of the songs that developed out of the collective genius of the ordinary people. Not only did the traditional ancestral music of Jamaica receive focus

Traditional kumina drummers have worked with the National Dance Theatre Company since 1970. In the foreground are (left to right) Obadiah Lewis, playing the kbandu (bass drum); Samuel Copeland, with the shak-shak rattle; and James Walker on the playing cast (treble drum).

The NDTC Singers serve as a choral orchestra for many Company works. Joyce Lalor, the first leader of the singers, is at far right.

through the sensitive efforts of Whylie; so have a few of the songs in the contemporary ska, rocksteady, and reggae styles. Obviously the Company has employed the music of the great reggae composers—such as Bob Marley (*Court of Jah*), Jimmy Cliff (*Tribute to Cliff*), and Toots Hibbert (*Backlash*)—but Whylie's imaginative talents have also been a contributing factor, particularly in the minor-key fight sequence of *Backlash*, catching the spirit of Toots Hibbert's original compositions.

Marjorie Whylie's understanding of traditional musical form and idiom has been of critical importance to the overall artistic direction of the Company. Whylie belongs to a distinctive group of formally trained musicians who have learned to speak with a voice that places them in harmony with the environment. Her extensive fieldwork in rural Jamaica, studying the rituals and customs of the people, has given her a special authority in this regard. Even in the process of distillation she realizes that the original spirit of the source material must be maintained; the adaptation of the Cuban Yoruba sequences that accompanied *Sulkari* is one of her most enduring achievements. In *Kumina* the Company also experimented with traditional musicians by including them in the actual performance. Pamela O'Gorman considered it a "stroke of theatrical genius . . . to bring the two traditional drummers into *Kumina* [since] authentic traditional drummers have a quality that other musicians don't have."[4]

Under Marjorie Whylie's direction the Company musicians and singers later tackled another dance reflecting profound native roots, *Gerrehbenta*, which utilized the benta (a single-string bamboo instrument), used among the people of Saint Mary's parish. When Nettleford experimented with Caribbean rhythms in *Drumscore*, it was Whylie who was able to translate them into viable musical material. Improvisations in the studio, which were initiated under the direction of master drummer Ronan Critchlow, were later carried out under Whylie's supervision; this was part of the Company's creative process. The dance works based on ritual, the dramas that move to the pulse of the Caribbean, the majority of the Creole suites that celebrate Caribbean life, as well as the works that mirror the dynamics of the region are all danced to Whylie's creative compositions or arrangements. Whylie herself has given a convincing analysis of her specific approach in the creation of a musical score.

In composing the music for *Ni—Woman of Destiny,* the exercise was not a simple one. The considerations stretched beyond the employment of tried and proven Western techniques. The creative impulse was given full rein, but it had to be informed creativity. Having been given a very clear scenario by the choreographer, the discussions began as to texture, density and dynamics, mood and balance. But that was only a first step.

The African presence had to be addressed. The African concept of music admits many sounds—the clatter of sticks, the noise of shells and seeds, foot-stomping, hand-clapping, sustained sounds as well as those that cannot be sustained. And always the central position of drums; the drummer exercises to the spirit of creation from whom the components of his drums are obtained.

We were then faced with instrumentation, which took note of this but had also to make concessions to Western ears. Research into the tonality of West African languages had to be undertaken, to ensure that melodies composed did not fall when they should rise and vice versa. Within the Maroon repertoire, however, one found a great many songs which could be lifted and used intact.

The music of *Ni* then is a mix of the traditional–ancestral and informed creation.[5]

There are many parallels in the music of the Caribbean islands, and in some instances the similarities are unexpected.[6] Legal sanctions against the use of the skin drum in the Caribbean encouraged many subterfuge methods of obtaining the same rhythmic effect—handclapping, foot-stomping, and, by extension, the use of steel drums, gourds, clappers, and stomping tubes. Stomping tubes are still found in Haiti (vaccines), Trinidad (bamboo-tamboos), and in Jamaica among the Mae River Kumina people.[7] There is also the similarity of goombay of the Bahamas, mento of Jamaica, and calypso of Trinidad—all genres of complaint, recrimination, ridicule, and humor.

Perhaps the most striking parallel is between the tambu dance of Jamaica and the bamboula dance prevalent in the French West Indies and the Virgin Islands—as well as in Louisiana till the end of the nineteenth century. The dance gets its name from the tambu drum, a large one-headed drum straddled by the player and beaten with the hands or at times with the feet. Kata sticks are played on the body of the drum by another player. The dance is done on the occasion of nine-night and last prayers.[8]

In the continuous search for music that depicts special moods and that has rhythms evoking appropriate body responses, the Company over the years has increasingly turned to native Caribbean music. Haitian drum rhythms and drumming technique were important in the early years, when the Company was unaware of the rich drumming heritage of Jamaica. Since then an indigenous style of drumming has been developed, incorporating modifications of traditional Jamaican ritual rhythms. As the experimental dance vocabulary grows, so does the repertoire of the Company's drummers. Consequently many rhythms derived from traditional African and neo-African utterances have also been incorporated into the music.

Caribbean songs were integrated into the early West Indian suites within the Company repertoire: arrangements of "Santa Foulle" from Saint Lucia for the *French West Indian Suite* and "Gee Bongo Lay" from Trinidad for the *Afro–West Indian Suite*. Later there were arrangements of traditional melodies for *Jamaica Promenade* and *Folkform*. *Celebrations* consciously deals with West Indian themes, and the finale of *Myal* is set to the Bahamian folksong "Letter from Miami."

The NDTC Singers, as a kind of choral orchestra which fits the Company's concept of total theater, have presented West Indian songs with great success. The situations related in the songs are familiar to everyone's experiences. The audiences understand perfectly the naughtiness of "Marle Lumbe" of Belize, the suggestiveness of "Chiffone" of Carriacou, and the songs involving the male and female tales of Sancho and Sitira of Guyana, as well as the wide range of emotions expressed in "Charlotte," "I'm a Better Woman Than You," "Shame, Marjorie Murdock," "Ogun Bele," and "Medelico" of Trinidad.

There is much to be said for the accomplishments of the National Dance Theatre Company in their music experimentations. The Company has helped to sustain for Jamaicans a consciousness of the musical integrity of rural Jamaica and has made many middle-class Jamaicans keenly aware of the beauty and vitality of African music, particularly in *African Scenario*. The NDTC Singers brought an African performing style into the performance of traditional Jamaican music. At the same time the Company has acknowledged reggae pop stars as legitimate artists in their own right. Local composers, such as Marjorie Whylie, Peter Ashbourne, Eddy Thomas, and Cedric "Im" Brooks, have been inspired to do some of their most extended work. Movement and music have been integrated in new ways: for example, the NDTC Singers have been organized as a choral orchestra or the dancers themselves have been the singers (as in *I Not I*). Another innovation has been coordinating the dance with established music so that audiences have often identified the music closely with the dance, such as in *Dialogue for Three* with the adagio movement of Joaquín Rodrigo's guitar concerto *Concierto de Aranjuez* and *The Crossing* with Quincy Jones's *Roots*.

5 · Technique, Vocabulary, and Style

The dynamic interplay between technique, vocabulary, and style is what has given the National Dance Theatre Company its special character as a group in formation. The definition of these three aspects of dance aesthetics is somewhat elusive, but an analysis of their general applications may help pinpoint the challenge facing the Company and affirm the urgency of the quest for an art form that is itself the art of discovery. The question becomes not whether European classical ballet is superior to American modern dance or to Broadway jazz dancing or whether Western dance expressions in general are better than other types of dance, such as the great dance theater traditions of Africa, India, and Asia. The questions were best posed in terms of the nature and meaning of definitive expressions developed by the genius of separate civilizations, especially if such civilizations are emergent ones. What then are the characteristic features of such expressions that make them different from one another so that they are separately identifiable? Yet what characteristics do they share that place them all within the realm of the art of dance?

Caribbean dance theater in its formation has drawn not only on the kinetic range and spiritual energies of the human body—the prime instrument of expression—but also on the region's social, religious, and historical experiences. The continuing exploration and invention in terms of movement, stage effects, music, and related aesthetic expressions are also important aspects of its development. The process is similar to dance theater formation anywhere. What then is the argument about the validity of dance expression by Caribbean groups much like Jamaica's National Dance Theatre Company?

Indeed the Company does not dance like the British Royal Ballet or like the New York City Ballet, George Balanchine's gift to the United States. Nor is it predicated on the artistic and political premises of a Dance Theater of Harlem, though the dancers of both companies bear obvious physical resemblances to one another. Although the National Dance Theatre Company shares stylistic similarities with the Alvin Ailey American Dance Theater, the Ailey company moves to the pulse of America, not to that of the Caribbean. Despite a shared vocabulary, the Company is not precisely modern in the sense that Martha Graham, Paul Taylor, Merce Cunningham, Murray Louis, or Alwin Nikolais is. The

According to Puerto Rican composer Hector Campos-Parsi, Caribbean dance fuses the "tradition of modern occidental music and the ancestral body wisdom of our forefathers." (*Owen Minott*)

National Dance Theatre Company is not even like the Guinea Ballet or the Ballets Africains of Senegal, for African continuities in the Caribbean produced new forms. What then distinguishes the work of Caribbean dance theater generally and Jamaica's National Dance Theatre Company in particular? How do Jamaicans and the Caribbean people themselves view their dance theater in terms of technique, vocabulary, and style? How do others see it?

When Europeans write about international dance, areas like the Caribbean, the Orient, and Africa, all great dancing regions of the world, are for the most part ignored—no doubt through genuine ignorance but also through ethnocentric arrogance. What is essentially one genre of dance theater becomes the unique representation of the art of dance. The concept of European classical ballet apparently permits no other qualification because presumably the European form is the only classical dance. For example, the classical dance traditions of the Orient are almost totally ignored.[1]

All civilizations by definition share certain modes of artistic manifestations, which are categorized broadly as ancestral–traditional, popular–contemporary, and classic. These three aesthetic modes interrelate symbiotically: traditional forms influence the classics, popular expressions eventually establish themselves as traditional, and the classics even draw on pop culture. The National Dance Theatre Company, conscious of the organic nature of such relationships, has been an instrument in shaping a classic mode of dance by utilizing the potentials of all other artistic manifestations. In fact being in command of such a process is a responsibility of any society that seeks to become civilized and invest its new-found power with human sensibilities that manifest themselves most urgently in the products of the creative imagination.

Therefore it is important to codify significant Caribbean discoveries in these areas. This is important for the society as a whole, which, as a society of severance, has been reared on the view that nothing it has created is of any real importance. Dance generally lends itself to this kind of philosophical approach. Yet documentation and acute analysis, which may be of universal importance to dance culture, is of special importance to developing countries like Jamaica, where the habit of recording the history of its people—as well as the deeds of its creative artists—is not fully explored. Cultural processes should not have to start from scratch with each new venture, and past experience can inform new policy and act as a guide for future action. A distinctive technique, vocabulary, and style constitute a sort of memory bank for the art.

Technique

The technical foundations of the National Dance Theatre Company naturally rest on the kinetic potentials of the human body. Therefore a class that prepares the dancer, sustaining his or her skills, employs common movements, such as jump, walk, run, glide, push, suspension, and swing. The dancers learn to spin into motion and cantilever into balances; they must contract and release to various tempi, alternately defying gravity and yielding to it with varying speeds of movement while they contrast energy forces with spatial emphasis. This language indeed suggests the influences of a modern American dance style. Company teachers such as Eddy Thomas, Neville Black, Bert Rose, and Barry Moncrieffe have definitely learned important aspects of their technique in the various schools of modern dance they studied at in New York and elsewhere. But teachers like Sheila Barnett and Barbara Requa—who take a different creative approach in molding the body's awareness of its potential in terms of alignment, kinetic range, and dynamics—have also been vital in building a technique consistent with the purposes of a native Jamaican dance theater. Other sources of movement, such as those exploited in recreation games, bring to the technique such specific gestures as the toss, pitch, pass, catch, long lunge, dribble, dive, or even backstroke. Exercises were devised to perfect these movements and invest them with a special eloquence that carries aesthetic weight in terms of dance vocabulary.

The iconoclastic spirit of modern dance was an inspiration in forging from traditional dance those technical elements that are not only viable but also transmittable as part of the system of training. The Company's artistic director along with other Company members found challenges in the repertory of traditional social dances, such as the quadrille, jonkonnu, and contredanse scarf dances. Indeed the experimentation with aspects of both modern dance techniques and European classical ballet principles has been part of the process of re-creation and revitalization, in order to retain the power of certain movements that will evoke the hidden realities of contemporary Jamaican and Caribbean life. Part of the research involved articulating the vast repertory of movements encased in ancestral rituals, ring-plays, and recreational dances, as well as in traditional songs and stories. Yet classical ballet also served as model since the national folk dances of Europe were absorbed by the classical dance theater.

When stripped of ethnocentric prejudices, the spirit of European classical dance theater has much to offer if only for its anatomically scientific foundations tested over a few centuries. A basic ballet barre with its potential for strengthening the limbs—especially the feet and legs—aiding body alignment, and facilitating stretches and extensions has served the Company well. But the unorthodox mix of contracting pelvises, supple spines, flexed feet, rippling torsos at the barre would be anathema to the purist, for whom the linear beauty of an arabesque is aesthetically more rewarding than a sculpted asymmetrical line of movement in three dimensions.

Thus the National Dance Theatre Company draws seriously on a wide range of technical sources, involving not only the heritage of European classical ballet

A basic ballet barre aids the dancer in body alignment and facilitates stretches and extensions.

and American modern dance but also the creative aspects of free-form dance and physical education exercises as well the repertory of movements inspired by ancestral rituals, social dances, and even contemporary street gestures. Significant technical possibilities have been experimented with utilizing these varied sources, which are now being shaped into a codified system of training. But unfortunately there is still a prevailing view among many Jamaicans that only dance theater with a European classical grounding is viable. This view is especially prevalent among the Jamaican privileged classes and the teachers of classical ballet. In their minds classical technique should be the basis for a dance theater tradition associated with cultural legitimacy and power in post-colonial Jamaica.[2]

With the diverse backgrounds of the founding members of the Company it was tactical to utilize the knowledge and experiences they had already gained. Special attention, naturally, had to be given to what Sheila Barnett has appropriately described as the "analysis of the traditional folk material of Jamaica and parallels in the Caribbean territories studied for commonalities and principles [which] had to be combined into cohesive expressive forms."[3] It was necessary at times to bypass individual variations and to accept the discipline of selected routines, demanding accuracy in movement and gestures from all performers.

The Company classes were organized into two categories: ballet–modern and folk. Ballet–modern classes were made up of four approaches: (1) ballet barre exercises, (2) center work, (3) floor exercises, and (4) progressions. The barre work emphasized traditional ballet exercises. The center work included complementary and compatible modern and ballet sequences. Floor work was strongly Graham at first but later incorporated aspects of Jamaican dance that stressed a characteristic way of releasing energy: the rib cage was free rather than fixed, and the hip less stable, permitting movement in all directions. Progressions combined kinetic and axial movements from Jamaican idioms and other sources.

The folk classes were also organized using the same four approaches. The barre work here was developed from elements native to Jamaican and Caribbean dance. Center work included various exercises that stress the low center of gravity, such as movements beginning from the hip, a stretched spine, and long curvature of the lower back, as well as movement of the torso over a moving base in order to create tilts and imbalances that project an asymmetrical illusion. Floor exercises utilized various body positions common to Jamaican folk dances. Progressions included a combination of steps and body movements that developed the dancer's ability to set up polyrhythms as the body travels through space.

Such a polarization into ballet—modern and folk was a shorthand way of dealing with the complexities of continuing experimentation. The versatility of the Company dancer is a function of this wide-ranging training. The demands for a codified technique meant special emphases in studio classes: coordinated placement of pelvis, shoulders, arms, legs, and feet to create three-dimensional designs in space; setting up of different rhythms in the body simultaneously in response to the polyrhythmic sounds native to the Caribbean; flexibility of the spine for rippling movement to the $6/8$ rhythm of the drumming, in contrast to the stately but stiff $3/4$ waltz time of the classical tradition; pliability of the rib cage for lateral isolations; strengthening of the pelvic region for rotational movement; articulation of the forward—backward thrust of the pelvis in contraction and

Floor work in the National Dance Theatre Company's early years of training was influenced by Martha Graham's techniques. Aspects of Jamaican traditional dance, which emphasizes a specific Caribbean way of releasing energy, were later incorporated into the Company's technical approach.

Spread, stretch, reach, recover—the basics of dance training.

release, which guarantees spatial progression. There is also the typically Caribbean hip sway often exploited for humor or for erotic expression.

Caribbean folk dances, particularly those still danced by an older generation, emphasize the body's center as if to celebrate life itself. These dances seem to recall a period when procreation and childbearing guaranteed men and women a sense of place and purpose. Building strength in the legs and feet is critical: strong feet and toes are needed for earth-centered movements, and sinewy calves will be resistant to the strains of marching and shuffling. Strong knees are requisite for attitudes of obeisance to the gods during ritual ceremonies, and strong thighs support a torso rippling horizontally while possessed of a particular spirit. The flexed foot is useful as symbol not only of hoe and pickax but also of resolution, strength, and earthiness. The arms, like other parts of the body, must be able to describe the curve of mountains, the flow of rivers, and the ebb and flow of oceans, just as in other traditions the movements of swans and the shapes of Gothic cathedrals, skyscrapers, and pine trees piercing the winter sky have found correspondences in dance attitudes. Movement in the Caribbean is outward and open; in northern environments it is more contracted and self-centered, perhaps as protection of one's body against the winter cold or as psychological retreat into the caves of the heart reflecting some kind of Freudian escape from a cruel world. Such spiritual imperatives are beginning to impinge on urban and middle-class life in the Caribbean, and Company dances have portrayed them, but the natural environment, even if now more fragile, is less eroded and peasant sensibilities still abound.

The flow from toe to crown imposes technical training that encourages coordination of the total body while it also allows for the isolation of different parts of the body to set up rhythmic counterpoint. There are many technical discoveries throughout the international dance world to aid Caribbean choreographers and teachers. It is not difficult to justify borrowing from established techniques of Western dance art to serve the special needs of the Caribbean dancer. But indiscriminate eclecticism must give way to an integrated system of technical training. Much of this will be accomplished by conscious efforts in schools and studios. But the most satisfying solutions will inevitably be developed by means of innovative choreography addressing technical needs. Caribbean dance culture must therefore speak with its own voice; that is, it must move with its own kinetic force and aesthetic conviction. That voice is the summary utterance of a vocabulary that is served by the technique.

The rib cage is free, rather than fixed, and the hip is fluid, permitting movement back and forth, from side to side, and in rotation.

Vocabulary

The vocabulary of Caribbean dance exists on a continuum, and its future is determined by the dynamics of that continuum. The intervention of a European classical ballet step into a sequence of an Afro-Caribbean dance rooted in hip-swaying, pelvic-propelled, earth-centered progressions may serve as pointed dramatic effect in a piece of choreography, whether or not the choreographer has formally studied classical ballet. The dancer is certain to be acquainted with the vocabulary of these forms as well as with certain variations of what is called modern dance, which developed in the United States. Yet there is a logic and inner consistency in the way Caribbeans move which give to the commonplace crawl, hop, skip, jump, walk distinctive aesthetic significance. This is closely allied to the structure of a country's musical forms as well as to the shared cultural values of creators, performers, and audiences alike.

If only for the sake of convenience, distinctive dance movements and gestures must have names. In the Caribbean the question immediately arises as to which language should be used. The European classical tradition settled for French, at one time the lingua franca and international diplomatic language, only recently eclipsed by English. Wherever Europe has colonized, the native population has been made to feel that the dance vocabulary must be French. Indians and Africans have held out, moving to Kathakali in India or to the different tribal

Progressions develop the dancer's ability to set up polyrhythms as the body travels through space. The flexed foot is symbolic of the hoe, pickax, earthiness, and resolve common to Caribbean traditions. (*Battle Vaughan, Miami Herald*)

The arms are expressive of the Caribbean experience, describing the curve of mountains, the flow of rivers, the ebb and flow of the ocean.

idioms throughout Africa. Because of colonialism the Caribbean area was less independent. The modern dance idiom in the United States has insisted on English terminology—such as spirals, relaxation–tension, contractions and releases, leaps, stretches, bends, falls, recoveries. But for many people concerned with tradition a plié seems to suggest a more profound technical feat than the bend, and rising on one's toes is best accomplished by means of a relevé. An extension carries less prestige than a développé, and the change of the back may be considered somewhat inelegant when an épaulement succeeds in carrying out the movement. In Jamaica the question of language presents a problem in dance communication, especially for those who settle for the use of French despite their lack of knowledge of European ballet technique.

Of course the terminology of American modern dance is also acceptable since English is Jamaica's official language. Yet there is no English word that describes the basic steps from kumina, dinkimini, tambu, and etu, all indigenous Jamaican dances. Thus dance steps derived from Caribbean rituals are best described by native names. The low back bend with pelvis forward and face up in the air on top of inching toes is called the limbo in Trinidad. In the Maroon community of Jamaica it is the masumba, which Sheila Barnett used effectively in *Ni—Woman of Destiny*. This inching movement using the toes on a flat foot firmly fixed on the ground has no name in traditional Western dance. Nor is there a word for the kind of port de bras where the arms are set akimbo—whether placed on the hips or overhead as if carrying a weight. There is no word for the extension—or twisted extension—of the spine into the shape of the letter S; in many ballet manuals this posture is even frowned upon. Nor are there terms for the countless movements of the feet or the pliant torsos of Caribbean dancers re-creating the throes of spirit possession or imitating the improvisations of recreational dances.

For the purposes of codification an analogy to Caribbean music may be instructive. The Trinidadians have added calypso to international music terminology to mean specifically the balladic musical forms that developed out of the ritual of pre-Lenten Carnival. Kaiso, the Creole term for calypso, is even more expressive.[4] The Jamaicans created reggae and gave it a distinctive name, which describes the music that emerged since the 1960s from the urban ghettos of Kingston.[5] It is also Creole in the strict sense of being native to a Caribbean country. Rhumba, samba, cha-cha, mambo, tango, and merengue have also been Latin America's contribution to the vocabulary of music and dance throughout the world. As with jazz in the United States, the imprint of the African diaspora on all of them is incontrovertible. The rituals of voodoo, kumina, pukkumina, santeria, and masquerade have lent their names to specific dance forms, especially Haiti's voodoo complex with its panoply of rites. Jamaica's dance theater tradition has drawn on the Haitian tradition as part of the sources of African continuities in the Caribbean.

The National Dance Theatre Company has developed its own emergent style, whereby symbols, like words, are characteristically linked together and performed in a way to communicate meanings in a specifically Jamaican and Caribbean way. Thus expressions of joy, sorrow, compassion, anger, fear are portrayed by movements mediated by Caribbean cultural perceptions.

Cheryl Ryman, a principal Company dancer and a dance researcher, has isolated a core vocabulary that evolved and sustained itself over the first two decades of the National Dance Theatre Company's existence and now also informs Jamaican dance activities independent of the Company.[6] She lists in detail many of the primary principles: contraction–release, rippling back or body waves, arched or hyperextended back, rib cage shifts (often with feet astride, as in second position), spiral and cross sit, flat back with side extension, low crouch turns, catch step, knee shuffles, off-balance leg extensions, slides to the ground, and hip side thrust, among others. She quite rightly identifies a strong modern dance influence on this terminology. But Europe's classical ballet is also part of the heritage and is retained primarily in adapted versions of jeté, fouetté, arabesque, attitude, pas de bourrée, pas de basque, sissonne, and so forth. Many steps based on traditional Caribbean movements are called by different names from one country to another, but Ryman has identified the kongo and the bambosche among others. Ryman also isolated the core forms in general terms: stretched, curved, and relaxed arms; held, stretched, cupped, flexed, and spread hands; pointed, flexed, relaxed, flat, inching, and "demipointe" feet. Patterns often occur in mass as a kind of visual polyrhythm, in columns of bodies deployed in straight or diagonal lines and circles, and in what she refers to as quadrille patterns, utilizing figure-eight weaves. Obviously the vocabulary also took into consideration certain peculiarities of dance expressions, such as the mechanical angularity of modern dance forms, developed in the industrial United States, which produce effects palpably different from the rounded, ebb-and-flow, and deceptively lethargic movements of the still largely agricultural seabound Caribbean.

Style

The predominant feature of the Company's emerging style is a cultural synthesis that reflects the diversity of Caribbean cultural realities. Synthesis does not refer to the simple linking of a variety of historical influences. It means the irreversible changes that resulted from the organic interaction of variant ingredients which produced something definably Caribbean—no longer purely European, African, East Indian, or Amerindian. Hence the central importance of the aesthetic articulation of Caribbean dance theater.

The popular and native dances in the traditional–ancestral mode are excellent examples of this organic mix of elements. The quadrille with its European basis and kumina with its obvious African elements are nonetheless native Caribbean forms of dance and music, but jonkonnu (masquerade) and pukkumina (revivalism) carry an even deeper stamp because they were not only developed in the region but were actually created there. In the popular mode, mento[7] and reggae are dynamic Jamaican forms of music with corresponding dance forms. But it is in the classical mode of expression that the National Dance Theatre Company is appropriately challenged not only to produce indigenously nurtured products of other cultures but more importantly to create artistic works that are specific to the imagination of the Jamaican and Caribbean people themselves. Cryptoballetic as well as American jazz and modern works have their rightful place in the repertoire and offer opportunities for certain innovations. They also relate to the heritage of the region. But the stamp of originality as a serious contribution to the mainstream world dance must come from those works which in the fusion of form and content with technique, vocabulary, and style offer an alternative way of seeing not only the art of dance but also cultural realities generally. It is in this sense that works like *Drumscore, Kumina, Celebrations, Myal, Pocomania, Mountain Women, I Not I, Ni—Woman of Destiny, Court of Jah, Backlash, Rockstone Debate, Sulkari,* and, to some extent, *Misa Criolla* and

The Crossing have made contributions in forging an indigenous style that gives the National Dance Theatre Company a special place in the world of dance.

Naturally there are other important works in the active repertoire—*Legend of Lovers' Leap* and *African Scenario* to name two—that have been invaluable experiments without staking out a definitive direction, and works such as *Dialogue for Three, The Rope and the Cross,* and *Switch* are creative gems that will remain in the repertoire for what they offer by way of enjoyment. No doubt these second and third categories of works continue to be questioned in terms of the Company's vision of an integrated Caribbean dance theater aesthetic. Yet in their own way they are influential in directing Jamaicans to an alternative way of looking at life and at themselves. Through a work like *Legend of Lovers' Leap* many Jamaicans would have encountered the Graham approach to dance for the first time, and they would have first experienced staged modern jazz dance through *Footnotes in Jazz. African Scenario* certainly prepared them for the ensuing appearances of the Ballets Africains in Jamaica and for the Company's own *Kumina* and *Myal* ten years later and *Gerrehbenta* two decades later. Such valid reasons will secure for these works a permanent place in the Company's repertoire. But these dances are qualitatively different from those works that more thoroughly achieve a unity of technique, vocabulary, and style in Caribbean terms. Without depriving itself of the rich and varied heritage of international dance, the Company realized that eclecticism, despite the obvious advantages of cultural pluralism, had to give way to a style that is less equivocal.

Style usually beggars description because of its elusive nature. Thus, despite the underlying unity and artistic coherence evident in the repertoire, the notion of eclecticism continues to be a handy tag for many critics attempting to pin down the National Dance Theatre Company. A number of foreign commentators have given useful accounts of their perceptions of the artistic profile of the Company, many of them targeting the cultural synthesis the Company exploits in its efforts at evolving a distinctive style.

The texture and diversity of the Caribbean cultural reality obviously presents problems not only abroad but also at home. Within the Caribbean itself the prominent Puerto Rican composer Hector Campos-Parsi observed that what the Company "has done is a distillation of the Antillean soul (this three-layered psyche born from the Amerindian, the African slave, and the European) of such rightness that all of us born in the Caribbean recognise as part of our most intimate self. Up to now our folk dance, our body attitudes and voices have been treated in the coloristic school, many times tainted with quaintness and quite frequently as a sort of exotic charm."[8] According to Campos-Parsi, the National Dance Theatre Company drastically changed this by creating out of native material a finely honed troupe of young people capable of transforming the Antillean soul into driving movement that surges with poetic drive, using the traditions of modern dance as well as the ancestral wisdom of body movement of

The Caribbean poet and playwright Derek Walcott has aptly described the style of the National Dance Theatre Company: "Two apparently different tensions become one ease, two cultures one metaphor."

the Jamaican people themselves. He felt that with the combination of music and modern theatrical devices the repertoire reflects a style that could be called Caribbeanism but comprehensible as well in terms of an international language. Derek Walcott, on seeing the Company, noted that a "work of art which is the last irony worth mentioning becomes itself by working against its mould. Mr. Net-

Dance critics Deborah Jowitt and Clive Barnes have both discussed the Company's achievements in terms of a resilient Afro-Caribbean style with a modern dance impulse.

tleford's belligerence, his revolutionary techniques lies in defying abstract movement. He strains to challenge and contradict it, and finally he absorbs it so that two apparently different tensions become one ease, two cultures one metaphor." Works like *Kumina* and *Pocomania* inspired him to a poetic description of the Company, which, he felt, manifested itself with "hair-pricking radiance of dignity, elation and cool asking for no conversions, is not out to convince."[9] For Walcott *Kumina* was imbued with authority and celebration.

The inherent authority and celebratory mood of the Company's style was also noted by non-Caribbean commentators. Clive Barnes writing in *The New York Times* felt that the Jamaican visitors danced with a "kind of insouciant vigor."[10] As with many commentators, he seemed to focus on the blend between traditional Caribbean sources and modern dance techniques. One sensed a feeling of triumph among the New York critics that American dance forms were sufficiently strong to influence a country like Jamaica. The blending of an indigenous style with modern dance made the Company unique according to *The New York Times* critic Anna Kisselgoff.[11] But it was Deborah Jowitt of *The Village Voice* who took the Company to task for their stylistic efforts: "How can you arrive at an aesthetic expression of black West Indies—past or present—by employing the very personal movement style created by a white American woman in the 1930s? Martha Graham's dance is taut, masochistic, neurotic in that every muscle seems braced against itself. The effect of such dancing can be stunning, but it is certainly inimical to the fluid, resilient Afro-Caribbean style."[12] Jowitt had clearly picked up on the burden of the inner conflict that characterized the Company's early artistic development. But she did not understand the enduring ambivalence of a richly textured and diverse society, which, though mostly black in color, is pluralist in cultural orientation. It is significant that Rex Nettleford and Sheila Barnett, the two choreographers who had the greatest influence on the Company's development, were not Graham-trained at all or out of the American schools of modern dance. While Jowitt found the singers and musicians excellent, she was uneasy with the variation of dance styles and technical levels and felt that the Company did not always live up to the promise of a distinctive style.

When the Company performed in Toronto in 1975, there were similar reservations about style put forward by *The Toronto Star*'s critic William Littler, who branded the Company's intentions of fusing disparate elements as bad art.[13] Maud Fuller was not daunted by the harsh review, which was evident in an article she wrote following the Company's 1981 visit to Toronto: "I had maintained all along that although the 1975 critique had been harsh, the amount of space allowed and the analytical tone of the piece were indicative of the fact that this critic was prepared to give more than a dismissively superficial commentary on the vim and vigour, the verve and vivacity of these naturally rhythmic performers. He had detected a potential for more than he had seen and six years later he was to witness the realization of that potential. In 1975 he felt: 'Choreographic

Everyday gestures and moods of the Caribbean experience often provide a vital source of ideas for Jamaican dance theater in its search for the fusion of form and feeling.

structure is clearly not a strong point. . . . They devise individual vignettes more successfully than they tie them together.' In 1981 his tune had changed to: 'They perform carefully worked out choreography—much of it heavily dependent on unison dancing.' A volte face? Not really! Just an admission of fact and a personal sense of justification for having invested some faith on the first visit. From seeing the Company as a 'curious mixture of good intentions and bad art, of the virtues of drawing on one's cultural roots and the dangers of misapplied sophistication' in 1975, Mr. Littler chose the 1981 review as the forum in which to educate his readers about the distinction between folk dance and dance theatre—arriving at the conclusion that this company has effected the successful fusion of the two."[14] More directly Littler caught on to the Company's approach to choreography in what he had to say about their dancing "carefully worked out choreography . . . and yet do so in the *spirit* of folk dancers."[15] In giving a full account of the Company's return to London in 1972, Peter Williams of London's *Dance and Dancers* felt that the Company had "found itself to a far greater extent compared to its first visit to London seven years ago."[16] Although the dance pieces seemed to coalesce when they involved narrative line or ritual, Williams felt there was need for a form of staging that binds together the disparate theatrical elements, including sets and costumes. Obviously the overall presentation of a dance theater company reflects its inherent style, and Williams's timely advice was well taken.

In Jamaica itself not many dance commentators paid much attention to the matter of style, although Norman Rae of *The Daily Gleaner* from the very beginning questioned the cultural meandering of the Company and suggested that an indigenous vocabulary served by an appropriate technical base could begin to develop.[17] Archie Lindo of the Jamaican *Star* seemed to have come to terms with the indigenous turn the Company's style had taken by 1975. Lindo made pointed reference to the Company's building "dance material which could be truly termed Jamaican and had fashioned 'things of beauty' in theatrical terms."[18] He felt that much of what the Company had been striving for through the years had now come to fruition.

As empathetic a commentator as the American critic William Moore, writing for the New York weekly newspaper *The Black American*, also found it difficult to come to terms with the reality of Africa in the Caribbean.[19] His expectations of artistic relevance seemed restricted to *Gerrehbenta,* which he praised without reservation. But he viewed the National Dance Theatre Company as a "major national folk company," which the Company has never intended to be. Here is yet another mainland metropolitan—a black one at that—advising Caribbean artists on how they should perceive their own cultural products. He disagrees with Caribbean commentators that the Company dances to the pulse of the region, even when the work, for instance, *The Crossing,* is performed to music that speaks universally to the sensibilities of those who survived the ravages and brutality of slavery and the plantation. His prudish outrage at a "woman doing a Caribbean pelvic roll to gospel music" no doubt emanated from his own limited aesthetic formula of appropriate movements for the sound of gospel. His dismissal of Eduardo Rivero's *Sulkari* as "nightclub African" in the style of Katherine Dunham or Pearl Primus was insulting to all three dance creators, and it shows a singular lack of appreciation of a tradition rooted in Afro-Caribbean realities on which Dunham drew heavily to create her dance utterances. Correspondences with modern dance are understandably disturbing to the purist. But Jamaica, like the United States, is infused with the influences from various worlds. The synthesis that finally emerges will indeed be the result of an arduous process of cross-fertilization of disparate elements. Moore will probably be surprised to learn that the contraction–release complex is not the invention of Martha Graham and neither are the approaches to movement now identified solely with American modern dance exclusive to that tradition. Thus much of the vocabulary of the Company's style can be observed in Jamaican schoolyards among children at play, in certain sports, in African-derived rituals, as well as in the limitless inventions of contemporary youth.

Moore's well-meaning advice is no doubt rooted in a mainland American reading of Caribbean sensibilities without due regard to the fact that the work of the National Dance Theatre Company is essentially conceived from homebase and not in exile. While one shares his enthusiasm for *Gerrehbenta,* there are many Jamaicans who believe that Caribbean life is a summation of more than the excellences that this dance work admittedly captures. Caribbean social and cultural realities, with references to Africa at its center, means more than simply Africa *in* the Americas. Therein lies the unassailable challenge to continue the search for a harmonious design for living.

Martha Graham's technique, which Moore considered worn out, and her "neurotic" contraction—release signature may not be directly appropriate to Jamaica's needs, as Beryl McBurnie herself long ago pointed out, but there will always be something to ponder in Graham's bold declaration of wanting, as a dancer, to be part of "the miracle that is a human being, motivated, disciplined, concentrated."[20] Such is the need of the ordinary people of the Caribbean, traditionally marginalized but with enough fighting spirit and sense of struggle to bequeath to an emergent society splendid gifts from the collective imagination. Such gifts include both the germ of a dance theater vocabulary and a way of moving that articulates a distinctive Caribbean style.

Alan Kriegsman of *The Washington Post,* without resorting to a patronizing acceptance of a folksy exoticism, noted with enthusiasm that when the National Dance Theatre Company performed, the "stage was vibrant with *rolling* shoulders, *swaying* pelvises, *flitting* feet, and torsos *rippling* like *windswept* vines."[21] The emphases are mine because the words denote signatures of an emerging style that communicates the pulse of the Caribbean heritage.

Yvonne daCosta in *All God's Children*.

6 · The Artists, Technicians, and Administrators

A definitive technique, vocabulary, and style was indeed impossible without the intensive collaborative work of a dynamic corps of artists working over an extended period of time. As with dance companies anywhere the Jamaican group was successful through the sustained creative efforts of its choreographers, dancers, singers, musicians, technicians, and administrators—all involved in the process of discovery and the act of self-definition.[1]

The Choreographers

Eleven Company members choreographed dances specifically for the National Dance Theatre Company, while three guest choreographers created original dances or passed on works from their home companies.

Rex Nettleford, as a choreographer, has had the major influence on the artistic style of the Company, especially since the end of the 1960s. He brought to Jamaican dance and to the Company itself an authentic sense of traditional Caribbean life as the basis for creating an indigenous dance theater. Nettleford grew up in rural Jamaica, where he gained firsthand knowledge of Jamaican folk customs early in life, which was later reinforced by extensive study of Caribbean history and folkways. Such works as *Caribbean Suite, Celebrations, Married Story, Kas Kas, Character Sketches*, along with the ritualistic trilogy of *Pocomania, Kumina*, and *Myal*, reflect Nettleford's artistic commitment to indigenous sources of energy for his creative work. Other important dances include *The King Must Die*, which explores the vagaries of Third World political power; *Lucifer Lucifer*, dealing with the Manichaean duality of good and evil; *Dialogue for Three*, about the eternal romantic triangle; *Masques of God*, exposing the entrapment of humanity in the act of living; and *Two Drums for Babylon*, which explores the fascination the Rastafarian movement held for middle-class Jamaican youths. These psychological themes were offset by pure dance works such as *Dance Andante, Gallandar la Pava, Synthesia*, and *Back to Bach, Viva*

Bach. The deep religious sensibilities of the Jamaican people found responses in such creations as *Misa Criolla* and *Homage.*

Cross-cultural experimentation produced *African Scenario,* created after extensive work with dance groups in Nigeria and Ghana in 1960–61. *Journeys,* danced to American spirituals, as well as *Ballad of a Lady, All God's Children,* and *Wonder Love and Raise* explored the rhythms of black American music, which reflects the concerns of all plantation America. In the 1970s Nettleford turned to contemporary popular music of Jamaica: reggae made up the striking scores offered in *Backlash, Court of Jah, Rockstone Debate, Tribute to Cliff,* and *Street People. Drumscore,* using traditional indigenous music, explores Caribbean dance forms with their interplay of polyrhythms, speech patter, and folk melodies. The taut and moving work *The Crossing,* which depicts the trials and triumphs of the middle passage during the slavery period, promises a long life in the Company repertoire, rivaling the perennial favorite *Kumina.*

During the twenty-one years of independence the Jamaican populace at last began taking their own ancestral riches more seriously. Thus a work like *Gerreh-benta,* which explored traditional themes, gained critical and audience appeal. Yet there was still room for such works as *Soulscape* danced to the music of George Gershwin. It spoke to the experiences of many individuals who yearned to exchange their loneliness for the protection of group membership. The strong commitment to ancestral and traditional sources, however, remains, bearing out what Peter Williams, as early as 1965, noted: "It would seem that Nettleford's strength, except for the dramatic approach shown in *Dialogue for Three,* lies with his research into ethnic backgrounds and his imaginative treatment of his findings."[2] Nettleford expanded his range as the need arose, especially in response to the realities of the varied existence of the Caribbean people. The Jamaican critic Harry Milner reflected on this in 1975: "The programme was a sort of retrospective for the choreographic work of Rex Nettleford and a very rewarding one. It indeed provided a dance concert of his work in all his moods and handsomely refuted those who sometimes accuse him of monotony and lack of variety. . . . But Nettleford's works and his generally expressive choreography has great variety."[3]

Eddy Thomas was among the choreographers who brought innovation and distinction to the Company's repertoire. It was natural that his work made the impact it did since, as codirector, he shared the vision of the National Dance Theatre Company, which he helped establish as a vehicle of experimentation and dance invention. He created works of real sophistication with a sense of theatrical form. His *Legend of Lovers' Leap, Footnotes in Jazz,* and *Games of Arms* were among the finest works presented in Jamaican dance theater in the 1960s. *A Time to Rejoice* and *Concert Suite* were essays into pure dance with dancers moving for the joy of movement itself. Thomas's own costume designs for his works gave them an integrated look that enhanced their visual impact.

And It Came to Pass, also an early classic, utilized elements of American modern dance, which he had studied at the Martha Graham School of Contemporary Dance in New York. Thomas's work with traditional folk idioms did not overshadow the stylishness and graceful linearity evident in pieces such as *Country Wedding, Parade Kingston 13,* and *Promenade.* His last dance work for the Company was *Omegan Procession,* choreographed in 1966 to Darius Milhaud's *Création du Monde.* Thomas left the Company at that time to concentrate on his own group, the Eddy Thomas Dance Workshop, and to choreograph for local musicals, including the annual Little Theatre Movement pantomimes.

Thomas's works for the National Dance Theatre Company were appreciated not only by Jamaican audiences. In 1965 Londoners responded warmly to his presentations, and *Dance and Dancers* magazine reflected seriously on his work: "It seemed as the entire touring repertory unrolled that in Eddy Thomas the Company has, as well as its principal dancer and designer, a notable choreographer of modern dramatic works. He has a very decided personal approach to modern dance forms and a strong dramatic sense; and although he must have been inspired by the modern dance creators with whom he studied in America, he has managed to weave enough of his native background into his work so that he has a very personal utterance."[4] Although the reviewer found the works with a folkloric background less satisfying, he felt that the choreographer's distinctive expression was undoubtedly shaped in large measure by the years he had spent experimenting with traditional forms.

Sheila Barnett is one of the most important choreographers to emerge in Jamaica since independence. Her *Ni—Woman of Destiny* and *I Not I* show a sensibility and artistic vision developed through her profound study of Caribbean cultural heritage as well as her continual experimentation with movement appropriate to this heritage. Her investigations into the legends of Jamaican mountain life produced the seminal work *Mountain Women,* a painterly presentation of peasant life in rural Jamaica. In terms of pure dance Barnett created rich inventions. *Foiled Encounter, Images,* and *Ring Hunt* revealed early attempts at exploring movement for its own sake, but by the time of *Shadows*—a dance drama based on the tragedy of Lady Macbeth—she was investing her vocabulary with dramatic eloquence. This sense of theatrical force was consummately realized in *The Rope and the Cross,* inspired by a dramatic poem about a religious dichotomy: the encounter between the mother of Jesus and the mother of Judas Iscariot. *In the Spirit,* performed to American spirituals, evoked religious worship, and *A Question of Balance* was a striking comment on the effects of the industrial age.

Barnett's work reveals not only a wide range of theme and texture but above all a personal utterance stated within the framework of a persistent quest for form. Her work is informed by a philosophical vision that inevitably draws on Caribbean cultural realities. Although Barnett never sacrifices her sense of form or aesthetic propriety for mere theatricality, she is quite capable of creative daring—for instance, exploiting such dramatic effects in the disco-inspired *Summer Is* as pouring rain, strobe lighting, and shimmering disco dancers.

Neville Black, like Eddy Thomas, was also trained in the American dance tradition, but, unlike Thomas, he lacked the years of experience in Caribbean dance traditions. Black worked with the Company between 1964 and 1968 and brought to the repertoire an infectious humor and skill in creating sharp-edged designs in the modern dance pieces he produced during those years. *Rites* was the most integrated of his Company works, although the natural humor of *Fables*, based on the tales of James Thurber, *Night Shelter,* and *Cantos*, a suite of dances to Jamaican folk melodies, made these pieces memorable. *Dance and Dancers* described *Rites* as "a work of great promise . . . [with] a strong and most effective sense of movement design which was well realised by his four dancers. It also had a very tidy construction and was simply but effectively designed by the choreographer himself."[5] Expert with the American jazz idiom, Black created *Bach, Brubeck, and Company* as a fitting sequel to Eddy Thomas's softer *Footnotes in Jazz.* Black's interest in electronic music provided the Company with *Legendary Landscape,* which offered exciting explorations in dance shapes. He also experimented with neoballetic idioms in such works as *Waltz Suite, Night Dances,* and *Sonata.* His work always bore the strong influence of American modern dance idioms, particularly the work of Sybil Shearer, Doris Humphrey, and Charles Weidman.

Bert Rose was also responsible for continuing the modern dance influence on the Company's repertoire. He began to choreograph seriously in 1973 while at the height of a distinguished performing career. His first Company work, the dramatic *Thursday's Child,* integrated modern dance forms with a Caribbean way of moving. He followed it with *Glory Road,* adding to the repertoire a clarity of form and plasticity for which he was also noted as performer. His *Reflections* explored the preoccupations of three emotionally disturbed women, but his best-remembered dramatic work is *Switch,* inspired by the legend of the white witch of Rose Hall. His skill at solo work, as well as the placement of bodies in dynamic spatial relationships in duets, produced *Moods, Ebb Flow,* and *Caro,* all of which challenged the Company dancers to virtuosity.

Before Bert Rose began to choreograph, two other Company dancers also made choreographic contributions. *Joyce Campbell* created the folk piece *Dance Time in Cascade*, a work that had a short life in the active repertoire. Her choreographic efforts are mainly concentrated in the two yearly offerings by her Jayteens Dance Workshop. *Thomas Pinnock* produced *Ballot,* about power and politics, and *Desperate Silences,* about the urban ghetto. *The Village Voice* critic felt that in *Desperate Silences* the choreographer's attempt "to show the kind of unhappiness that is released in wild Saturday night sprees . . . got sidetracked by the fun and the funniness."[6] But Pinnock understood the structure of this piece, and another view, from the London critic Peter Williams, who had seen the work at Sadler's Wells, was more discerning: "Pinnock has a good sense of movement and no small amount of typically Jamaican humour." Williams found the snatches of reggae music too brief—much of the dancing was done in silence—"but the idea is original and the Jamaican audience loved it." [7] Even in a major London theater Pinnock knew how to communicate with his own people.

Barbara Requa appears to be of special interest to the choreographic future of the Company. As a former principal dancer, she contributed her first choreography to the Company in 1982, although she had choreographed extensively for the juniors in the School of Dance. The work, entitled *Fantasy,* utilized the music of Chick Corea, popular among the Jamaican urban young, and dealt with the fantasies of a young man about love and the kind of woman he yearns for. A year later the emphasis on youth was revealed again in *Trio,* an even more successful choreographic offering, which explored form and kinetic force through the use of alternate casts: three male dancers or two males and a female. The youthful athleticism of the piece, in a period when physical fitness was becoming the rage, was timely. This expressive piece was warmly received by both audiences and critics,[8] giving Requa the kind of encouragement a choreographer with an independent voice needs. Her strength is rooted in a deep understanding of the dancer's instrument and the possible range of movement in space.

Patsy Ricketts was another Company dancer encouraged to take up choreography in the late 1970s and early 1980s. Ricketts first produced the light and airy *Someday,* following it with the dramatic dance play *The Brothers* to music by Ernest Bloch. She became concerned that the music to this dance, undoubtedly her most successful work, was not indigenous Jamaican music. Thus a solo, danced to reggae, which she choreographed for the longer work *Elements*, revealed the new interest she was taking in Rastafarian-inspired cultural forms.

Jackie Guy, on the other hand, found Albinoni's Adagio in G Minor, in a sung version by Morgana King, just the right touch for *Solitude,* the solo he created for Judith Pennant. As a first work for the Company, it showed promise for more substantial work. In his contribution to *Elements* Guy's distillation of theatrical forms through the use of mento music pointed toward serious development in this genre. But he left the Company before this direction was realized.

Tony Wilson contributed a solo, *Just Time,* in the style of *Solitude,* but Guy's departure probably opened the door sooner for Wilson's work entitled *Phases,* which was welcomed for the kind of jazz dynamics associated with the Company's aesthetics. It obviously revealed the influence of certain American choreographers whose work Wilson was exposed to during his four-year stay in the United States. In 1983 he mounted *Progeny,* a small dance drama about family relationships, also using Albinoni's Adagio in G Minor but this time in the original instrumental version. Wilson's sense of movement and spatial awareness are natural gifts, but after his initial contributions he faced the challenge of addressing the rich store of material from his own environment to create distinctly innovative dances.

Guest choreographers also brought new challenges for the Company dancers. *Clive Thompson* introduced *Recollections* from the repertoire of his fledgling New York company, based on Staten Island; this duet permitted Melanie Graham, whom he partnered, to reach new heights of lyricism and musical phrasing. Thompson's choreographic credits include the Emmy Award–winning *Pueblo Incident,* dances for "Sesame Street," and Leonard Bernstein's *Mass* for the Kansas City Philharmonic. *Eduardo Rivero,* a founding member of the Danza Nacional de Cuba, introduced *Sulkari,* originally choreographed for the Cuban company. Both this dramatic work and his love duet *Romance* remain in the active repertoire. Rivero brought to the Company an articulation of technique, vocabulary, and style rooted in Afro-Caribbean forms with which the Company had been working for eighteen years. As a dancer-choreographer, he was a major contributor to the development of an indigenous Cuban dance theater. *John Jones* had extensive performing experience with the Katherine Dunham Company, Jerome Robbins's company Ballets: USA, and the Dance Theater of Harlem. In the early 1970s Jones had been working in Philadelphia when he created his choreographic work for the Company, leaving behind the pioneering pieces *Resurrection, Windsong,* and *Supernova,* the last work performed to the music of the innovative American jazz musician Sun Ra. All three guest choreographers understood and respected the artistic objectives of the National Dance Theatre Company and were able to work with the dancers in classes before embarking on choreography that complemented other Company work.

The Dancers

Through the choreographers' inspired collaborations with the dancers—the instruments of creative expression—performing artists of unquestionable talent have emerged who have been sensitive interpreters of the Company's vision. The dancers have also been a source of energy for a wide-ranging repertoire. In the beginning the need to keep the group together encouraged an ensemble approach to choreography, and the no-star system was the inevitable result. Yet this approach did not lead to anonymity for dancers of great ability. The public has a way of isolating its favorites, and, despite the fact that much of the Company's choreography encourages collective endeavors rather than solo virtuosity, most Company dancers somehow managed to reveal their individuality to the viewers.

In the early period the Company was often considered an ensemble of soloists, and indeed the specific performing strength of many of the performers was a matter of record. Yet those who soloed in one work might dance in the chorus in the next. This was also true of the Company codirectors, although their experi-

Barbara Requa in *Reflections*.

Sheila Barnett in *Homecoming*.   Joyce Campbell in *Legend of Lovers' Leap*.

ences in both theater and dance perhaps gave them an edge over their colleagues. This advantage was short-lived, and soon the names of Yvonne daCosta, Sheila Barnett, Maureen Casserly, Gertrude Sherwood, Barbara Requa, and Joyce Campbell among the women and Audley Butler and Bert Rose among the men were added to those of Eddy Thomas and Rex Nettleford as prominent dancers who contributed their talents throughout the 1960s.

Yvonne daCosta came to prominence between 1962 and 1972, bringing to the Company special gifts of concentration, stage command, style, and versatility. Some of the most ambitious roles in the repertoire at that time were created for her—the other woman in *Dialogue for Three*, the spinster in *Masques of God*, the queen mother in *The King Must Die*, the Spirit of Good in *Lucifer Lucifer,* the hostess in *All God's Children,* and the lady in *Ballad of a Lady*. But she also danced in the chorus of the other works in the repertoire. Pliable and articulate, she responded quickly to the choreographic impulses that drove all the dance creators working with the Company in those early years. Dramatic power, coupled with a keen emotional understanding of a role, marked her as a major dance artist of the new Jamaican dance theater after 1962. Her early training in the Fay Simpson School of Ballet and later at the University of the West Indies summer schools gave her the appropriate technical foundation, but it was her musicality and dance intelligence that gave her a legendary mastery over her roles and established her as a consummate artist. Illness forced her to retire from active performing after the Sadler's Wells season in 1972, but she later returned as ballet mistress, a position that forms a critical link between the generations of dancers working in the National Dance Theatre Company.

Sheila Barnett with her strong stage presence brought dramatic power to the roles of the wife in *Dialogue for Three,* Mary in *And It Came to Pass,* the woman in *Omegan Procession,* and the spinster in *Masques of God.* Before retiring at the peak of a distinguished performing career in favor of choreography, research, teaching, and cultural administration, Barnett gave a moving portrayal of the mother of Jesus in one of her own works, *The Rope and the Cross.* A noble carriage and innovative interpretations of her roles set her apart as a performer of major significance in Jamaican dance theater, attracting devoted fans.

Barbara Requa won critical acclaim[9] as the "flaunting queen" in the role of the other woman in *Dialogue for Three.* Stately and self-possessed, she brought elegance as well as energy to everything she danced in, whether she was the spinster in *Masques of God,* the bride in *Country Wedding,* the disturbed woman in *Reflections,* or simply one of the dancers in the scores of works she appeared in until the late 1970s, when she retired from active performing and concentrated on teaching in the Jamaica School of Dance and on choreographing for the Company. Requa retired from performing with the expressive role of the mother in *The Brothers.* Her articulate feet and superb line were special attributes that served her well as a dancer, and her phenomenal stamina made her a consistently outstanding performer in difficult dance situations.

Joyce Campbell, who still performs with the Company, developed through her work with the Ivy Baxter Creative Dance Group a vivacity and a grasp of kinetic movement in the traditional mold. Her forte was undoubtedly that of investing a folk character with dimensions of reality, giving her work an edge of artistry over others who danced similar roles. Her characterization of the Christadelphian Sister in *Street People,* the yard woman in *Kas Kas,* the other woman in *Married Story,* the water spirit in *Pocomania,* and the mother protector in *Myal* all indicate admirable talent as an interpreter of Caribbean ancestral lore. Yet she was also capable of the demands offered by the character of the matriarch in *Resurrection* as well as anchor roles as member of the chorus in ensemble dancing. She remains Jamaica's foremost advocate of community dance and directs the Jayteens Dance Workshop.

Maureen Casserly had gained an early reputation as a performer with the Soohih School of Dance and in the annual pantomimes. She had a clean line, sharp movements, and a vitality that graced such Company works as *Footnotes in Jazz, Plantation Revelry,* and *Two Drums for Babylon.*

Gertrude Sherwood, in contrast, displayed soft, flowing movements in her dancing and won audience and critical approval for her roles as the initiate in *African Scenario,* the wife in *Dialogue for Three,* and Eve in *Omegan Procession.* As the downtown hostess in *All God's Children,* she showed the dramatic and expressive powers she brought to dance from the beginning. She immigrated to the United States in the early 1970s, continuing her studies with Eleo Pomare in New York, but returned for a short stint in 1975.

During the Company's first decade there were two prominent names among the men, in addition to the codirectors. *Audley Butler* was known for his solid dancing and physicality. He became an audience favorite, established through the strong dance personality he brought to his various roles: the authoritative Rasta chief in *Two Drums for Babylon,* the imperious second shepherd in *Pocomania,* the calculating rival in *The King Must Die,* the powerfully visceral young warrior in *African Scenario,* the boyish schoolyard brat in *Games of Arms,* the jealous slave traitor in *Legend of Lovers' Leap,* and the passionate simple suitor in *Dialogue for Three.* His roles were enhanced by a finely sculpted form and muscularity as well as concentration and seriousness of interpretation. He worked for all the Company choreographers between 1962 and 1974, when he stopped performing with the Company and emigrated from Jamaica to work in the United States.

Bert Rose had gained a strong stage presence through constant performing in musicals, dance workshops, and lecture demonstrations before he joined the

Maureen Casserly in *A Time to Rejoice.*

Gertrude Sherwood in *Reflections.*

Company. Through his gifts of technical facility, theatrical flair, as well as a lyrical quality, he attracted critical attention from the beginning. He also exhibited skill at dramatic work and partnering. Graced with a quick intelligence and an impish wit, he was also capable of emotional intensity and expressive plasticity of form. He won praise for his portrayal of the plantation owner in *Legend of Lovers' Leap* when he was one of the youngest members of the Company. The most memorable roles in which he made a lasting impression were as the man in *Dialogue for Three*—a role he took over from Eddy Thomas on short notice and later mastered as his own—the young man in *Two Drums for Babylon,* the angel in *And It Came to Pass,* Lucifer in *Lucifer Lucifer,* and the oppressed one in *Tribute to Cliff.* He danced in most of the major works created between 1962 and 1977, after which he retired from active performing to concentrate on teaching at the School of Dance. His lyricism, emotional reach, sense of form, and excellence in partnering are reflected in the choreography he executed for the Company.

Eddy Thomas as a dancer had a grace and cleanness of line which made him an audience favorite and a prime model for later male dancers. His best-remembered role was the man in *Dialogue for Three,* which he developed with intelligence and artistry, placing an almost indelible stamp on the interpretation. But he also brought vitality and authority to the male chorus in a number of

Bert Rose in *Homage. (Owen Minott)*

Audley Butler in *Rites.*

Rex Nettleford in *Myal*.

Eddy Thomas in *Gallandar la Pava*.

ensemble works. His presentation of the celebrant in *Misa Criolla* and the witch doctor in *African Scenario* bore his own personal mark, and his special virtuosic gifts made him the obvious choice for the solo part in *Diarist in Sand* and for the jazz duet in *The Awakening*. On leaving the Company in 1967, Thomas continued to perform, with his own company, the Eddy Thomas Dance Workshop (later Jamaica Dance Company), but he began to concentrate more on teaching and choreographing until he switched completely to theatrical designing.

Rex Nettleford attracted attention as a dancer because of his unique personal style and stage presence in such roles as Herod in *And It Came to Pass,* the celebrant in *Misa Criolla,* the king in *The King Must Die,* and the messenger in *Wonder Love and Raise,* all works which have a strong modern dance and jazz orientation. But a strong musical sense, described by one critic as a "su-

Bridget Casserly in *Murals*.

Monica McGowan in *Lucifer Lucifer*.

Barry Moncrieffe
in *Switch*.

perb and very African way of playing around within a given rhythm—making counterpoint or subtle delays in the ripple of a shoulder or the fall of his weight,"[10] was undoubtedly revealed most fully in the many roles he portrayed in the traditional–ancestral mode of expression, for example, the king in *Kumina,* the yard thief in *Kas Kas,* the bongo dancer in *Afro–West Indian Suite,* the rich suitor in *Married Story,* the Obeahman in *Myal,* and a shepherd in *Pocomania.*

By the early 1970s other dancers became prominent and began to be looked at more closely by both audiences and critics. Monica McGowan, Bridget Casserly, and Pansy Hassan, all founding members of the Company, were among those. Later other dancers came to the forefront, such as Noelle Chutkan, who had alternated several roles with Yvonne daCosta; Dorothy Fraser, with a strong classical ballet technique; and Patsy Ricketts, returning to the Company from her studies and performing experiences in New York.

Monica McGowan, a stylish and intelligent dancer with dramatic power and an impeccable gift for phrasing, had made a success with *Legend of Lovers' Leap* in the role of Liza. But it was not until the 1970s, with such works as *Lucifer Lucifer* (in the role of the woman), *Shadows* (the protagonist), *Ni—Woman of Destiny* (Nanny), *The Rope and the Cross* (Judith), *Mountain Women* (the third generation woman), and *Wonder Love and Raise* (as soloist) that she emerged as an artist of major stature. Her concentration and details of performing are still fresh, despite her many years of experience in over fifty of the works in the

Noelle Chutkan in *Reflections*.

Pansy Hassan in *Kumina*.

repertoire. She teaches at Kingston's Holy Childhood School and at the Jamaica School of Dance. She guides several community dance groups and choreographs as well.

Bridget Casserly had scored a success in *Two Drums for Babylon* in 1964, but in general she functioned in strong supportive roles until the early 1970s, when her quickwittedness, analytical powers, and lyricism were revealed in the duet *Murals* as well as in *Dialogue for Three,* in which she portrayed the wife. Responsive in her grasp of movement, she remained a gift for choreographers until she voluntarily went into semiretirement to give, according to her own statement, the younger dancers an opportunity to grow.

Pansy Hassan, who appears in fewer works now than she did in the 1960s, has danced in over forty Company works. Her work impressed Jamaican audiences, particularly with her brilliant portrayal in 1971 of the queen in *Kumina*. A decade later she showed a similar quality of understatement and linear clarity in movement inspired by traditional forms in *Gerrehbenta*, especially the etu section. She was also one of the first Lizas in *Legend of Lovers' Leap*. She now doubles as Company costume coordinator, and teaches aerobic dancing in Kingston as well.

Noelle Chutkan came into prominence with the Company in the 1970s. After a long period performing ensemble work and understudying major roles, she took on such challenging portrayals as the queen mother in *The King Must Die,* the wife in *Dialogue for Three,* the mother in *Mountain Women,* the earth goddess in *I Not I,* the mother figure in *The Crossing,* and one of the women in *Tribute to Cliff.* Chutkan was a self-assured Company dancer with a strong stage personality, exhibiting real intelligence in the shaping of a character.

Dorothy Fraser returned to Jamaica in 1969 after several years of professional dance work in Great Britain. She had studied from childhood in Hazel Johnston's studio before she went to London, where she became a founding member of the Experimental London Dance Theatre and later joined the London Festival Ballet. The role of the protagonist in *Shadows* was created for her, which brought her critical acclaim, as did the role of the woman in *Lucifer Lucifer.* Her speed and clarity of execution suited the role of the rival's girlfriend in *The King Must Die.* Her easy adaptation to the traditional portion of the repertoire quickly made her a principal artist. She continued for a time teaching in the Rowe ballet studios and in the Jamaica School of Dance before returning to London to settle with her husband.

Patsy Ricketts rejoined the Company in 1972 after four years' absence—in New York, where she danced with the Dance Theater of Harlem, and in Spoleto, Italy, where she taught dance. She had left the Company at the peak of success, following appearances in such works as *Plantation Revelry* and *Bach, Brubeck, and Company,* but her professional experiences away from the Company had greatly improved her technique. On her return she expressed an ambition to be a dance teacher, but for the next five years she focused on performance, giving special articulation to major roles created for her in such dances as *Homage, Windsong, Tribute to Cliff, Glory Road, The Rope and the Cross, Court of Jah, Supernova, Ni—Woman of Destiny, Moods, Wonder Love and Raise, Switch,* and *The Crossing.* Like Yvonne daCosta of the previous decade, who was an inspiration for her, Ricketts performed in every type of dance and displayed great versatility and plasticity. After the 1978 season she withdrew from performing to raise a family, but she continued to teach. She resumed performing in 1983 but decided to work only on a fee basis, which obviously ruled out further work with the National Dance Theatre Company.

Among the male dancers who became prominent during the second decade, Thomas Pinnock carved a niche for himself, filling the gap left by such promising dancers as Derek Williams, who remained in the United States after his studies with Martha Graham and the Harkness Ballet school, and Dennis Scott, who retired from dancing to concentrate on theater, poetry, and teaching. But above all it was Barry Moncrieffe who emerged as one of the most important lead dancers.

Dorothy Fraser in *Shadows*.

Patsy Ricketts in *The Rope and the Cross*.

Barry Moncrieffe developed as a performer of distinction, partnering Patsy Ricketts in many important works. His early training in Jamaica and in the United States, particularly his experience with the Anna Sokolow Dance Company prepared him for the unrivaled position he commanded by the end of the 1970s as the Company's lead dancer. A long list of credits of leading roles began with the boy in *Two Drums for Babylon* and has continued to the present time. He placed a distinctive mark on such works as *Masques of God* (the clown), *Lucifer Lucifer* (Adam), *Murals* (duet partner), *Thursday's Child* (the child), *Tribute to Cliff* (duet to "Many Rivers to Cross"), *Court of Jah* (the Jah figure), *Ni—Woman of Destiny* (Cudjoe), *Caro* (duet partner), *Switch* (the field hand), *The Crossing* (the father figure), *The Brothers* (one of the brothers), *Back to Bach, Viva Bach* (duet partner), *The Gospel According To* (solo to "Buk'd and Scorned"), and *Progeny* (the father figure). A majestic carriage and an enigmatic but authoritative detachment have characterized Moncrieffe's presence in Jamaican dance theater. Very much a dancer's dancer, his clean line and effortless style of moving continue to be his greatest strengths. He doubles as the artistic coordinator of the Company and teaches in the Jamaica School of Dance.

Thomas Pinnock first drew attention for his humor and impeccable timing in such works as *Kas Kas* and his own *Desperate Silences*. Technical strength and speed, coupled with his training at the Martha Graham school and performances with the Rod Rodgers Dance Company in New York, were recognizable assets when he returned to Jamaica in the early 1970s to participate in the Company's annual seasons. Commitments in New York, particularly his appearances on and off Broadway, prevented his continued participation in the Company's work. His later exploration of reggae and Rastafarian forms shows a continuity of effort with his earlier association with the National Dance Theatre Company.

Derek Williams, like Pinnock, also remained in the United States to work professionally. His early training was in the Eddy Thomas Dance Workshop and the National Dance Theatre Company. Williams had drawn attention as a dancer in *Rites* and *Misa Criolla,* but during his stay in New York he placed his talents at the service of the dance workshop of the Harkness Ballet. Following that, he became one of the first members of the Dance Theater of Harlem, which he left because of injury to teach in Oregon and in Europe. Subsequently he returned to the Dance Theater of Harlem.

Dennis Scott achieved distinction through the strength and intelligence he brought not only to lead roles but also to ensemble work. Joseph in *And It Came to Pass,* the brute bachelor in *Masques of God,* and Adam in *Omegan Procession* were all memorable portrayals. Scott's discipline, analytical powers, and dramatic sense served the Company well until postgraduate work in the fine arts

Thomas Pinnock in *Desperate Silences*.

Jackie Guy in *I Not I*.

caused him to leave Jamaica. His early dance training is reflected in the choreographic sense of design he always brings to his productions of plays for the Jamaican legitimate theater in the eastern Caribbean and in North America.[11]

Thomas Pinnock's departure left a gap in respect to comedy, easy characterization, and a natural dance sense among the newer recruits. *Jackie Guy* filled that gap in the 1970s. He had come to the Company from Alma Mock Yen's Harbour View Community Workshop in Kingston. He had a strong stage presence and a natural feel for traditional movement. He drew attention to his dancing through substantial lead roles in *Ni—Woman of Destiny, I Not I, Two Drums for Babylon,* and *Drumscore,* all of which challenged both his dramatic sense and his ability to shape abstract movement. He was also prominent in such works as *Kumina, Street People, Tribute to Cliff, Court of Jah, Backlash,* and *Character Sketches.* Guy also has to his credit a long list of works in the modern dance idiom in which he appeared since the late 1960s, including *Images, Lucifer Lucifer, Journeys, Resurrection, Homage, Windsong, Glory Road, Peace Offering, Wonder Love and Raise,* and *The Gospel According To.* He left the Company in 1982 to continue work with the many ventures he was involved in as choreographer, teacher, performer, and artistic coordinator.

Guy's departure focused greater attention on *Tony Wilson,* who returned to the Company in 1982 from a four-year period working in New York and Chicago. As a performer, Wilson brought to the Company dramatic power, a natural love for dancing, and an energetic magnetism, which showed to advantage in a work like *Backlash.* He first joined the Company in 1970, subsequently dancing in over twenty-five works. He took a leave of absence in 1976 but returned four years later to take over the role of the messenger of death in *The Visitor.*

During Wilson's four-year absence two talented and accomplished dancers, Melanie Graham and Judith Pennant, came to prominence. Thus leadership was leaning toward the younger recruits, especially after the departure of Patsy Ricketts from the Company.

Melanie Graham had studied classical ballet with Madame May Soohih from an early age and was no stranger to dance theater when she joined the National Dance Theatre Company. She grappled with the Company's style, and through dedication and hard work emerged as a major dancer. Since becoming a full member in 1975, she has appeared in over forty works in the repertoire, with lead roles in such works as *Tribute to Cliff, Glory Road, Peace Offering, The Rope and the Cross, Switch, The Crossing, Chainlinks, Dialogue for Three,* and *Two Drums for Babylon.* Her plasticity makes her an ideal instrument for a choreographer, as Clive Thompson discovered with his *Recollections.*

Judith Pennant was also trained in classical ballet. Over the past decade she developed into a soloist of stature, inspiring the solos *Solitude* and *Just Time* as well as the "If It's Magic" sequence in *Wonder Love and Raise* and the extended opening passage in *Summer Is.* She brought deep feeling to the role of Mary in *The Rope and the Cross* and the half-caste in *The Crossing.* In *Back to Bach,*

Melanie Graham in *Two Drums for Babylon*.

Tony Wilson in *Celebrations*.

Viva Bach she executed a finely etched duet with Barry Moncrieffe as she also did with Christopher Morrison in Clive Thompson's *Recollections*. She was a featured dancer in *Tribute to Cliff* and other works in the repertoire. Her many assets include a keen professionalism and technical power as well as sensitive interpretation and strong attack. Her early training was with the Barbara Matalon School of Dance in Jamaica and later with the National Ballet school in Canada and at Havergal College in Toronto. Pennant recently had taught at the Jamaica School of Dance.

Yvonne Ffrench, recruited from the Jayteens Dance Workshop, came to prominence by the end of the 1970s. Immigration to the United States robbed the Company of her distinctive gifts, such as a natural dance sense, an ability to define movement, and a deep understanding of a style rooted in Jamaican folk forms. Her portrayal of Bag-and-Pan in *Street People* revealed some of the wittiest dancing that has appeared in a Company work, and a long list of credits as a featured dancer include *Celebrations, Myal, Tribute to Cliff, Ni—Woman of Destiny, The Crossing, Woman Song, The Brothers, Drumscore,* and *Chainlinks*. She expressed a quality that captured the special spirit of Jamaica, which has not been seen in the Company since her departure.

During the first two decades of the Company's existence, from 1962 to 1979, a number of dancers came to prominence over a period of time. Among the women were founding members Shirley Campbell, Rosalie Markes, and Mavis Stoppi, as well as Madge Broderick, Carol Miller, Jean Summers, Dorothy McFarlane, Andrea Nash, and Judy Wedderburn. As a dancer, Cheryl Ryman, whose research studies have been discussed elsewhere, provided a special link between the end of the 1960s and the beginning of the 1980s.

Shirley Campbell was an established stage personality even in her early years with the Ivy Baxter Creative Dance Group, due in particular to her infectious vitality. As the saucy hen in *Gallandar la Pava,* she brought a sense of humor to the dance and, as Mary in *And It Came to Pass,* she received her greatest challenge. Before retiring from active performing, she ran her own dance workshop at the University Dance Society and assisted with the costuming of her sister's Jayteens Dance Workshop.

Rosalie Markes possessed special qualities of lyricism and restraint, which won her the part of the initiate in *African Scenario* as well as roles in other works before she left the Company to pursue postgraduate work in chemistry abroad.

Mavis Stoppi served the Company faithfully while raising a family. She imprinted her sense of lyricism and wit on many Company works such as *Rites* and other dances in which she appeared during the 1960s and the first half of the 1970s, until her sudden death in 1975.

Madge Broderick personified the slinky goddess in the ghetto-inspired *Des-*

Yvonne Ffrench in *Street People*.

Judith Pennant in *Summer Is*.

Shirley Campbell in *Plantation Revelry*. (*Bruin Photographs*)

Rosalie Markes in *African Scenario*.

perate Silences, but her tall athletic frame highlighted several other works in the repertoire with a special touch of statuesque elegance.

Carol Miller brought unusual strength and attack to the emergent Company vocabulary during the late 1960s and earned success in the part of the revolutionary rival woman in *The King Must Die,* which was not followed up because immigration to the United States, where she raised a family, ended her career with the company.

Jean Summers through her beauty and quiet charm gave immense pleasure to audiences who saw her as the village girl in *Married Story.* Her presence was also memorable in many other dances until the early 1970s, when marriage also terminated her relationship with the Company.

Dorothy McFarlane was remembered most for her natural feel for movements based on traditional–ancestral patterns as well as her humor and dramatic sense of characterization in works such as *Cantos* and *Street People* and particularly as the downtown hostess in *All God's Children.*

Andrea Nash lent her petite frame and striking good looks to many works between the late 1960s and the middle 1970s, when she moved with her hus-

Dennis Scott in *Rites*.

Mavis Stoppi in *Celebrations*.

band to Australia, where she practices law and still dances. She returned briefly to Jamaica to dance in the Company's twentieth-anniversary season.

Judy Wedderburn was a young supporting dancer in the 1962 *Roots and Rhythms* show, but she left the Company at a critical point of her dance development and lived abroad for a number of years. She returned to the Company but left once again in the 1970s for a career in Jamaica's diplomatic service overseas. Yet since 1980 her statuesque bearing has reclaimed its place in such works as *Ni—Woman of Destiny, Court of Jah, Married Story,* and *Celebrations*.

Cheryl Ryman, who continued to perform into the 1980s, joined the Company as a supporting dancer in the late 1960s. She left in the 1970s to study at York University in Canada and later studied African dance forms in Ghana. When she returned to the Company, she was armed with a greater understanding of the aesthetic integrity of the African-derived dances of her native Jamaica. She brought to such dances as *Ni—Woman of Destiny, The Crossing,* and *Drumscore* not only articulation and an ability to mold sculpted forms but also an authority based on the fusion of form and feeling. She has danced in over forty works of the Company's repertoire. Since 1982, research, the pursuit of a gradu-

Cheryl Ryman in *Someday*.

Derek Williams in
A Time to Rejoice.

Judy Wedderburn in
Ni—Woman of Destiny.

ate degree in dance, and raising a family have taken her away temporarily from performing.

Besides dancers discussed earlier, such as Derek Williams and Dennis Scott, other male dancers of note working with the Company before the change in membership at the beginning of the Company's third decade were Noel Hall and Neil Summers. *Noel Hall* joined the Company after much performing experience in Jamaican studios and in the annual panto-mimes. Later he went to New York to further his studies, working with the Rod Rodgers Dance Company and other American ensembles. He also taught at Oberlin College in Ohio after acquiring a fine arts degree. *Neil Summers* was an extremely competent dancer who married another Company member, Jean Summers, who is discussed earlier. Their departure to the United States in the 1970s ended their relationship with the Company.

Other names are deserving of mention for the attributes they brought to the Company: Fredericka Byfield, Sandra Monroe, and the American Beverly Kitson, as well as provisional dancers such as Joan McLeod, a nutritionist by profession, Michael Richardson, a medical doctor, Karlene Samuels, the first Jayteens alumna to join the Company, and Michael Binns. These dancers did not remain long enough to make the kind of impact they might have. The same could be said of a host of supporting dancers, at least two of whom continued in dance: Frank Ashley, who later worked with Eleo Pomare and taught dance in summer schools in Europe, and Cathi March, who went into dance therapy for paraplegics in Jamaica before immigrating to the United States.

The year 1980 marked the changing of the guard among many of the dancers and other artists of the Company. There had been a prolonged period of transition, with its uncertainties and unevenness in artistic output. Some dancers were clearly accomplished technicians without being consummate artists. The change was peaceful, but the competitive and talented new tribe already showed their impatience with the status quo as early as 1976. But by 1980 the profile among the membership had definitely altered. Eighteen years had brought many changes in the Company personnel, but the brunt of the artistic burden was generally borne by the founders and those seasoned performers whose membership dated back to the 1960s. This was as true of dancers like

Recruits for the 1973 season include (from the front, left to right) Melanie Graham and Eleanor Ferguson; Yvonne Ffrench and Judith Pennant; Marilyn Sanguinetti and Sandra Monroe; Michael Richardson and Fitzroy Hunt.

Carson Cumberbatch

Alaine Grant

Samuel Bailey

Adrian Fletcher

Noelle Chutkan and Barry Moncrieffe, who were supporting dancers in the early 1960s, as it was of founding veterans like Monica McGowan, Rex Nettleford, Pansy Hassan, and the indefatigable Joyce Campbell. Due to the maturity of the dancers, the Company had always avoided the disadvantages of rapid turnover; this kind of continuity was appreciated abroad and drew positive critical comment.[12] The need for consolidation was inescapable, but new challenges in the performing arts are important for artists and audiences alike.

Happily the need for change was anticipated. Some founding members voluntarily retired or concentrated their efforts on teaching. The Jamaica School of Dance, in which some of them taught, promised revitalization and further development. Beginning in 1976, a new crop of supporting dancers was being recruited, while dancers of the second decade, such as Melanie Graham, Judith Pennant, Jackie Guy, Cheryl Ryman, and Yvonne Ffrench, developed steadily. Patsy Ricketts brought an aesthetic focus to the female performing style of the Company in the 1970s, as Yvonne daCosta had in the 1960s. The ambience of a deepening tradition, combined with greater attention to a sound knowledge of the art, helped considerably. By 1980 the members from the middle years who remained became the frontliners, with support from veterans like McGowan, Moncrieffe, and Hassan and assistance from the coaching skills of daCosta.

The new generation could by then be identified as Denise Robinson, Sandra Minott, Arlene Richards, Jacquie Smith, Duran Hylton, Samuel Bailey, and George McGann—all products of the National Dance Theatre Company training system and the School of Dance, receiving the school's five-year certificate in technique. They had also traveled the route of supporting, provisional, and full membership. The certificate course demanded not only proficiency in technique but interpretative skills as well. Supporting dancers Carson Cumberbatch, Christopher Morrison, and Adrian Fletcher were also students at the school. The year 1980 offered these newcomers excellent opportunities since several Com-

Gabrielle Harban

Fitzroy Hunt

Duran Hylton

Sandra Minott

pany members—eight dancers and five singers—were on leave of absence. Gabrielle Harban, Alaine Grant, Alison Symes, and Fitzroy Hunt also became full members of the Company.

It was the new generation of dancers—bolstered by the efforts of Moncrieffe, McGowan, Hassan, and frontliners Melanie Graham, Judith Pennant, and Tony Wilson—who prompted from Clive Barnes the comment that "it would be hopelessly inaccurate to call these Jamaicans amateur dancers."[13] With the strong technical facility acquired through years of training and dance education, these young recruits will in turn challenge the choreographers to further inventions and discoveries.

Samuel Bailey received his early training under Jackie Guy at the Cultural Theatre in Spanish Town, Jamaica, and with the University Dance Society. He was a student at the School of Dance and appeared in their annual concerts. He joined the Company as a supporting dancer in 1978 and appeared in over twenty works in the repertoire, assuming lead roles in *The Brothers, The Crossing,* and *The Gospel According To.*

Alaine Grant, who started dancing at the age of four at the Rumsey School of Ballet in Kingston, continued ballet training until sixteen at the Fay Simpson School of Ballet and the Marywood College in Scranton, Pennsylvania. After her return to Jamaica she joined the Eddy Thomas Dance Workshop and appeared in several of his concerts. She is a graduate of the Jamaica School of Dance and also teaches at the school. She joined the Company as a supporting dancer in 1978 and appeared in the Company's 1979 season. She has taken part in a number of stage productions as a singer and guitarist. Noted for her clean line, Grant has danced in musicals and has taught movement to the internationally acclaimed performing group Sistren Theatre of Kingston. Her Company triumphs have been in *Sulkari* and *The Visitor.*

Gabrielle Harban received her dance training under Bert Rose and at the

Jamaica School of Dance. She appeared in her first season with the Company in 1979, and as a provisional member she performed in eighteen works, assuming feature roles in such dances as *The Crossing, Rockstone Debate, Sulkari,* and *Tribute to Cliff.* As an actress and singer, she appeared in a number of productions with the Jamaica Playhouse and in the annual pantomimes. A graduate of the Jamaica School of Art, Harban has also designed costumes for a number of stage productions. She became a full member in 1983, appearing to critical acclaim in five of the six new works created for that season.

Fitzroy Hunt, who joined the Company as a supporting dancer in 1971, had trained for years at the Jamaica School of Dance. He has attained full Company membership and was a featured dancer in *Gerrehbenta* in 1983. His strength lies in his natural feel for Jamaican contemporary dance forms, which was used to advantage in such works as *Street People* and *Tribute to Cliff.*

Duran Hylton began dancing in 1976 under the tutelage of Jackie Guy at the Cultural Theatre in Spanish Town, and between 1976 and 1978 he attended classes at the University Dance Society, appearing in some of their annual presentations. He also attended the Jamaica School of Dance. Becoming a full member in 1980, Hylton has appeared in over twenty works in the Company's repertoire, taking leads in such dances as *The Brothers, The Crossing, The Gospel According To, The Visitor, Soulscape,* and *Gerrehbenta.* He brought to his portrayals intense energy, a sense of comedy, and a sharp articulation of movement, often reminiscent of the earlier work of Pinnock and Guy.

Sandra Minott, who began her dance training under Alma Mock Yen at age seven, was one of the pupils at the Jamaica School of Dance when it opened in 1970, remaining there until 1978. A founding member of the school's workshop, she appeared in several of its annual concerts. She was made a full Company member in 1980, and in the tradition of many of the Company's founding members she displayed dedication and attention to detail in the crafting of a role, whether a leading one, as in *The Crossing, Moods,* or *Soulscape,* or a member of the ensemble, as in *The Gospel According To, Wonder Love and Raise, Tribute to Cliff,* and *Litany.* She is a graduate in mass communications from the

Pauline Monroe (left) and Carol Murdoch

Christopher Morrison

University of the West Indies and wrote a history of the National Dance Theatre Company for her Caribbean Studies paper.

Arlene Richards first studied dance under Tony Wilson at the Saint Andrew Technical High School dance workshop in Kingston and later attended the Jamaica School of Dance. She became a full Company member in 1980 and has appeared in over twenty dances, including *Street People, Ni—Woman of Destiny, Myal, Rockstone Debate, Sulkari, The Crossing,* and *Back to Bach, Viva Bach.* Her strong technique and disciplined approach guaranteed her a firm foundation for her budding artistry in such works as *Gerrehbenta, Summer Is, Progeny, Litany,* and *African Scenario.* A stenotypist by profession, she works with the island's Industrial Relations Tribunal.

Denise Robinson began her early dance training under Neville Black—while she was still in high school—and under Cathi March and then continued at the Jamaica School of Dance. She started taking Company classes in 1973 and made her first appearance in the 1975 season. Presently a full member of the Company, she has appeared in over twenty dances, taking lead roles in *Court of Jah* and *The Crossing* and appearing in Bert Rose's solo piece *Moods.* Having graduated with distinction from the Jamaica School of Art, Robinson has taught art at Saint Andrew High School. She brings to her performances stylishness and gutsiness, which is already turning her into an audience favorite in such works as *Summer Is, Sulkari,* and *Moods.*

Jacquie Smith, a secretary by profession, also trained with Neville Black, Cathi March, and at the Jamaica School of Dance. Now a full member with the Company, she has appeared in over twenty works, taking on important roles in *Two Drums for Babylon, Chainlinks,* and *Back to Bach, Viva Bach.* With a fine line, accomplished technique, and sense of elegance, she brings to certain dance works that insouciant grace which is the hallmark of the Company's style.

Alison Symes, who began her dance career in the Eddy Thomas Dance Workshop, appearing in its annual concert performances in rural Jamaica as well as in the pantomimes, joined the Company in 1975 after brief study at the Jamaica School of Dance. Now a full Company member, she has appeared in

Arlene Richards

Denise Robinson

Jacquie Smith

Alison Symes

A set of young dancers from the 1980s generation in Rex Nettleford's *Soulscape* (1983).

twenty-five works in the repertoire, including *The Brothers, Ni—Woman of Destiny, The Crossing,* and *Tribute to Cliff.* A graduate of the University of the West Indies, Symes is a journalist by profession. Dedication and perseverance have resulted in greater dance technique and artistry, evident during the Company's twenty-first anniversary season in such works as *Summer Is* and *Progeny.*

Carson Cumberbatch came to the Company via the Jamaica School of Dance. A Barbadian, he started his early training under Rosemary Wilkinson of the Barbados Dance Theatre Company and later became a member of that company. In Jamaica Cumberbatch attended the annual summer workshops run by the School of Dance and started taking Company classes in 1979, appearing with the Company for the first time in its 1980 season. He has danced in over a dozen works, including *Sulkari, Tribute to Cliff,* and *Elements.* After appearing with the Company in New York, Cumberbatch returned in 1983 to his native Barbados to dance.

Dancers drafted as full Company members in 1980 include (front row, left to right) Sandra Minott, Jacquie Smith, Samuel Bailey; (back row) Fitzroy Hunt, Duran Hylton, Denise Robinson, Arlene Richards, Homer McGann.

Young dancers from the 1980s generation, performing in Tony Wilson's *Progeny* (1983), include (left to right) Alison Symes, Samuel Bailey, Arlene Richards, and Gabrielle Harban.

Adrian Fletcher is a product of the Jayteens Dance Workshop and later of the Jamaica School of Dance. He joined the Company as a supporting dancer in 1980 and has appeared in ten works, taking over leads in *Drumscore, African Scenario,* and *Pocomania.* Enterprising and ambitious, he runs the Jamaica In-

Judith Pennant (center) lead 1980s generation dancers in Sheila Barnett's *Summer Is* (1983). Monica Potts-Lawrence, the newest recruit from the Jamaica School of Dance, is at extreme right.

Namron and Celia Hulton (*Anthony Crickmay*)

Neville Black

stitute of Dance, which shared one of the top dance awards in the 1982 dance competition of the annual festival.

    Christopher Morrison, one of the newer Company recruits, started dancing with the company known as the Self-Theatrical Group in Spanish Town under the leadership of Eisenhower Williams. He also attended classes with the Dinthill Technical Dance Group in rural Jamaica, and later attended the Jamaica School of Dance on a scholarship awarded through the annual festival dance competition. Morrison, who began taking classes with the Company in 1980, brings youthful exuberance to his dancing; his increasing technical competence and sense of form won for him in 1983 the position of understudy, to Clive Thompson, for the role of the suitor in Thompson's love duet *Recollections.*

    George McGann was also a student of the Jamaica School of Dance and the Company's own training program. A promising virtuoso with an impressive energy level, he did not remain long enough to make the impact his peers did.

    Completing the list of new recruits are Glen Dhyll, Carol Murdock, Paula Monroe, Sita Dickson, and Monica Potts-Lawrence, all of whom studied at the Jamaica School of Dance. *Glen Dhyll,* a physiotherapist by profession, is a product of the Self-Theatrical Group of Spanish Town and has spent two years with the Company as a provisional dancer, following his training at the School of Dance. *Carol Murdock* had her early training with Neville Black before she gained her certificate in technique from the School of Dance. *Paula Monroe* gained a diploma in dance from the School of Dance after training at the Jayteens Dance Workshop and spending a summer season at Jacob's Pillow at the encouragement of its administrator, Liz Thompson; an annual summer dance festival at Lee, Massachusetts, Jacob's Pillow was originally organized in the 1930s by Ted Shawn. *Sita Dickson,* who also trained at the School of Dance, gained her early performing experience in the school's workshop. *Monica Potts-Lawrence* had her early training with Joyce Campbell and later worked with Eddy Thomas in his various ensembles before she attended the School of Dance, excelling in the school's 1982 workshop performance. In that appearance she danced the lead in *The Gospel According To,* which was on loan to the School of Dance. She was also featured in *Summer Is,* originally choreographed by Sheila Barnett for the School of Dance but subsequently mounted by Barnett for the Company. Such exchanges of works, which was not unprecedented, facilitated the induction of dancers into the Company from the School of Dance or studios like the Jayteens Dance Workshop and the Jamaica Institute of Dance, which are sympathetic to the Company's stylistic orientation. Two of the most recent apprentices—Delroy Rose and Glenford Brown—have been introduced from the institute and the school, respectively.

Clive Thompson (*Kenn Duncan*)

John Jones (*Horst Schröder*)

Eduardo Rivero

Lois Requa, a provisional dancer who took a leave of absence from the Company to study in New York, returned to perform during the twenty-first anniversary season, resuming her role in *The Crossing.*

Besides Neville Black—who later joined the Company as a choreographer and is discussed previously in those terms—there have been four important guest performers who danced with the Company.

Clive Thompson is a Jamaican from the same background as the Company's founding members, many of whom he worked with either in the Ivy Baxter Creative Dance Group, the Soohih School of Dance, or as a member of the Jamaican group of dancers and singers who toured Washington, D.C., and Baltimore in 1961. Later he worked and studied outside of Jamaica, first with the Martha Graham school in New York and in her company of dancers and later in the Alvin Ailey company, where he gained even greater prominence. Thompson first performed as guest artist with the National Dance Theatre Company in 1975 at the Commonwealth heads of state gala in Kingston and then in 1976 during the normal dance season. His third stint was during the nation's twenty-first anniversary, when he danced the lead in *Court of Jah* and appeared in his own duet *Recollections.*

Namron (formerly Norman Murray) was born in Jamaica and went to England when he was thirteen years old. He became an apprenticed mechanical engineer but decided instead to enroll at the Ballet Rambert school in London, also taking classes at the London School of Contemporary Dance. He became a founding member of the London Contemporary Dance Theatre, later returning to his native country as guest instructor at the Jamaica School of Dance.

Celia Hutton studied at London's Royal Ballet school and later at the London School of Contemporary Dance. Hutton has been partnered by Namron, and the two of them received critical acclaim for their collaboration.

Eduardo Rivero, from the Danza Nacional de Cuba, presented another version of a native Caribbean impulse to Jamaican audiences. Dancing in his own *Okontomi*—which did not remain in the active repertoire—Rivero cleverly personified the spirits of Yoruba gods, the haughtiness of Hispanic pride, and the vigorous muscularity of New World youthfulness.

The Singers

The watershed year 1980 was significant not only for the dancing segment of the Company but also for the singing division—the NDTC Singers. *Joyce Lalor,* the group's vocal soloist and founding leader, was ailing and gave up active performing after the Russian tour. Marjorie Whylie, the Company's musical director, became the leader of the group in 1981, following Lalor's death. Since 1962 Lalor had been a guiding force and something of a Company institution. Her experiences in many areas, including choral music, musical theater, school teaching, educational broadcasting, and the promotion of literacy, gained her considerable public respect. Her rendition of the song "Evening Time"—the Barbara Ferland and Louise Bennett classic—was a personal statement; her particular stamp, revealing an unrivaled poignancy, made her name synonymous with the song. Her musical personality survives in the Company not only in the active repertoire of songs she once led but also in the continuing presence in the ensemble of a number of the talented singers she considered her protégés, recruited from the choirs she worked with in Kingston. These are represented by the following names, which make up the core group of singers.

Paula Johnson, one of the founding members of the NDTC Singers, performed in the 1962 *Roots and Rhythms* show. She has been involved in over twelve pantomimes and in addition has performed in concerts as a member of the Eddy Thomas Dance Workshop, as both singer and dancer. Johnson, who was a member of the Canboulay Singers and the Saint Andrew Singers, also sings with the Saxthorpe Methodist Church choir in Kingston. She ranks as one of the most accomplished performers among the singers.

Vin James, a businessman and farmer in private life, is also a founding member of the NDTC Singers. Beginning his singing career as a choirboy at Saint Michael's church in Kingston under George Goode, James became the lead

NDTC Singers in their program *Traditional Songs of the Caribbean*.

baritone soloist in the choir while still very young. Under George Goode and Hazel Lawson Street, he became a member of the Diocesan Festival Choir, singing solo parts in large works like the *Messiah, Israel in Egypt,* and Mapletoft Poulle's *Folk Mass*. He also performed as soloist with the Saint Andrew Singers under Lloyd Hall as well as with the Spanish Town Cathedral choir and the National Chorale. He is presently in charge of the choir of the parish church of Saint Andrew and also trains students in various secondary schools. His rendition of the folksong "Medelico" as prologue to *Drumscore* is yet to be surpassed.

Vivienne Dewdney, an accountant by profession, started singing at primary school under the tutelage of Mrs. Vidal Smith at the Institute of Jamaica. Dewdney later turned to dancing, and in this capacity she traveled internationally for the Jamaica Tourist Board on promotional tours. She returned to singing in 1968 with the Saint Mary's choir. In 1971 it was on the invitation of Joyce Lalor, who also led the Saint Mary's choir at the time, that she joined the NDTC Singers, which augmented her classical and ballad singing experience by encompassing folk singing.

Stan Irons, a printer by profession, joined the NDTC Singers with a wealth of experience in local theater. A former student of Marian Nowakosky, he has been choir master at Saint Matthew's, Saint Mary's, and the Duke Street Christian Church. In addition he has been heard in such notable choirs as the Saint Andrew Singers, the Diocesan Festival Choir, and the Ivory Club Singers. He has been a lead singer in the pantomimes and has also performed in several dramatic productions and made radio and screen appearances. He made a success as the vocal soloist for the Company dance work *I've Been Buk'd,* which was danced by Barry Moncrieffe.

Carole Reid, an executive with the Bank of Jamaica, is a leading soprano with the singers. Trained in the Jamaica School of Music under Jeanette Cross-Holder, Reid has received diplomas in voice studies from London's Royal School of Music. She has performed with major choirs in Jamaica and is currently a soloist with the Diocesan Festival Choir.

Carl Bliss, who works in the life insurance field, is a former member of the Kingston College choir and during his undergraduate years performed with the University Singers. He trained under Dawn Marie Virtue, Robert Williams, and David Reid and has sung with the Tuesday Singers of Mandeville and in various productions of the Jamaica Amateur Operatic Society. He joined the NDTC Singers as a tenor in 1977 and doubles as the Company's treasurer. His collaboration with Vibart Seaforth in *Misa Criolla* was a tour de force, and he has shown a similar quality in the tenor singing for *Gerrehbenta*. A good stage presence is one of Bliss's performing assets.

Louraine Emmanuel joined the NDTC Singers in 1977. She sang her first solo performance at age seven at a church concert. During her undergraduate years at the University of the West Indies she was a member of the University Singers and toured with them in Jamaica as well as overseas. She was also a member of the Dramatic Society and appeared in their presentations. She is a librarian by profession and works at the Mona campus of the University of the West Indies in the main library.

Wesley Scott, who is an accountant by profession, joined the Company singers as a tenor in 1978. He received his musical education while a member of the Kingston College choir. He has had considerable performing experience with groups like the Jamaican Folk Singers and the National Chorale, of which he is still a member. Scott brings to his performances a keen wit as well as an impec-

NDTC Singers in *Songs from the Pantomimes*.

NDTC Singers in *Mento Suite*.

cable sense of comedy and timing, especially in songs that require dramatic characterization and a facility for movement.

Carmen Gordon, a cosmetologist by profession, started singing at an early age in junior choirs and later in church choirs. She joined the NDTC Singers in 1968 and then left for a few years but returned in 1979.

Marlene Buckeridge has rejoined the Company singers after a leave of absence of some years. She is a member of the Christ Church choir in Vineyard Town, Kingston.

Vibart Seaforth completes the list of full members. A former member of the Jamaican Folk Singers, he has been with the NDTC Singers since the middle 1970s, bringing especially to his interpretation of the *Misa Criolla* a fine musical intelligence. He has worked extensively in Jamaica's musical theater as singer, instrumentalist, and musical director. He plays the clarinet with the National Chamber Orchestra of Jamaica and is a voice instructor at the School of Music. Seaforth is a Guyanese by birth.

Provisional members of the singers include bass Charles Wright, soprano Claudette Allen, and tenor Henrick Hamilton. Both Wright and Allen are alumni of Noel Dexter's Kingston Singers and former participants in the once-active choral-music scene of Ardenne High School, a secondary school in Kingston at which Dexter taught. Hamilton's background is with church choirs in Kingston. Other singers performing in 1983 were soprano Pauline Davis, also from a choir background, and soprano Sandra McKenzie, who had been involved in singing since high school days. Between 1980 and 1983 a number of supporting singers performed periodically with the Company, such as tenor Cecil Cooper, a painter and teacher at the School of Art, and bass Roy Hall, a public relations executive.

Past singers for the Company include four tenors—Lloyd Hall, a music educator and choirmaster; Noel Heron, a former trade unionist and a journalist; Rob-

Carl Bliss

Marlene Buckeridge

Vivienne Dewdney

Louraine Emmanuel

ert Dunkley, a salesman; and Leo Tyson, an educator—and two contraltos—Hope Foreman, a founding member of the NDTC Singers; and Marie Cunningham, a radio and television broadcaster and music teacher.

After 1980 the NDTC Singers received international acclaim in their travels with the Company in Great Britain, Russia, the United States, and Mexico. They performed on their own in New York at Carnegie Hall and went on Jamaican tourist promotion tours to Missouri and Illinois. "If you don't go to watch the National Dance Theatre Company . . . you can just as profitably go to listen to it," mused William Littler of *The Toronto Star*.[14] Anna Kisselgoff also expressed enthusiasm for the group: "The Company's singers . . . are first-rate and they led off with an infectious and good-humored suite of folksongs."[15] The ensemble's origins naturally influence its interpretations of the folksongs that accompany the dances. In its efforts to remain faithful to the spirit of the originals it has settled on a dynamic and robust style of presentation, which serves the dances well.

The NDTC Singers are an integral part of the National Dance Theatre Company. The singers, as a choral orchestra, conform to the Company's concept of

Henrick Hamilton

Vin James

Carmen Gordon

Stan Irons

Carole Reid

Wesley Scott

Charles Wright

Paula Johnson

total theater. Like other members of the Company, the singers offer their services free while making a living at other vocations. They rehearse weekly, and before each dance season they prepare themselves carefully for the suites of songs they present independently on the dance program as well as in their own concerts either in rural Jamaica or abroad. Apart from the traditional songs of Jamaica and the Caribbean, the singers have exposed Jamaican audiences over a decade and a half to American spirituals, chants and social songs from Ghana and Nigeria, Yoruba chants from Cuba, Jamaican mento songs of the 1940s, ska and rock steady songs of the early 1960s, reggae classics from the late 1960s and the 1970s, and songs from the annual Little Theatre Movement pantomimes.

Out of the dance repertoire itself has come a set of works challenging the singers to concentrated efforts. For example, the *Pocomania* suite gives soprano Paula Johnson an opportunity for virtuoso solo work as successor to the

Recent singers include (left to right) Sandra McKenzie, Pauline Davis, and Claudette Allen.

Vibart Seaforth

NDTC Singers in *Love Songs of Jamaica*.

dynamic Joyce Lalor, who created the suite for the Company dance of the same title. *Sulkari,* Eduardo Rivero's collection of Cuban Yoruba chants, was brilliantly adapted by Marjorie Whylie and led by her as both solo singer and drummer. The dancers waited fourteen years for the NDTC Singers to sing Ariel Ramírez's *Misa Criolla* in a live performance, replacing the recording of Los Fronterizos Singers which accompanied the dance between 1967 and 1981. Under Marjorie Whylie's leadership the dream was realized, and ironically the work was first sung by the singers at the funeral service for Joyce Lalor. This was followed by an unforgettable rendition at the 1981 Easter Sunday morning concert at the Little Theatre. The tonal richness of Carl Bliss's tenor and the well-regulated timbre of Vibart Seaforth's bass offered a vocal blend of unique musical pleasure. In 1983 in Venezuela this Spanish-sung work was enthusiastically received by the audiences there.

The NDTC Singers have produced three long-playing records: *NDTC Singers* (Dynamic Sounds), *West Indiana* (Dynamic Sounds), and *Traditional Songs of the Caribbean* (Organization of American States). The OAS recording turned out to be the most popular in the organization's series of music from Latin America and the Caribbean. Music critic Charles Fowler praised the album, describing it as a treasure for public schools in the Americas.[16]

The Musicians

THE MUSICAL DIRECTOR

Linking the singers with the musicians and drummers is *Marjorie Whylie*, the Company's musical director who also presently leads the NDTC Singers. Whylie is one of the most accomplished musicians working in the Caribbean today. Her contributions to the Company cover a wide range: composing original scores for many of the dances, such as *Ni—Woman of Destiny, Shadows, I Not I,* and *Litany;* arranging traditional songs and rhythms for other works; leading the singers; directing the musicians; playing the piano and drumming; and even performing in *Sulkari.* Her participation dates from the founding of the Company, when she performed as a pianist for *Legend of Lovers' Leap.* Whylie has been the musical director since 1967.

A graduate of the University of the West Indies, Whylie taught Spanish at Kingston College before switching to a full-time career in music—playing with studio bands, leading the orchestra for many Little Theatre Movement pantomimes and other musicals, performing on television and radio, judging the annual festival competitions, scriptwriting for educational broadcasting, and researching Jamaican traditional music. She is head of the research department devoted to folk music at the Jamaica School of Music. She brings to the Company deep musical creativity and a knowledge of Jamaican folk forms, but another important asset is her background of dance training with the Barbara Fonseca School of Ballet as a child and later with the Eddy Thomas Dance Workshop and the Jamaica School of Dance. She appears on Jamaican television, informing the public on Afro-Jamaican musical forms, and she has participated in a number of conferences at home and abroad, presenting various papers on Jamaican musicological studies.

THE NDTC ORCHESTRA

The orchestra comprises congo and kumina drummers as well as pianist, flutists, trumpeter, guitarist, and bass player. In the past, many instrumentalists worked with the Company on a fee-paying basis: the most notable were the pianist and arranger Mapletoft Poulle—the first Company musical director who also voluntarily supported the Company during its seedling years—clarinetist Peter Hudson, trumpeter Ossie Williams, and bassist Herbert Nelson. There were other professionals who played for the Company on a fee basis, such as Flo Wilson on violin, David Madden on trumpet, Cedric "Im" Brooks on flute, Ernest Ranglin and Irvine "Allah" Lloyd on guitar, and Boris Gardiner on bass.

Marjorie Whylie, Company musical director and leader of the singers.

The orchestra as a distinct entity must be dated, however, from 1976, when the members waived their fees and joined the Company on the same basis as dancers, singers, technicians, and administrators. The core of the orchestra, who became full members at that time, was made up of Lloyd Mason, Minky Jefferson, Barbara Boland, Leighton Johnson, Jeffrey Cobham, and Steve Golding. By 1983 they still constituted the core, with Lloyd Mason being replaced by Laury Woolery, a provisional player between 1982 and 1983; Steve Golding also left the Company to work with leading orchestras and music groups.

Lloyd Mason, like Woolery and other players, was a product of the Jamaica Military Band, which along with the band of the First Battalion of the Jamaica Defense Force served as a primary source for musicians who worked with the National Dance Theatre Company. Between 1962 and 1982 the military provided no fewer than eight key instrumentalists. In this regard the defense force's chief of staff and the bandmasters of the respective bands generously cooperated by allowing the soldiers leaves of absence so that they could participate in the annual seasons and the overseas tours. Lloyd Mason was a versatile musician, playing bass, flute, and clarinet. Besides working with the Company, he led the orchestras of several musicals. After he retired from the army, Mason immigrated to New York.

Minky Jefferson, a flutist with the orchestra, began playing the flute in her native Trinidad and later trained at the Jamaica School of Music. She has also played with the Jamaica Philharmonic Orchestra and the Jamaica Amateur Operatic Society. A professional librarian, she is presently chief librarian at the Mona campus of the University of the West Indies. She also chairs the university's Musical Advisory Committee and is a member of the National Chamber Orchestra of Jamaica.

Barbara Boland, the other Company flutist, is like Jefferson a Trinidadian. After graduating from the University of the West Indies, she taught sociology at the Mona campus while pursuing music studies at the Jamaica School of Music, working with Melba Liston, the jazz trombonist, among others. She has a wide range of musical experience in classical, jazz, folk, and pop and has been active in recording studios, providing flute background for reggae performers and for commercials. Boland is presently an economic planner with a doctorate from the University of Pennsylvania.

Leighton Johnson plays trumpet in the orchestra. Before joining the National Dance Theatre Company in 1974, he performed with the orchestra of the National Chorale of Jamaica. He is also a member of the National Chamber Orchestra of Jamaica. He is employed as a sales representative with a multinational firm operating in Jamaica.

Jeffrey Cobham is the guitarist in the orchestra. He joined the Company in 1980, after serving as classical guitar instructor at the Jamaica School of Music and the Creative Arts Centre at the university. A Barbadian, he is a radio producer and announcer turned banker.

Steve Golding, who succeeded Irvine "Allah" Lloyd as guitarist, brought vitality to the orchestra pit. He left the Company to work with popular groups, such as Bob Marley's. He remains a leading instrumentalist with reggae bands, both in live performances and in recordings. His natural interest in traditional folk music and lore was greatly enhanced by his experiences with the Company.

Jeffrey Cobham

Ronan Critchlow

Minky Jefferson

Leighton Johnson

Keith Reid, who studied at the School of Music, has played since 1982 with the orchestra as flutist, replacing Barbara Boland while she studied abroad.

THE DRUMMERS

The drummers have a special place in the musical setup of the National Dance Theatre Company. Traditionally led in performance by the master drummer—founding member Ronan Critchlow—they have been led by first drummer Billy Lawrence since 1983. There are also two traditional kumina drummers, Obadiah Lewis and James Walker, who have worked and toured with the Company since 1971. The drummers play under the general direction of Marjorie Whylie, herself a drummer and teacher of drumming.

Ronan Critchlow, the master drummer, was the first major male dancer to emerge on the Jamaican creative dance scene; thirty years ago he created the hero in Ivy Baxter's *Rat Passage.* At the founding of the National Dance Theatre Company Critchlow decided to give up dancing and work instead in the orchestra pit, where he has kept a professional rein on the drum corps.

Billy Lawrence, the first drummer, also sings and once studied dance, actually performing in the pantomimes. Lawrence, who studied with Marjorie Whylie, is an accomplished congo drummer. He plays the shak-shak rattle for the Company dance *Kumina* and the benta for *Gerrehbenta.* In the classroom he is able to respond to the demands of Company teachers for ever-changing rhythms. He also accompanies classes at the Jamaica School of Dance.

Leaford McFarlane, a congo drummer who also studied drum technique under Marjorie Whylie, earned his place in the Company because of his quickness and natural gift for innovation. Besides accompanying Company classes as well as those at the School of Dance, he has taught drumming to rural youths for the Jamaica Social Development Commission.

Richard Cunningham—the son of the Company's sound director, Clyde Cunningham, and a contralto formerly with the NDTC Singers—accompanied his

Drummers Leaford McFarlane (left) and Billy Lawrence.

The Company musicians include (left to right) Steve Golding, Barbara Boland, Antonio Henry, Marjorie Whylie, Minky Jefferson, Irvine Jarrett, and Ronan Critchlow.

parents to rehearsals. Through this exposure he began to play the drum, ending up as a supporting congo drummer for the Company. He was later replaced by *Henry Miller.*

The two kumina drummers, Obadiah Lewis and James Walker, brought to *Kumina*—considered the Company's signature piece—the authenticity and magic of a traditional art developed over years of practice and actual involvement in the ancestral kumina rite. *Obadiah Lewis,* who is a farmer by profession but is profoundly involved in music, actually dances the role of the king in the kumina rites in his native village of Seaforth in Saint Thomas. He also plays the kbandu (bass drum), which keeps the regular beat, with hypnotic concentration. *James Walker,* who is a blacksmith by profession, performs on the playing cast (treble drum), adding vigorous complexity to the polyrhythmic structure of the kumina music that results from pounding two drums, beating kata sticks, and shaking the shak-shak. Both men reside in one of the Jamaican parishes in which African traditions are still prominent.

The present corps of Company congo drummers are the beneficiaries of the accomplished drumming of a number of former players with the Company. *Carl Messado,* probably the most technically deft of all of them, left the Company to live abroad after becoming the first of the young drummers to achieve the status of first drummer. Trained by his brother, Ronan Critchlow, Messado developed into a fine musician and was selected to perform before Queen Elizabeth and

Prince Philip when they visited Jamaica in 1975. Messado returned to the Company temporarily to play for the twentieth anniversary dance season. Other former drummers include Milton Osbourne, a sculptor now residing in New York; Lloyd Patterson, who died in 1976; Horace Wedderburn, a young drummer with a masterful grasp of traditional rhythms; John Walker; Antonio Henry; and Irvine Jarrett, who later won international recognition as a founding member of the innovative reggae band Third World.

The Technicians

Supporting the performing artists is another group of people who are no less talented, with a full appreciation of the Company's aesthetic ideals.

George Carter, the lighting director, was a founding member of the Company. His sustained efforts in designing the lighting for most of the Company's dance works over twenty-one years is a significant part of his career. His general management of Kingston's Little Theatre and the creation of lighting designs for other shows also has won him wide public recognition. Carter exploited a wide range of lighting effects in his designs for Company dances, such as the memorable luminosity he gave to the design for *Lucifer Lucifer,* the eerie foreboding that lends *Kumina* and *Myal* their power, and the uninhibited theatricality and sense of fun he brought to *Summer Is.*

Assisting Carter is *Rufus McDonald,* who works professionally as a data center operations manager. His sensitivity and clockwork precision was of great advantage in 1976, when he directed the lighting by himself on the Company's tour of Australia during Carter's absence. Since the late 1970s McDonald in his articulate and creative responses to lighting designs has become indispensable to the lighting director during Company rehearsals. McDonald himself later had the assistance of Bertram Thompson, a graduate of the Jamaica School of Drama and a technical assistant at the Little Theatre.

In an age when electronically reproduced music is critical to dance theater, particularly for economic reasons, a sound director with up-to-date technological knowledge and the ability to exploit that knowledge creatively is important. *Clyde Cunningham,* the Company's talented and knowledgeable sound director, is an electronics engineer by profession. He supervises the complex sound systems required for the annual seasons and other local performances and also tours extensively with the Company abroad. He succeeded *Baldwin Lennon,* a jazz enthusiast and electronics buff who worked as an accountant professionally. Lennon concocted musical scores for such works as *Two Drums for Babylon* and *Masques of God* by arranging various prerecorded pieces into one composition. Cunningham himself manipulated taped music, originally assembled by Freddie Borough, for *The Rope and the Cross.*

George Carter,
lighting director.

Clyde Cunningham,
sound director.

Barbara Kaufmann,
wardrobe mistress.

Anthony Locke,
stage manager.

The wardrobe mistress in a dance company has a tough job, requiring an analytical mind. *Barbara Kaufmann,* starting from scratch, developed an innovative approach to the classification, storage, and easy retrieval of hundreds of costume items for the more than one hundred dance works in the Company repertoire. She has had to make difficult and ingenious decisions to find substitutes in critical moments or to make do when serious financial limitations put constraints on ambitious design plans. Trained as a dancer at Eddy Thomas's studio, she had performed in the 1962 show *Roots and Rhythms.* Kaufmann assumed the role of wardrobe mistress during the Company's early years, building up a wardrobe management system unmatched in current Jamaican theater operations. Her backstage expertise is also the mainstay of the annual pantomimes, when she is not engaged in her civil service job with the Ministry of Finance or in the annual Company seasons and on overseas tours.

Since 1980 Kaufmann has had the invaluable support of *Pansy Hassan,* the costume coordinator, in the purchase or creation of the costumes. Hassan contributed creatively not only to the administrative side of the job but to the design side as well. Her assumption of these coordinative functions, which were performed first by Eddy Thomas and later by Rex Nettleford previous to 1980, was responsible for a palpable artistic improvement of the Company's presentations.

The ballet mistress's job also involves routine administrative duties, but there are important creative demands in the remounting of earlier dance works as well as the rehearsing of current and new repertoire. *Yvonne daCosta,* who became the ballet mistress in 1969 and returned to the position after a leave of absence during the early 1970s, is well suited to the job. A keen memory, strong analytical sense of movement, fine knowledge of music, which she studied formally, and an innate grasp of the Company's style allow her to keep revivals fresh and as near as possible to the originals. *Footnotes in Jazz, African Scenario, Two Drums for Babylon,* and *Dialogue for Three,* among others, have managed to survive because of her sharp eye and creative spirit.

Rufus McDonald,
lighting assistant.

Barbara Gloudon, Company public relations
director, presiding over the Company's twentieth
anniversary awards. (*Delmar*)

Barry Moncrieffe, the artistic coordinator, assists the artistic director by scheduling classes and rehearsals and, with the ballet mistress, devising suitable engagement schedules. Moncrieffe's position is critical because he also interprets Company policy for the younger dancers.

The stage manager's responsibility is to find innovative solutions to technical snags the Company encounters both at home and on overseas tours. *Anthony Locke,* who has been serving in this position since 1977, started out with the Company as a lighting technician and later acted as assistant stage manager. His extensive knowledge of the theater is the result of many years' experience with straight plays, pantomimes, and other musicals. Professionally he works at the Jamaica Citizens Bank. After a short stint by the theater director Noel Vaz, when the Company was first organized in 1962, the stage managing was supervised by Felix Barnett, Sheila Barnett's husband, and then by *Frederick Hickling,* following his premed undergraduate studies at the University of the West Indies. It was Hickling who gave the job definitive shape, readying it for Anthony Locke. *Donat Buckner,* who served as stage manager for only one season, completes the list of persons who have brought their talents to this technical job. As a designer, Buckner became a significant Company collaborator; his costume and set designs added important dimensions to such works as *Kumina, Ballad of a Lady, Backlash,* and *Gerrehbenta.*

Perhaps the greatest demands on the technical staff of a theater company, in terms of creative ingenuity, fall on the public relations officer. In 1981 *Barbara Gloudon*—journalist, playwright, and public relations consultant—formally took over the Company's public relations. No stranger to the nation's artistic ambitions following independence, Gloudon with the support of her mentor Theodore Sealy, editor of *The Daily Gleaner,* had made the effort to examine seriously the cultural expressions of the new Jamaica—music, dance, art, and theater. The National Dance Theatre Company was one of her beats, and she covered their tours to Stratford, Ontario (1963), Atlanta (1969), and Georgetown, Guyana (1972). Supportive of the Company's essays in dance but equally concerned about its future, Gloudon has been careful to project an accurate image of the Company, mindful of her obligations to address a younger generation sometimes unfamiliar with its history. With a deep knowledge of Jamaican life and Caribbean traditions, sensitivity toward the human condition, and an appreciation of the need for cultural self-definition, along with her impeccable taste, Gloudon's approach is invested with original ideas about communicating the artistic goals of the National Dance Theatre Company as well as other aesthetic concerns of the nation. Gloudon has written four pantomime musicals as well as children's plays, and presently she chairs the Management Committee of the Little Theatre Movement.

Heather Royes, a communications consultant, had preceded Barbara Gloudon as public relations officer. Royes had emphasized the history, philosophy, and future planning of the Company, an approach that seemed viable by the time of the Company's tenth anniversary. Her concerns with the profound implications of dance as a serious art form were reflected in her Company releases. *Roy Burns* was the very first public relations officer, but he was able to serve for only a year before returning to his native Canada. During that year he had attracted the valuable assistance of the artist Eugene Hyde, who continued to work for the Company after Burns's departure.

Foremost among the artists working behind the scenes is *Maria LaYacona,* the Company photographer, who is a naturalized Jamaican born in the United States. Working on the same basis as other full members of the Company, LaYacona has made a considerable contribution to the Company's public image through her photographic representations. The pictures she took between 1964 and 1969 illustrated *Roots and Rhythms,* a primarily photographic history of the Company published initially in London in 1969. In 1972 she mounted an important exhibition of photographs on the National Dance Theatre Company, which was both a public and critical success. The dramatic power and simple truth of her photographs have inspired many other Jamaican photographers to work with dance imagery. Her pictures taken during performance have an immediacy that enhances the artistic interpretation. During the 1960s and early 1970s LaYacona spent hours at classes and rehearsals attuning herself to the complex creative processes involving choreographer and dancer. Her interests revolve around the power of movement, the magic of shapes defining empty space, and the mystery of interior patterns being apprehended in outward forms.

Many times having garnered the gold medal in the annual festival competitions, LaYacona received the special citation of Champion Photographer in the 1983 "Jamaica 21" competitions. She has been a source of inspiration for the work of such Jamaican artists as Eugene Hyde (series of black and white paintings), Barrington Watson (his "Pocomania" series), Susan Alexander (numerous works depicting the Company repertoire), Cecil Baugh (dance figures on ceramic objects), and Kay Sullivan (figures for her Company-derived sculpted works *Myal* and *Street People*).

Before coming to Jamaica, LaYacona had worked in New York with *Life* magazine and *Sports Illustrated;* she also journeyed extensively with travel writer Lowell Thomas. Since coming to Jamaica, her work has covered the gamut of natural imagery, from personalities—such as government ministers, sports greats, and entertainers—to the beauty of the Jamaican countryside and the harsh

Maria LaYacona, Company photographer.

realities of factories, mines, and industrial works. But it is the dance that has been her most satisfying challenge and her enduring passion.

The Administrators

There are often questions about how a company like the National Dance Theatre Company is actually run. The voluntary nature of the enterprise dictates many of the operational arrangements, and the persons described above perform the major administrative duties involved in mounting the annual seasons and mini-seasons and arranging the overseas tours. These tasks were manageable until the problems of increased assets and liabilities demanded more structure in the overall management of the Company.

The artistic product itself and the process of achieving consistent quality remain the central concerns of the administration of the National Dance Theatre Company. Therefore, besides the chairman, secretary, and treasurer, the Management Committee comprises the artistic director, musical director, ballet mistress, artistic coordinator, leader of the singers, sound director, lighting director, stage manager, Company photographer, dancers' representative, and public relations officer. With the establishment of the Jamaica School of Dance representation also came from that institution; another institutional presence was provided by the Little Theatre Movement, whose theater has served as the Company's home. In order to avoid the problems of in-breeding, interested outsiders have served not only on the Management Committee but also on ad hoc and standing committees. Like the Company's artistic corps, the Management Committee revitalizes itself by a process of self-elimination. No one is fired or requested to leave.

From the beginning the founders were convinced that cultural institutions

Verona Ashman,
Company secretary.

Maurice Stoppi,
Company chairman
from 1972–1983.

should be run by the artists themselves or by persons with a genuine love for the specific art form. Thus the frustrations of bureaucratic maneuvering are avoided although not at the expense of a structured management. Besides the artistic personnel constituting the Management Committee of the National Dance Theatre Company, the chairman, secretary, and treasurer should also be described.

The young lawyer *Joseph Cools-Lartigue,* the first chairman of the Management Committee, gave effective leadership in the Company's early years, but he died in 1969, too early to accomplish his goals for the Company. *Maurice Stoppi,* succeeding Cools-Lartigue as chairman, presided over Company affairs from 1972. As the husband of Company dancer Mavis Lai, he took an early interest in the Company's operation, giving sound advice and administrative support throughout the years. Stoppi is a quantity surveyor by profession, with the firm of Stoppi, Cairney and Bloomfield, and is especially known for his work in urban renewal projects and social services. Giving up the chairmanship in 1983, although not membership on the committee, Stoppi was succeeded by John Cooke, a young Jamaican businessman.

Verona Ashman, a founding member, has served the Company since 1962 as secretary, as well as front house manager for its annual dance seasons; she has also served as liaison administrator on the international tours. Knowledgeable about Jamaican social and cultural history, Ashman has had an important career as cultural administrator: she was registrar for the Jamaica School of Art, where she studied sculpture, and an executive assistant for the Institute of Jamaica. She has had extensive experience as an actress on both television and the stage, collaborating with Orford St. John throughout the 1950s on a number of plays for the Repertory Players.

Carl Bliss, one of the NDTC Singers, has been the Company treasurer since 1979. Despite his accounting skills, Bliss had to learn the job while actually doing it. He encountered difficulties associated with the changing of the guard, as it were, but because he represented the new generation himself, he was able to appreciate some of the necessary changes. In the very early years Verona Ashman held the position of treasurer as well as secretary. Ashman was soon succeeded by Baldwin Lennon, who was sound director of the Company but lent his accounting skills to its management. Succeeding him was Paul Breen, an Englishman working with the firm of Stoppi, Cairney and Bloomfield. By then there were increased chores to the position and Breen contributed professional efficiency until 1979, when work away from Jamaica prevented him from giving full attention to these duties and he was succeeded by Carl Bliss.

Thus besides the artistic and technical personnel that made up the management of the Company, there were also important contributions from the fields of business, social work, education, banking, law, and medicine. The absence of rural representation within management was considered a serious deficiency. Ad hoc representation covering appearances outside Kingston had been effective in the past, but direct representation is obviously a requisite, as is full resumption of Company appearances, in towns other than Kingston, Mandeville, and Montego Bay, the three major cities on the island.

The Development Fund, established in 1982 with a standing committee, is intended to rationalize the financial administration and to maximize whatever resources the Company retains. Chaired by Carl Bliss, it includes within its membership the Company's guitarist, Jeffrey Cobham, who is a banker, as well as the lawyer and businessman Pat Rousseau, who was a member of the Management Committee in the 1960s. There is also a committee that administers an apartment block, which was negotiated for the Company under Maurice Stoppi's direction. Any profits from the rents will go to the Development Fund. With heavy mortgages and inherited liabilities the Company has discovered that ownership of this kind of real estate [17] belongs to the bank rather than the registered owner, at least at the beginning. Admittedly a new experience for a traditionally impoverished Company, the enterprise involved many anxious moments for the management. The presence on the Management Committee of the young attorney Harold Brady, himself a man of the theater, is to help ease such anxieties.

The agenda for the future includes such priorities as the education of Company members who may need further education in basic reading and mathematics skills or supplementary training for careers in dance or related theater arts. A system of rewards on a cooperative basis for long-time Company members and an upgraded health and accident insurance policy are also important priorities. The regularization of these concerns as a matter of policy is advisable in the absence of any realistic hope of making the Company professional, in the sense of providing regular and adequate salaries in the foreseeable future for a group of sixty or more persons who work with the Company from year to year.

The search for a long-term operational framework and a rational administrative structure is the present challenge of the Company. The administrators must now build courageously on the strong foundations laid by those who gave their services voluntarily in the spirit of a tradition that has informed dance companies, both professional and amateur, in many parts of the world—but which has had a special meaning for the National Dance Theatre Company, itself conceived as a voluntary institution for the development of arts and culture in independent Jamaica.

Unity in Diversity

During the first twenty-one years of its existence the National Dance Theatre Company has involved the participation of over five hundred individuals working directly for it in various capacities as choreographers, dancers, singers, musicians, composers, designers, stage technicians, dance instructors, photographers, filmmakers, wardrobe attendants, administrators, and box-office personnel. These individuals, as well as those recruited from the private sector and government agencies, have offered their voluntary services in the name of artistic discovery and cultural self-definition in order to shape a new society.

The ability of Jamaicans to achieve high standards of performance through discipline and commitment and the mobilization of creative energy into effective action had been clearly demonstrated. The implications of what is possible in the wider society cannot be overemphasized. For generations the people of the Commonwealth Caribbean had been brought up on distorted perceptions of themselves held by their colonial masters and encapsulated in views reflected by such intellectuals as Robert Charles Dallas, a nineteenth-century authority on the Maroons, when he made the pronouncement that the "notion of a free, native, negro republic does not seem to have any reasonable foundation."[18] Today such an arrogant view seems more cynical than condescending, even in the historical context. How else would one interpret the following statement from another English historian, James Anthony Froude, who visited the Caribbean in the late nineteenth century? "As a body [the population has] shown no capacity to rise above the condition of their ancestors except under European laws, European education, and European authority. . . . Give them independence, and in a few generations they will peel off such civilization as they have learnt as easily and as willingly as their coats and trousers."[19] Froude obviously had internalized his own culture's naive assumptions about class restrictions and racial proprieties and accepted without question the colonial status quo.

It is the work of groups like the National Dance Theatre Company which helps to alleviate these aberrations of perception on the part of foreign observers who were burdened by preconceived notions about the capabilities of Caribbean people to manage anything or to govern themselves. Rather than peeling off "such civilization as they have learnt," the Jamaicans have enriched their civilization through their creative activities not only in terms of appropriately pre-serving, while selectively rejecting, much of what they learned but also in terms of the new dimensions they have added through their own creative imagination. Much of this has taken place with the advantage of a continuity of effort on the part of succeeding administrations pursuing cultural policies that share a signifi-cant place with other priorities of public management.

The continuity on the part of the artists, technicians, and administrators of the Company, all of whom subsidize the work of the Company by contributing their talents voluntarily, is responsible for the quality of the artistic product showcased in the annual seasons in Jamaica and on the numerous tours overseas. That the society has responded at all, whether by attendance at the Company perform-ances or by critical comment on the dance work, points up the dynamics of a society that is conscious of its responsibilities in integrating culture into its na-tional life—a fact also borne out by the rich outpourings from the mass of the population in the area of music. Music and dance after all transcend boundaries set up by class or race.

The creative arts in general and the National Dance Theatre Company in particular have challenged class–color barriers by fostering the shared creative experience between urban ghetto-bred and peasant-born, on the one hand, and scions of the middle and upper-middle strata, on the other, or between the highly educated and the minimally literate; their efforts have also linked small farmers with urban professionals, low-income wage earners with members of the salariat, and the securely employed with those marginally employed. The Com-pany artists, technicians, and administrators have forged a coalition of collab-orators who have managed to promote the primacy of talent and creative achievement over such arbitrary determinants of status and self-worth as mate-rial wealth, genealogical pedigree, and color. It is in this respect, as well, that the Company has assisted in exploding inherited myths about the preordained in-feriority of things Caribbean that are not anchored unequivocally in European civilization. Those who have worked with the National Dance Theatre Company represent a varied group that speaks at once to the specifics of the Jamaican reality and the universality of the human condition.

7 · The National Dance Theatre Company as Catalyst

The role of the National Dance Theatre Company as a cultural force in the Caribbean has been a positive one. The influence has been most evident in five areas: (1) dance as an art form practiced in the wider community; (2) the approach to dance training; (3) research into ancestral dance and the connections between traditional forms and dance as a sophisticated art form; (4) the delicate collaboration between choreographers, composers, and set designers; and (5) the nascent tradition of criticism in the Caribbean which speaks to the aesthetic realities of Caribbean dance theater.

Not everyone agrees that the influence has always been positive. For example, the attempts at reproducing the Company's choreographic style by apprentices competing in the annual national festival have been criticized by those who insist on greater originality. Yet imitation in a dynamic situation is not necessarily completely negative, since it frequently leads to adaptation and thus to genuine creativity. There is already ample evidence that these annual offerings have stimulated originality throughout the island, and the influence of the National Dance Theatre Company in such cases has not been detrimental. The singularly positive effect the Company's work has had on dance as an art in Jamaica and the English-speaking Caribbean has been acknowledged in many quarters. The work has altered the perceptions of many Jamaicans not only about their natural ways of moving but also about the capacity of their own ancestral sources to give energy to aesthetic creations.

Community Outreach

The National Dance Theatre Company's effective work in the wider community was accomplished primarily under the auspices of the Jamaica Cultural Development Commission (formerly known as the Festival Office). This was not coincidental. The senior dance officer for most of the twenty-one years since

This terra-cotta bas-relief by Edna Manley, Jamaica's leading sculptor, celebrates the dance as typified by the National Dance Theatre Company. Mrs. Manley has often acknowledged the Company's influence on her work. (*Yvonne daCosta*)

independence was Joyce Campbell, one of the founding members of the Company. The policy committee that guided her program was headed during the first twelve years by Rex Nettleford, the Company's artistic director. Many Company members voluntarily trained the teachers who created dances for the annual competitions. Some of the judges were also drawn from Company membership. Insistence on the highest standards within the competitions was reflected in the paucity of gold medals awarded to festival contestants in the early years. But the high standards did not deter participants, and the dance grew in popularity to a premier position, overshadowing all other arts competing in the annual festivals. The figures for schools and communities taking part in the competitions drastically increased over the years. In 1964 nine primary schools, one high school, and one all-age school sent contestants; whereas in 1978 seventy, forty-nine, and ninety were sent, respectively; community groups increased from thirteen to sixty-one. To date thousands of children and hundreds of adults have competed in a variety of categories, including traditional dances, Jamaican and Afro–West Indian folk, modern, jazz, popular, and European classical, as well as national dances of other countries. Encouraging young people to accept traditional forms as a basis for creative dance was one of the approaches of the National Dance Theatre Company, which was building a repertoire on precisely these premises.

There was an organic interaction between the work in dance in the wider community and the work in the Company's studios. Joyce Campbell brought her experience from investigative fieldwork. In the 1960s the Company's artistic director shared with her the responsibilities of recording traditional dances on film. This exploratory work made possible Campbell's *Dance Time in Cascade* and Nettleford's various dances based on traditional lore. These works in turn inspired the teachers entering the competitions, thus new ground was broken in the exploration of form and content in dance. An interest in traditional rituals and recreational dance—kumina, bruckin party, gerreh, maypole, jonkonnu, and dinkimini—emerged, and the Company incorporated aspects of these movements and concepts into their formal dances. As a result of the catalytic role of the National Dance Theatre Company and its cultural interactions, there has been a greater appreciation of the dance and, by extension, of the overall cultural potentials of the Jamaican people. By the end of the first two decades of Jamaican independence there was greater acceptance of a black Caribbean aesthetic compared to the Eurocentrism that formerly dominated cultural perceptions. Through dance the Company has indeed helped Jamaicans to interpret themselves to themselves.

The catalytic influences of the Company are also evident in other areas of the Caribbean. For example, the Barbados Dance Theatre Company was inspired by the Jamaican experiment. In the early years Rex Nettleford taught classes in Barbados, and Bert Rose and Jackie Guy not only taught there, they also created short dance works for the Barbadian company. More important has been the work of Carson Cumberbatch, one of their own members, who pursued a four-year course in dance education and choreography at the Jamaica School of Dance. His return to Barbados dance theater will be valuable. In Guyana a national school and company also drew its inspiration from Jamaica's National Dance Theatre Company following its appearance in Georgetown in 1962 at Carifesta, and Noelle Chutkan, a Company principal for many years, taught dance at the National School of Dance in Nassau in the Bahamas. Even Bermuda, despite its North American orientation, was inspired by the Jamaican example to form a national dance group after the Company's appearance in Hamilton in 1972. In fact the entire English-speaking Caribbean has drawn on members of the National Dance Theatre Company for teaching and consultation. Company principals and choreographers have taught dance in Grenada, Dominica, Antigua, Montserrat, Barbados, the Cayman Islands, and Trinidad; others have participated in judging dance festivals in Belize and the Bahamas. Through fellowships sponsored jointly by UNESCO and the Organization of American States, a number of dancers and dance teachers from the eastern Caribbean have studied at the Jamaica School of Dance and have had direct access to the Company. The Company's appearances in the Caribbean islands have convinced many of what is possible—despite limited resources—with boundless energy and a belief in the indigenous culture of the region.

Training and Research

Other areas in which the National Dance Theatre Company has had direct and positive influences on the development of dance are in training and research. Before the Jamaica School of Dance was established, Company members were training dancers in the outreaches of Jamaica and in other parts of the region and employing Company approaches to foster dance technique. It was natural for individual Company members to concentrate on their own particular strengths, but the habit of experimenting with new approaches to training was second nature to each of them.

Sheila Barnett held a pivotal position in the Saint Joseph's Teacher Training College, where teachers were encouraged to exploit body movements in creative ways not only to produce dances for the showcase offered by the annual festival competitions but also to stimulate students to cultural knowledge. Many who were exposed to Barnett's systematic training joined the Contemporary Dance Centre, directed by Barnett and Barbara Requa, who at the time was teaching dance-oriented physical education at the secondary school level. The names of Gloria Grandison, Barbara Edwards, Barbara Robinson, Maria Smith, and Grace Hamilton are identified in Jamaica not only with the creative work that emerged from their pupils in the festivals but also with dance education.[1] It's a fact that a high percentage of students from primary schools participating in the Cultural Development Commission's dance competitions are also successful students in the common entrance exams. Parents now request that their children be included in the dance groups participating in the festival. Gloria Grandison, who works in Kingston's depressed area, has observed fewer incidents of teen-age pregnancy among the girls who dance. An increase of teachers committed to dance in education could make a serious impact on the educational system if the Ministry of Education were willing to cooperate with the Jamaica School of Dance and the Company's training program.

The Company's training system has now been taken over by the Jamaica School of Dance. The school has a concentration of the best teaching talent in Jamaica, although the strongest classical ballet training remains in private studios. Company members who have been engaged to teach in the school found themselves much in demand as instructors at other studios. The new dance group Movements (made up of a few members of the former Jamaica Dance Company, led by Eddy Thomas) engaged both Patsy Ricketts and Jackie Guy as instructors even while they were principals with the National Dance Theatre Company. Guy, who for years had directed the University Dancers, became the artistic coordinator for the Movements group. Under the direction of Joyce Campbell the Company's training system was incorporated into the Jayteens Dance Workshop, which in turn provided the Company with many recruits.

Several other small groups run by Company members throughout the first twenty-one years extended the Company's influence beyond its Kingston studios at the Little Theatre. Bert Rose and Barry Moncrieffe taught effectively for two years in the tourist resort towns of Montego Bay and Ocho Rios; one result was a dance group now transferred to Chicago; under the name Caribbean Dance Theatre, it is directed by Fred Baker. The Company's training system was also beneficial in several social projects in Kingston institutions: the system was modified for programs involving the prison inmates at the Gun Court Rehabilitation Centre and the mental patients at Bellevue Hospital as part of the new curricula devised primarily by Sheila Barnett. In July 1978 Barbara Requa and Sheila Barnett, attending the first International Conference on Dance and the Child in Edmonton, Canada, delivered a paper based on work they were accomplishing in Jamaica. Moira Logan, writing in *Dance Magazine,* cited the discussion by these two Jamaican dance educators as among the most memorable of the conference's presentations and then concluded that their important work "focused on dance as a traditional part of Jamaican society and its potential for playing an even more vital role in Jamaica's cultural and educational life."[2]

Many individual Company members developed their own specialties as teachers. Bert Rose's method showed a strong identification with modern dance

This drawing, representative of the sequence in *The Crossing* that describes the slave coffle during the middle passage, was executed by New York artist Richard Barclift during the Company's 1980 appearance at the Brooklyn Academy of Music.

techniques; whereas Sheila Barnett and Barbara Requa blended these techniques with a creative approach to body awareness which would be beneficial to teachers in the educational system. Jackie Guy utilized his skills in developing traditional dance, and Barry Moncrieffe also experimented with folk forms, which gave his classes a special intensity. Fitzroy Hunt was responsible for developing movement suitable for contestants in body-building and beauty competitions. Dancers like Judith Pennant and Monica McGowan prepared young students for examinations in the Cecchetti ballet methods. Over the years Company members or dancers trained in Company methods were identified with several performing groups, such as Movements, the University Dancers, the Jamaica Institute of Dance, Black Image, the short-lived Western Dance Theatre, the Jayteens Dance Workshop, as well as a cross section of school groups that have excelled in the annual festival competitions.

In terms of the cultural perceptions of a new generation, an even more important legacy of the National Dance Theatre Company is related to ideas of self-definition. For until recently anything produced from indigenous sources has been denigrated by the society. Even though the former masters and the upper classes often found delight in the minstrel performances of the slave or, after

The Company's influence on other art forms is revealed in these three works. Kay Sullivan's sculpted figure *Myal* was inspired by a Company work. Maria LaYacona's striking photograph of the Company shows members in traditional costume. The vase, showing a dancer's stately pose, is by Cecil Baugh. (*Yvonne daCosta*)

emancipation, of the poor black populations, these performances were regarded as subcultural diversions rather than creative contributions to a civilized society. Despite the efforts of Britain's Sadler's Wells and the Royal Ballet—both of which assumed responsibility for students from the colonies through the Royal Academy of Dance examinations—the dance was relegated to third place, behind drama and music. Both subjects were offered in the region's educational system long before dance was considered appropriate as a serious educational tool. Yet dance remained a natural source, aching for imaginative integration into the educational system.

The negative attitude toward dance was reinforced because it was identified in the popular imagination with upper-class sophistication. Except for character portrayals, hip movements—particularly lateral sway and contraction–release patterns—were looked upon as vulgar despite the fact that this type of movement was characteristic of indigenous religious and recreational dancing. Nobility and grace were acceptable only in terms of a straight spine on demipointe or in an arabesque position. Many middle-class Jamaican youths wanted to imitate these stances exclusively, which they regarded as the only appropriate cultivated image, lending a special kind of social power. Anatomical requirements set forth by the Royal Academy of Dance manuals naturally disqualified many Jamaicans, who were deemed unsuited to classical dance. But this approach to movement was obviously unnatural under the circumstances, and the National Dance Theatre Company set out to be a catalytic force to change this perception of the dance. In this way we hope to offer the world of dance a contribution that will be taken seriously, one that will be genuinely respected not only by Caribbean peoples but also by the world and at the same time that will heed Derek Walcott's warning against accusing "great art of feudalism and [excusing] poor art as suffering."[3] This change were best achieved through a profound knowledge of traditional Caribbean and Jamaican music and dance as well as the region's religious beliefs and social customs.

Thus research into indigenous forms has been supportive of the technical development of dance and the training systems within the Company. The need to mount dances that gained authority through their authenticity sent choreographers and dancers into the field. What had begun as the simple ferreting out of traditional dances for the festival showcase opened up possibilities not only for dance researchers but also for the collection of musical data. Some of the research studies in traditional dance and music—particularly the work of Sheila Barnett, Joyce Lalor, Marjorie Whylie, and Cheryl Ryman—have been discussed in previous chapters. Ryman, who studied dance research methods as part of her undergraduate degree at York University in Toronto, has done critical work in this area over the years. By 1983 she was able to point out that the pattern of research has settled into one of greater analysis rather than simply the collection of data: "Most recently the research has focused on two main areas of practical application: (1) the development of a methodology and curriculum, using dance as the major source and stimulus, for communicating Africanisms and effecting black self-actualisation; (2) the identification and analysis of the core dance vocabulary in both traditional and contemporary dance with a view to developing and refining the respective techniques—that is, systems of training. Specifically

David Boxer, a Jamaican artist who is also an art historian and director of the National Gallery in Kingston, paints the backdrop he designed for the Company work *The Gospel According To*.

a rudimentary methodology and the nucleus of a black dance technique has already emerged."[4] The debate surrounding the Company's aesthetics sharpened Ryman's research concerns, allowing her to focus on a somewhat neglected area of dance research; that is, the philosophical considerations of dance. Subsequently she developed a course that emphasizes the historical–aesthetic–philosophical perspectives of black dance, both traditional and contemporary. This is a long way indeed from the immediate objectives of 1974, which involved the identification and location of all traditional dance forms in Jamaica.

By the 1980s the appropriate language in which to communicate graphically the movement patterns evident in traditional work began to emerge. For example, Ryman's description of dinkimini—the basis of much of *Gerrehbenta*—bears this out:

The dinkimini dance is characterised by two main styles, which tend to be male-dominated: (1) a "corkscrew" (up and down and around simultaneously) action in the upper torso and a rotation in the hip, with the feet placed one flat in front and the other behind on the ball of the foot, and (2) a turned-in knee, drop and brush (to the side) step, which may be extended into an alternating brush to the front and the back while the arms and shoulders "pump" on each brush. Both variations carry a subtle but distinct "impulse and suspension" or syncopated quality. The equally characteristic impulse and "break" turn, with an inclination of the upper torso to one side, may be interchanged with sharp pelvic contact between couples.[5]

Thus research investigations into the dance offered choreographers, performers, and audiences alike several insights into the totality of Jamaican life. Although the National Dance Theatre Company has stimulated the identification and analysis of persistent areas of African and European retentions in the Jamaican dance culture, there must be continued work to test emerging hypotheses through various methods: academic as well as practical teaching-environments, exhibitions, lecture demonstrations, audio-visual media, and books and magazines. But dance communication is basically nonverbal, and the choreographic efforts themselves will benefit directly from such research. Thus, if the Company is to remain true to its original mission, its work must continue to be informed by the very investigations it has inspired.

Art and the Dance

The Company's work naturally has had a deep influence on related arts, particularly scenic and costume design and musical composition. But the influence has also extended to arts independent of the dance, including painting, sculpture,

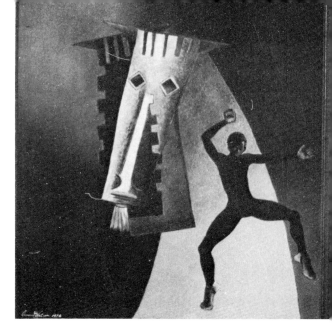

Dolls representing the king and queen in the dance work *Kumina* were created by Company dancer Pansy Hassan. (*Yvonne daCosta*)

Osmond Watson, a leading Jamaican artist, pays tribute to the Company in *Tribute to Rex*, a painting of a dancer poised in a dramatic movement in front of a jonkonnu mask. (*Yvonne daCosta*)

photography, and film. This interrelatedness of the Company's efforts and those in other cultural areas was the subject of the impressive exhibition "Art and Dance," organized in January 1983 by the National Gallery of Jamaica. Celebrating the twentieth anniversary of the National Dance Theatre Company, the exhibition sought to show the dynamic interaction between the various disciplines of the plastic arts and the dance.[6] Over 130 works of art were exhibited in various categories, such as painting, sculpture, ceramics, prints, photography, and costume and set designs, among others. Jamaican painters, such as Susan Alexander, Stanley Barnes, Valerie Bloomfield, David Boxer, Ralph Campbell, Eugene Hyde, Osmond Watson, and Barrington Watson commemorated the Company directly in their work; Malachi Reynolds (Kapo) and Albert Huie, for example, celebrated dance in general. Sculptors Edna Manley and Kay Sullivan modeled from life, but Cecil Baugh worked from photographs of the Company by Maria LaYacona for his expressive figures on stoneware vases.

Company dancers and choreographers —such as Eddy Thomas, Bert Rose, Denise Robinson, Gabriel Harban, and Pansy Hassan—have provided creative decor and costumes for Company works, but from the very beginning professional artists and designers collaborated with the Company in producing dramatic design environments for the repertoire. As early as 1963 Eugene Hyde and Milton Harley designed backdrops for dances: Hyde for *Dialogue for Three* and Harley for *Games of Arms.* Lloyd van Pitterson accurately captured a Kingston neighborhood on his backdrop for *Parade Kingston 13,* and Howard Parchment designed not only the backdrop but also dramatic sculpted forms as part of the decor for *Masques of God*; Parchment also produced the set and costumes for *The King Must Die.* Moira Small provided the decor for *Omegan Procession,* and Susan Alexander both the decor and costumes for *Fables.* Jerry Craig, former director of the Jamaica School of Art, designed *Celebrations.* Colin Garland, who had designed costumes and set for *Lucifer Lucifer,* covered the stage with a backdrop dominated by the figure of a lion for *Court of Jah;* his costumes for this work also appropriately utilized the black, green, and gold colors of the Rastafarian faith. Kofi Kayaga lent his talents to *Ni—Woman of Destiny* and *I Not I.* David Boxer created a powerful backlit backdrop for *The Gospel According To.* Other collaborators on set and costume designs include Donat Buckner, Richard and Sally Montgomery, Michael Bryne, Claudia Robinson, Easton Lee, Garth Robinson, and Bruce Jones.

In the area of music the Company was influential in inspiring important com-

Before mounting his 1966 exhibition in Kingston, Jamaican painter Eugene Hyde discusses with Rex Nettleford his works representing dances in the Company's repertoire.

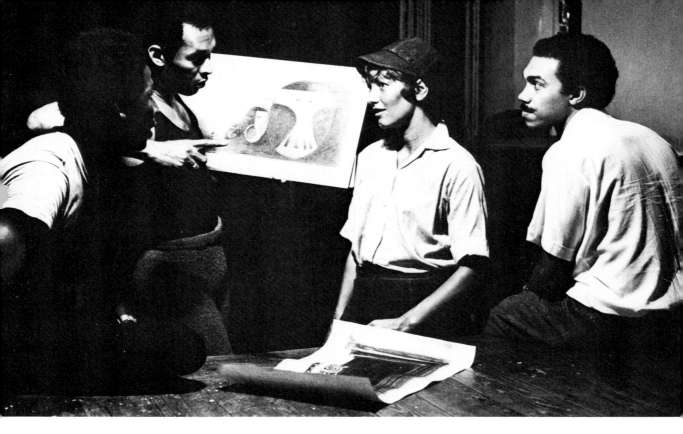

Prior to the Company's 1966 dance season in Kingston, Rex Nettleford (sitting at left) and Eddy Thomas confer with painters Moire Small and Howard Parchment about their respective set designs for *Omegan Procession* and *Masques of God*.

positions from Oswald Russell, Carlos Malcolm, Peter Ashbourne, Cedric "Im" Brooks, Bob Sinicrope, and, of course, Marjorie Whylie, the Company's musical director. But it was not simply this aspect of the theater arts that felt the Company's impact on music. The musical theater began taking dance seriously and engaged the services of many Company members. Rex Nettleford had choreographed and directed Little Theatre Movement pantomime musicals since 1959, changing the character of dance in those annual shows during the 1960s and 1970s. Eddy Thomas, Sheila Barnett, Bert Rose, Joyce Campbell, Jackie Guy, and Tony Wilson also choreographed for them.[7] Some became favorite choreographers for small revues and transplanted Broadway hit musicals. Cheryl Ryman assisted in the premiere of *Maskarade,* written by Sylvia Wynter and Jim Nelson. Choreographers are now regarded as important members of production teams of such undertakings.

The National Dance Theatre Company has been an influence on the annual musicals produced by the Little Theatre in Kingston. Company singer Joyce Lalor and musician Marjorie Whylie perform in the 1974–75 pantomusical *Dickans for Fippance*, written by Gloria Lannaman, directed by Norman Rae, and choreographed by Rex Nettleford. (*Daily Gleaner*)

Unexpected developments underscore the catalytic effect the National Dance Theatre has had on cultural life in Jamaica. In 1978 a new expression in popular musical theater burst on the scene. Known as *Explanitations,* the show was a reggae event featuring the acclaimed musical group Third World. The event was organized by Frederick Hickling, the Company's stage manager. Former Company dancer Thomas Pinnock returned from New York to stage the show. Irvine "Carrot" Jarrett, a former Company drummer, cited Company experience and influence in helping to sustain the long and demanding hours of preparation for the show.

In September 1983 Hickling again assembled Third World, representing the reggae expression of the popular music of the 1970s and 1980s, as well as the Skatalites, a musical group that originated during the ska period of the early 1960s; the event took place at the Zinc Fence in Kingston. Among the dancers engaged for the performance's was Patsy Ricketts, a former Company principal, who had begun to explore the reggae idiom for its theatrical potential. The Company's influence has also been acknowledged by Irvine "Allah" Lloyd, a moving spirit behind the reggae group Chalice.

Richard Barclift, a gifted black American artist from Brooklyn, captured in his dance drawings the special movements associated with the Company. Barclift was a frequent visitor to the Brooklyn Academy of Music and the City Center Theater on the Company's last two visits to New York. Poets too have been inspired by Company works, the tributes of Leebert Bethune and Mervyn Morris being especially moving.[8]

Film and video were also challenged by the Company's work. The names of Freddie Borough and Donat Buckner became identified with dance presentations—not only those of the National Dance Theatre Company—on television and in films. Buckner, a film producer with the Jamaica Broadcasting Corporation who was also a costume and set designer for the Company, won an award from the Jamaican Press Association in 1981 for the presentation of the National Dance Theatre Company on his popular "Spectrum" series. During the 1970s the Jamaica Broadcasting Corporation recorded the dances and rituals of rural Jamaica, which the Jamaica Information Service had begun to do in the 1960s. Under Buckner's direction extensive footage of traditional revival, etu, tambu, gerreh, and dinkimini were recorded with the assistance of Cheryl Ryman, Joyce Campbell, and Marjorie Whylie. An increased awareness of the need for the collection and storage of this valuable indigenous material has been encouraging to all Company members.

Company dancers in rehearsal, a sketch done in March 1970 by Mexican muralist Raul Anguiano while engaged as artist in residence at Kingston's University of the West Indies.

Above: Originally presented in 1964, *Two Drums for Babylon* was given a new production in 1980. This new version also explored the conflict of a Jamaican youth in choosing between marriage and affection or the vitality of a Rastafarian cult.

Below: In *Elements* (1978) the affirmation of Caribbean movement patterns is emphasized as well as the sounds and rhythms that shape those patterns.

8 · The Company and the Critics

One area in which the National Dance Theatre Company is yet to have the sort of catalytic effect appropriate to the art of dance is that of serious criticism. A tradition of vibrant, sensitive, and intellectually sound criticism is crucial. Understandably initial efforts were influenced by criteria established for Europe's classical form of dance theater. Notions of line, aesthetic harmony, and underlying artistic philosophy were dictated by received values from European and colonial critical traditions. Despite some rave notices in the popular press, there is still a great need for a body of genuine critical assessments that speak to the cultural realities of Caribbean dance theater or to the iconographic framework of dance. Yet there has been some important progress. The vigorous critical debates of the 1960s were precisely what this author would wish for the dance. After all, West Indian literature had to wait decades before it attracted the serious attention of scholars and critics. Ironically the few notable critical responses to dance developed in the Caribbean literary circle of poets like Derek Walcott, Edward Kamau Brathwaite, and Dennis Scott.

Brathwaite's deep concern that the Caribbean citizen view self and society independently rather than through the colonial experience has brought him naturally toward a serious assessment of the National Dance Theatre Company and the place of dance in Caribbean culture. Brathwaite's early doubts about the Company's intent were not unknown, and he came to accept the Company's direction only with the creation of *Kumina* in 1971. At the Caribbean Dance Seminar held at the Jamaica School of Dance in 1979 Brathwaite shared a schematic assessment he felt was necessary for any serious expression of Caribbean dance.[1] He stated that efforts to establish a Caribbean dance theater must be organized around six crucial elements: *rhythm,* one of the basic elements of African life[2]; *kinesis,* the special use of energy evident in West Indian drama, poetry, jazz, sex, and gospel; *possession,* the dominant power of the mind which transcends boundaries; *icon,* the creation of a recognizable Caribbean image; *nommo,* the ability to find one's own vocabulary to describe not only individual realities but also the universality of human experience; and *nam,* the irreducible kernel that holds the essence of Caribbean culture or any emerging culture. There would be much to object to in Brathwaite's schema by those who believe that legitimate Caribbean dance must subject itself to Eurocentric aesthetics.[3] The critics who adhere to this line find unacceptable the premise that the National Dance Theatre Company has created a new vocabulary and a different aesthetic. They lose sight of the fact that Caribbean heritage has historical roots in a plurality of sources. Yet some of the critics are beginning to understand the implications of the continuing debate over why the marginalized elements of Jamaican cultural life—predominantly derived from Africa—should be given a central place in the ethos.

As early as 1970 Dennis Scott had lamented the fact that nowhere, at home or abroad, has there been a critical probing into the meaning of the works:

One does not expect foreign critics to be aware of, or interested in, the intimate connections between the dance and the society's experience of itself. One does keep hoping that Jamaicans who discuss the Company will think it worthwhile to analyse seriously the intention which increasingly dominates the dancers' efforts to reflect our society. . . . But in this time of catchwords like "relevance," "eurocentrism," and "black," we do ourselves an ironic disservice if we continue to apply to our creations the critical methods of cosmopolitan centres. However sympathetic, those foreign critics can know nothing about the particular situation against which we must measure the validity of our own arts. It is time now to create new ways of perceiving and judging our dance, by revealing a new depth of insight into our society.[4]

Scott had anticipated Derek Walcott's assessment by a year. Walcott also had no patience for catchwords that would saddle the Company with a narrow sense of identity. Following the August 1971 performances in Trinidad at Port of Spain's Queens Hall, he praised the Company's artistic interpretations of the dilemmas of a groping society.[5] Walcott targeted the intentions and the overall orientation of the Company's work. He asserted that the road to whiteness (his phrase) was not the route for the Company and credited the artistic direction of the Company with a recognition of this. Walcott was struck by the deeper meaning of creative work reflecting the cultural realities of an entire society. He had addressed Brathwaite's *nommo*—the adamic urge—and *nam*—that irreducible kernel of Caribbean reality. The assertion of blackness in the dance was the celebration of culture not of skin. It is an intensely Caribbean reading of a Caribbean language of dance theater.

Despite Walcott's praise, he also challenged the Company to continue to dare to be true to itself. Walcott's critique addressed process, philosophy, aesthetics, and the relation of art to society. It took the Company seriously and we were grateful: it was a view liberated from the boredom of ignorance, malice, and the gossipmongering of the critical cocktail circuit.

It was a decade before comparable in-depth criticism revealed the merits of Jamaican dance theater, when Wycliffe Bennett began to study the National Dance Theatre Company and local dance seriously. He attended Company classes, rehearsals, and performances and interviewed dancers, choreographers, and scenic designers. He concluded that through the efforts of the

Company the dance in Jamaica had become a valid expression of a specific country and time. On the occasion of the Company's twentieth anniversary, Bennett decided it was necessary to place the work in its proper perspective, to look at the sources of growth, to examine the Company's strengths and weaknesses, and to note some of the challenges that lay ahead.[6] He was forthright about the occasional lapse of authority in a few pieces, but his criticisms were accompanied by empathy with the Company's direction. Bennett's careful and concerned study of the repertoire made him a serious commentator. The Company could obviously benefit from his trenchant insights and criticism.

Useful criticisms were also communicated to us by way of correspondence from discerning audience members. In August 1976 the film producer Lennie Littlewhite sent the artistic director a valuable summary of audience responses to the use of reggae in the Company's repertoire. He was positive about the way this type of indigenous music was employed in *Street People, Tribute to Cliff,* and *Backlash,* but with *Court of Jah,* danced to music by Bob Marley, Littlewhite felt that, "set against the three earlier works, it gives the impression that Marley's music is the least important."[7] Despite this impression, Littlewhite was now "convinced that the NDTC is a Jamaican dance company and not just a dance company featuring Jamaicans."

Also in August 1976 we received a welcomed critique from the Nigerian playwright Wole Soyinka, who was on a scouting mission for talent to attend the African Festival of Arts and Culture (FESTAC). Caught up in the audiences' enthusiasm to the Company's offerings at Carifesta '76 held in Jamaica, Soyinka wrote in his letter that he hoped the audiences in Nigeria "will also be able to partake of the transformations in dancing concepts which have taken place in the diaspora."

In September 1980 the Barbadian novelist and essayist George Lamming wrote a letter from Barbados analyzing his responses to Company performances he had seen while in Jamaica. Lamming was particularly taken with the 1980 version of *Two Drums for Babylon,* which had been remounted with original music by Peter Ashbourne: "One of the most exciting things about my recent visit was my discovery of a peculiar marriage: the way Rastafarian 'metaphysics' has grafted to itself a form of Socratic interrogation . . . with results that are quite novel. . . . I came away with the feeling that I was bearing witness to a new type of intellectual formation. . . . This could have a profound creative influence on the future writing of social history, and its importance for prose fiction is very great."

As early as the 1960s there was at least one professional theater reviewer who took an intelligent and tough-minded approach. Norman Rae's notices in *The Daily Gleaner* from 1963 to 1966 often rankled, but they revealed a potential for serious criticism once he was convinced that eclecticism in the repertoire did not necessarily prevent artistic unity, whatever the range of subject matter. Rae regarded the Company as the most important organized artistic group in Jamaica, but in the early days he challenged the Company to make good its intentions of producing a vocabulary, technique, and style that accurately reflected Caribbean cultural realities.[8] His insistence on profound complex movement over superficial assembling of steps indicated a genuine concern on his part for the development of Jamaican dance theater. But because of his own involvement in the production of plays and musicals in the Jamaican theater, Rae lost some credibility about his capacity to criticize fellow artists in the press, and he gave up dance reviews during the late 1960s.

Beyond the serviceable but useful offerings of Archie Lindo of *The Star,* Harry Milner of *The Daily Gleaner,* and Verena Reckord of Jamaica's defunct *Daily News,* the field has been wide open since, yearning for far more meaningful evaluations. Archie Lindo, a playwright and photographer, revealed a genuine love for the art of dance. Harry Milner was more emotionally attuned to drama than to dance, as he often admitted. He had a longer track record of evaluating Jamaican productions in the press, but he found it difficult to depart from criteria rooted in a Eurocentric aesthetic. Milner's main contribution to Jamaican dance was as dialectical foil to the Company's work in its quest for self-definition. Of these three established Jamaican dance critics Verena Reckord, with the advantage of formal music training, showed an analytical gift which often went beyond the commonplace opinions of the casual observer.

The book *Roots and Rhythms,* published in 1969, took issue with the level of criticism suffered by the Company during its first seven years.[9] We felt that the critics too often reflected their personal temperament in their writings rather than a genuine concern for the art. Some critics were naturally offended by these remarks, but Winnifred Risden, in a thoughtful review of the book, was not to be intimidated: "I don't think the Company needs to worry about its critics—most artists are, or ought to be, their own and most severe arbiters. In any event, I think it is right that its most severe examiners should be those at home. The critics, certainly, need constant educating in what the Company is about."[10]

Risden—herself a former dancer with the Ivy Baxter Creative Dance Group and a costume designer for dance and musicals as well as a sophisticated literary scholar—knew exactly what she wanted, not only for the dance but also for the Company. The difficulty lay partially in the nonprofessional status of the Company. She felt that there was clearly no lack of talent or raw material and, if so much had been achieved by part-time dancers working against great odds, the possibilities seemed unlimited. For the National Dance Theatre Company, as for other branches of Jamaican theater, some way must be found to enable talented performers to be nurtured under ideal conditions. She was clearly challenging Jamaica to foster the growth of its arts if the culture were not to stagnate in purely amateur conditions.

Risden had other sharp insights about the Company's existence as a dance ensemble. The designation of the Company as a dance theater revealed a celebration of the "common origin of dance and drama as ritual expressions of what one might call the tribal experience." Such tribal experience was indeed regarded by Company members as the indispensable source of energy for any true classicism in Caribbean dance. Risden also had strong ideas about the art of dance, and she stated them with the elegant clarity typical of her writing. She saw dance as inescapably sensual: "Classical ballet or belly dancing, the instrument is the body and the first target is the senses. The dancer's body is trained to defy the limitations of nature—whether in the disposition of its angles or its resources of breath. This is simply because the dance, above all other arts, is a celebration of the life principle itself. The popular attraction of pyrotechnic and virtuoso dancing is not an indication of defiant taste as is sometimes snobbishly claimed but an unconscious and healthy recognition that the more one defies the restrictions of the body the more one affirms the joy of life."[11]

Yet Risden's reductionism restricting dance to sensuality and stripping it of its social context as well as its complementary dramatic elements is in a deep sense alien to the Caribbean sensibility. Insofar as they prompt man's communion with nature, those very ritual expressions she cites as part of the tribal experience are no less a celebration of life than what she claims for the defiance of nature through virtuoso dancing. The inherent philosophy of the Company does not accept the two approaches as mutually exclusive, as the work following Risden's review clearly demonstrated. The National Dance Theatre Company's raison d'être in terms of dance theater certainly was not to hide under the umbrella of eclecticism, as implied in her review. Rather their intention was to reflect the totality of life in all its textured diversity.

Risden's reservations about dance theater itself turned on her claim that companies frequently place what is basically sensual at the disposal of the cerebral, which thus poses a delicate challenge; she felt there was a danger that ideas might overtake the body's resources, resulting in something inflated. Although she found this fault with certain works, such as *The King Must Die* and *Two Drums for Babylon*, at least *All God's Children* and the early *African Scenario* seemed to her consistently integrated in sensuality and idea.

Risden's review is an excellent example of serious analysis working at the service of recollected experience. Admittedly it came just prior to the second decade of the Company's existence, before some of its most important dance works were created. Many of the subsequent works will no doubt have allayed her fears. Dancers, it is now clear, must learn to *think* as well as *move* and *feel*. Movement without feeling is a kind of minstrelsy parading as celebration of life.

Another critical appraisal of the book *Roots and Rhythms* was refreshing because it accepted on its own terms the Company's insistence on integrity and credibility. Andrew Salkey, the Jamaican-born writer and broadcaster working out of London, appreciated the challenge to the critics when he reviewed the book on the BBC: "The maverick quality of the work performed by Jamaica's

National Dance Theatre Company allows for total freedom of artistic expression, imaginative flights of content and technique, and continuing surprises which delight and disturb the theater's audiences everywhere. I took particular pleasure in the bafflement of the critics, in this country, at the time of the Commonwealth Arts Festival, when they confessed their lack of contact with the essence of the dance theatre's history and development."[12] Salkey went on to explain that the reason the work did not meet the critics' rigid approval was not so much because it seemed tangential but because it was indeed rebellious. The Company's dances were particularly challenging because they went beyond the safe national expectations imposed upon them by the critics.

Some of the foreign critics have obviously tried to be fair. Peter Williams, the former editor of *Dance and Dancers,* on seeing the National Dance Theatre Company for the first time in 1965 at the Scala Theatre in London, introduced the Company to his readers with the following remark: "Not that professional or nonprofessional consideration should affect judgment of anything that is shown before a paying public; on the other hand, it is, I think, essential to place companies of this kind against their own background and not to overlook the climate in which they normally play."[13] Williams made an effort to see the Company's entire repertoire presented in the short London season and was therefore able to offer an incisive analysis and evaluation of all the dances. He harbored no ethnocentric conceits or bigoted prejudices against aesthetics that did not follow preconceived notions. He took the Company seriously while pointing out its weaknesses: "It was obvious from the first programme that Jamaica's National Dance Theatre Company is working toward the goal set by Nettleford and Thomas. What it still has to find is a way of integrating its sense of movement with a more cohesive form of theatrical presentation. . . . The material is all there and so are the dancers, who have an ability not often seen in highly professional dance shows. At the moment the repertory is too large and they should concentrate on building up a greater unity of conception overall and pay far greater attention to the lighting. . . ."[14] Such advice was constructive and reflected Williams's deep love for the very art he was criticizing

Seven years later, when the Company gave a three-week season at Sadler's Wells, Williams again took the trouble to see every program before he wrote his critical appraisal: "Contact with the audience is particularly vital to the success of any enterprise of this kind, and the importance of this could be seen in the different performances of the Jamaicans at the Wells—with a typical London dance audience there was a slight flatness, when the London Jamaicans were there in full force and finery, it became quite another thing, vibrating and stimulating. Obviously, one shouldn't judge anything by audience reaction, yet to assess what Nettleford is trying to do, it is essential to pay attention to the reactions of the people for whom it was primarily intended."[15] Such a courtesy from a metropolitan critic was welcome. Williams found thematic and structural correspondences between certain works in the Jamaican repertoire and works from the world of European classical ballet on which he was brought up. *Married Story* was to him a Caribbean *Fille Mal Gardée,* a work which the Jamaican choreographer had never seen. *Dialogue for Three* suggested to him the idea behind Jean-Paul Sartre's *Huis Clos,* while *The King Must Die,* despite its African influences, seemed to have "certain overtones of Graham technique; in fact the Graham emphasis is made even stronger owing to [Yvonne] daCosta [as the queen mother] bearing uncanny resemblance to Graham herself." Williams was less happy with *Murals,* danced to the music of Bach, Scarlatti, and Villa-Lobos, because he felt an overemphasis on classicism. He thought the suite was especially well written and praised the duet danced by Bridget Casserly and Barry Moncrieffe to the Villa-Lobos music. But, he asserted, "there is no escaping the fact that, although the dancers are well trained, they do not quite attain the standards that an audience steeped in classicism has every right to expect, particularly when most of the music is associated with ballets from more established masters. I would think that *Murals* is more for home consumption."

Williams clearly had a sharp insight into some of the problems faced by the Company in its journey toward a style of its own. For instance, he was fully aware of the problems of selecting the appropriate programs for international tours and the concessions that must be made for different audiences: "The answer would seem to lie in the fact that it is better to do what you do rather than doing what you feel others may want." [16] Yet the problem persists: many of the most popular works at home would be less appealing to many metropolitan audiences abroad, although the Company is resolved not to compromise itself in order to satisfy a folksy exoticism foreign audiences expect from Caribbean cultural ensembles.

The critics in both New York and Moscow have certainly appreciated the Company's objective of forging classic forms out of its indigenous realities. The Russian writeups during the tour of the Soviet Union in 1979 revealed a particularly sensitive awareness of the Company's intentions. The former Bolshoi dancer Marius Liepa, as critic, conscientiously attended a Company class in Moscow to evaluate the training system before he even attended the performance. [17] The 1983 performances at the City Center Theater in New York were also greeted with critical respect by the two most important daily critics—Clive Barnes and Anna Kisselgoff. Barnes was at pains to establish what he perceived as the legitimate influences of the Company, making pointed references to other companies that have dealt with the black experience—such as Katherine Dunham's and Alvin Ailey's as well as the work of Trinidad's Geoffrey Holder—and to the modern dance techniques of Martha Graham and the combined folk–ballet style of Mexico's Ballet Folklórico. He was quick to assure his readers that the Jamaicans were different from all of these. He acknowledged the technical competence of the dancers and the Company's international reputation. His parting advice to his readers was instructive: "Go in the mood for a *show* and a demonstration of national identity . . . and you should find it rewarding."[18] Barnes's perception of Caribbean dance aesthetics seems to result from a tradition of criticism that segments dance in ways that the African sense of the totality of life and art would reject. Yet he at least showed a willingness to judge the Company on its own terms.

Anna Kisselgoff's assessment revealed an especially sharp eye. Despite her partiality to European classical ballet, Kisselgoff was capable of a certain aesthetic tolerance. The authority of her opening review of the Company's 1983 New York tour was the result of a fairly incisive analysis, which also included the background of the Company's growth and development and an examination of its artistic policy.[19] The effort to judge the Jamaicans on their own terms without making patronizing allowances came through in the criticism. Above all, it revealed a profound knowledge of the art, appreciation of the creative process in its various expressions, and respect for the validity of the Jamaicans' efforts.

The other New York dailies at the time were somewhat at odds in their appraisals. Jane Rigney of *The New York Tribune* was ecstatic: "The National Dance Theatre Company of Jamaica presented a visual feast of color and an aural feast of island tunes."[20] But Rod Baker of *The New York Daily News* found the program unsuccessful. His profound ignorance of both dance and culture was divulged when he debited the deeply ritualistic work *Gerrehbenta,* based on definite Jamaican cultural realities, with "borrowings from Alvin Ailey's *Revelations.*"[21]

This author stands firm in his conviction that the Caribbean people can create something of value out of their experience and that the products of their creative imagination are worthy of evaluation on their own terms and not necessarily by the criteria developed within the tradition of European culture. It should be an accepted fact that professional critics possess not only deep knowledge but also sensitive insight into the very art they criticize.[22] We demand excellence of the critics just as the society and the critics themselves expect artistic excellence from the Company's dance work. The critics must be part of the process of creative construction, enriching the art form and at the same time helping choreographers, performers, designers, and composers to fulfill their gifts. If the National Dance Theatre Company has erred in demanding high standards from those who purport to be the critical guardians of dance, then it will have made yet another valuable contribution. It was Edward Kamau Brathwaite who, in responding to the voluntary surrender of the Company to public debate in 1969 at the University of the West Indies, expressed his appreciation and sympathy for such exposure to criticism:

On behalf of the Caribbean Artist Movement . . . I'd like to thank you and the Company for what you did, and *how* you did it, on Sunday. It was, as I was telling you, the second time in my experience that I have watched creative artists take their ticking hopes, dismantled, into public. It is a rare and rewarding experience, well worth it, no matter how harrowing. What I fear is that some of the younger members of the group might have thought themselves exposed to unskilled jewellers. Please assure them for me that this was not the case. Every word that was spoken on Sunday came with love and with a real concern for dialogue of understanding. In face of the present evident failure of our playwrights to catch our dreams within a network of communal experience, the burden of your dancers and the movements that they make will be, for many of us, more grave, more heavy, than they think they ought to bear or have to make. But, as long as we think that the act is completed only by its audience, this will be the case. Your answer and justification—not that that is needed—was not only in the grace and discipline displayed, but in the simple willingness of the Company to be there, to be present. This seems to me to be, in part at least, what "socially committed" means; from this home it begins.[23]

It is through this willingness "to be there, to be present"—both physically and mentally—that the National Dance Theatre Company, growing out of its native soil rather than out of foreign metropolitan mores and aesthetic preferences, retains the promise of a life beyond mere survival.

9 · Beyond Survival: The Company as Model

Twenty-one years in the life of a dance company may be considered a long time. But for a cultural movement that seeks to discover its own aesthetic logic and consistency as part of society's wider process of self-definition, it is a short time indeed. Seedling years are significant, however, and the first twenty-one years of the National Dance Theatre Company of Jamaica—which operates as part of the movement of self-definition, even giving it shape and articulation—could be of interest not only to dancers and other performing artists all over the world but especially to performers in developing countries who share common concerns about their people's material well-being and creative potential.

The development and survival of the National Dance Theatre Company is the story of a voluntary action group operating continuously in a poor Third World country over a period of twenty-one years. The Company's very existence is based on collaborative management as well as the dynamic interaction of all its participants, with creative skills and leadership being mutually reinforcing. This group has succeeded in making a deep impact on the cultural life of Jamaica. Its unpaid members, who have occupations as teachers, doctors, lawyers, civil servants, farmers, and bankers, among others, are dedicated to the view that their efforts in the area of dance will contribute discipline as well as a sense of process and cultural awareness to the task of nation building.

Objectives and Achievements of the Company

The original objectives of the National Dance Theatre Company were: (1) to provide a vehicle for well-trained dancers and other dance theater artists, such as choreographers, composers, and musicians, who want to participate in the creation of works of excellence rooted in Jamaican and Caribbean cultural realities; (2) to help create an informed Jamaican audience critically responsive to works of excellence in the theater arts; (3) to experiment with various dance forms and techniques; (4) to develop a style and form that faithfully reflect Carib-

The naturally graceful movement of a young Jamaican exemplifies the creative activities that make up the instruments of survival in the Caribbean. The technical foundations of the National Dance Theatre Company are based on the kinetic potentials of the human body. (*Richard Montgomery*)

bean movement patterns; (5) to encourage serious research into the indigenous dance and music forms of Jamaica as well as the Caribbean.

Each objective has had evidence of success. Besides gaining an international reputation for dance performance through its many tours, the National Dance Theatre Company during two decades of continuous work by its highly skilled and dedicated members has spawned not only a distinctive style of Caribbean dance theater but also a training system and a national School of Dance as well as a framework for community activities, particularly in the area of traditional dance, which since the 1960s has become an indispensable source for research into dance and folklore in general. In a wider sense more has been achieved. For example the Inter-American Foundation, based in Washington, D.C., funded this cultural agents project in the Jamaica School of Dance and facilitated the development of the curriculum for the diploma program as well as the core course of Caribbean studies in the Cultural Training Centre in Kingston. In recognition of the special achievements of the National Dance Theatre Company the Ford Foundation, based in New York, has funded this valuable documentation of the Company's work.

But what specific qualities have made the Company succeed where it has? To begin with, it is fair to state that there has been a high level of satisfaction on the part of individual members. Despite the relatively low turnover of members over a period of twenty-one years, there have been some unavoidable negative factors that have caused a few individuals to withdraw from the group. These factors turn on such issues as the limits imposed on personal ambitions because of group obligations; the inability of having certain economic needs satisfied; or the inevitable personality clashes. Yet there has been continuous membership by the majority as well as residual goodwill expressed by most individuals who have left for whatever reasons. The basic reasons for such loyalty involve not only the nature of the task in which all members are engaged but also the internal dynamics of the group's operations.

The nature of the task must be analyzed in the wider context of the creative process. The making and performing of a work of art is a complex process involving the mobilization of individual skills to effect collective action. Dependence on individual effort ensures the fullest collaboration of all members of the group. In this sense there is more worker participation in the process of creation than in a typical industrial operation.[1] The participants gain satisfaction from the knowledge that their separate contributions are essential to the whole.

Thus the emphasis on social recognition, ego satisfaction, and self-actualization within one's work takes precedence over economics and other practical needs. Performing arts companies are likely to offer more of this kind of intrinsic satisfaction than other marketplace endeavors, and thus chronic tension and resentment against management are lessened. When tension occurs, which is inevitable in the competition over roles or the persistence of personal points of view, it is likely to be resolved in creative compromise, since ego satisfaction and self-actualization are made possible through actual performance.

At this point I want to elaborate two propositions that I believe account for the survival of the National Dance Theatre Company: (1) the Company has maximized for the majority of its members the possibility of high levels of intrinsic satisfactions and at the same time has promoted minimum concern for practical needs; (2) the Company retains a leadership structure that perceives management power not as a case of property but one of relationship.

The first proposition, the maximizing of satisfactions, has involved a number of factors, such as the very nature of the creative process; the relative economic independence of most Company members;[2] the members' commitments to the ideals of nation building; and the scope that individuals are offered in order to gain national recognition from related careers in dance education, research, community development, and freelance choreography. Another factor that has tended to augment satisfaction within the group is the networking of individual responsibilities, which are organized in subtle intermeshing arrangements rather than in a hierarchical pattern. Thus the concept of the direct line of authority from the top, common in conventionally structured organizations, is secondary to the semiautonomous subdivisions of the group.

This takes us to the second proposition, involving the Company's leadership structure as one of relationship rather than property ownership. This definition of power, which is brilliantly elaborated in James MacGregor Burns's book entitled *Leadership,*[3] is rooted in a perception of management in all organizations as the leader–follower process of dialectical and symbiotic relationship. This dimension of power as relationship rather than absolute control is an important consideration of the effective management of cultural institutions like the National Dance Theatre Company.

Although the Company's management is predicated on these very assumptions, there exists outside the Company the erroneous view that absolute leadership obtains on the part of the artistic director. Naturally an artistic director's strong sense of leadership must be in evidence. There is no doubt that he should be pivotal in every aspect of a company's operations, responsible for major policy decisions regarding administration, funding, and the group's public image. But he is something like the conductor of an orchestra rather than absolute commander. He succeeds in retaining loyalty because of his own dependence as a leader on the consent and trust of the group. The decisive personality of the artistic director must also be taken into consideration. Self-discipline and persuasive leadership must be by example rather than precept. Members need to be motivated by a belief that the objectives set by the group are worth working for and that it is necessary to reinforce the vision and perception of the group as a whole. In the final analysis moral authority will be demonstrated by the successes of the leader's artistic initiatives.

There certainly should be no delusions about the leadership role in terms of a group like the National Dance Theatre Company. Like any leader, the artistic director becomes the target of criticism as well as praise. Not all decisions will please everyone, but the decisions should be made in good faith and for the benefit of the whole group. Not only personal integrity but also respect for those being served is necessary. Self-pity cannot be indulged. Disloyalties and recriminations are all part of the deal.

Strong charismatic leaders of theater groups are not infrequently regarded with a certain awe, almost as if they were political dictators. At the same time these leaders may attract inordinate admiration. But even affection is likely to be transformed negatively when certain decisions of the artistic director's are resented by a particular theater member. In such situations veiled threats of withdrawal are not uncommon. But the most that any leader should strive for is the acknowledgment of the values informing the vision shared by everyone in the group. These values must be emphasized even while everything else appears to be peripherally chaotic, as frequently happens in theater productions.

The Company Leadership

Beyond the personality and talents of the artistic director, there are important patterns of the overall management of the National Dance Theatre Company that have guaranteed the survival of the group. Many of these patterns turn on the view that leadership is best defined, according to James MacGregor Burns, in terms of "leaders inducing followers to act for certain goals that represent the values and the motivations—the wants and needs, the aspirations and expectations—*of both leaders and followers,*" since "the genius of leadership lies in the manner in which leaders see and act on their own and their followers' values and motivations."[4] The way the leadership of the Company is organized, as well as the manner in which it responds to demands of the creative process, satisfies this definition in an applied behavioral sense.

Above all, the composition of the Management Committee is based on task-oriented membership. Except for the chairman, and two or three persons drawn from the wider society to avoid in-breeding, the Management Committee includes the following Company members who perform specific functions in the Company's day-to-day operations while they are also involved in the actual production of dance theater: artistic director, musical director, lighting and sound directors, ballet mistress, artistic coordinator, stage manager, Company photographer, public relations officer, a representative of the dancers, as well as a representative of the Jamaica School of Dance. The present treasurer is a principal NDTC Singer, and the secretary is a founding member of the Company. The inclusion of an outside lawyer and a businessman rounds off the complement of persons responsible for the executive management of the Company's business. Therefore committee representation covers all Company divisions and gives to key persons a sense of involvement, which ensures mutual trust.

Leadership performance is based on the fact that the management's needs and goals are inseparable from those of the rank and file. The committee leaders all share the same goals as the persons they are responsible for. With so many of the performing artists and technicians in management there is little chance of alienation between management and workers. The concept of transactional leadership, also described by Burns, comes into operation: "Each party to the bargain is conscious of the power resources and attitudes of the other. Each person recognizes the other as a *person*."[5] This type of leadership need not be enduring, and in fact many members do not have relationships with one another outside their theater activities.

There is another form of leadership, besides transactional leadership, by which Company goals are achieved in a more lasting way. Known as transformational leadership, this type of guidance has also been cogently defined by Burns: "Such leadership occurs when one or more persons *engage* with others in such a way that leaders and followers raise one another to higher levels of motivation and morality. . . . Their purposes, which might have started out as separate but related, as in the case of transactional leadership, become fused. Power bases are linked not as counterweights but as mutual support for common purpose."[6] The organic connection linking the Company, the School of Dance, and community work under the auspices of the Jamaica Cultural Development Commission is a case in point. Many of the participants in these organzations have become the authorities in dance education. The undisputed leader in the field of community dance is a founding dancer of the Company. The Company's musical director is an authority on traditional music. Other members have independent careers in dance research and related areas.

The authority of the Management Committee is rooted not only in the members' proven skills but also in their recognized achievements within their specific fields. But it is best to keep in mind that the authority of any leadership structure is nothing more than legitimized power. That power works most efficiently in human terms when it is mandated by those being led. The mandate must be continually reinforced by renewed trust and mutual respect from both sides. A voluntary group depends a great deal on this; otherwise nothing gets done or is allowed to be done.

Lessons from the Past

If the National Dance Theatre Company has utilized what could be called behavioral science methods to produce stated objectives, it may be useful to analyze the lessons that have been learned and how viable are the Company's claims of being a model for organizations seeking mutual benefits for its members.

There are three variables by which the operations of any organization must be evaluated: intent of objectives, capacity to perform, and actual accomplishment in terms of promised change. The Company's intent was articulated by clearly stated objectives realistically related to existing conditions, particularly within the framework of the country's independence and the concomitant enthusiasm of national pride.

The National Dance Theatre Company had the capacity to perform and operate, since it was organized by a group of disciplined and highly motivated founding members. It also had an authoritative leadership with thorough knowledge of the dance and dance theater, which helped gain the confidence of group members. Added to this was institutional support from the University of the West Indies, the Ministry of Development of Welfare, the Ministry of Education, and the Cultural Development Commission. There was also support from the media, including the Jamaica Information Service, which publicized the Company's work and accomplishments. The capacity to operate was enhanced by a program of activities—systematically implemented by all members—which comprised regular classes and rehearsals, an annual season of dance held during independence celebrations, overseas tours, performances in rural Jamaica, and research into dance, music, and folklore. The capacity of the group was determined by rational planning organized around long-term needs. Members internalized Company objectives, personally planning their own activities to fit in with their voluntary contribution so that there were no undue pressures on jobs and family obligations. Finally the capacity to operate was also a function of sensitive leadership, which does not push members beyond their capabilities to contribute voluntarily.

The achievement of promised change can be assessed in various ways: by the impact the Company has had on the nation's perceptions of dance and dance theater; by the increased popularity of creative dance among the young; by the establishment of a national School of Dance, which provides expert training in Jamaican dance; and by the development of a unique style of dance rooted in Jamaican and Caribbean realities. Achievement of change is also evident in the emergence of an institutional model for Third World performing arts organizations which is community-oriented in objective, national in scope, international in recognition, professional in standards, and amateur in status. But perhaps the most significant evidence of promised change resulting from the

Company's mobilization of performance skills in its first twenty-one years is revealed in the alteration of attitudes among key personnel with respect to dance aesthetics and cultural realities in the Caribbean. Indigenous cultural forms are now considered crucial for instilling cultural confidence and a deeper understanding of the social dynamics of the society.

The Future: A Question of Professionalism

Much of the foregoing analysis constitutes a somewhat clinical review of an organization's performance in terms of the goals it sets itself from the beginning. This naturally leaves questions about the years ahead. The first question that comes to mind is whether or not the Company should become professional. We do not mean a narrow interpretation about standards of excellence, since the National Dance Theatre Company has a proven record in this regard, but simply the engagement of performers and other creative personnel on a paid full-time basis. There is nothing illogical about the Company's wishing to go professional in that sense, but harsh realities must be faced: the theater arts in Jamaica are plagued by the country's economic woes and in addition the small population base finds itself incapable of supporting paid theater companies.

Judged against the unpromising dance environments in metropolitan centers like New York, where more dancers are out of work than are fully employed and many fail to find performing jobs after years of arduous training, the Jamaican situation needs to be looked at more closely. In 1983 an experienced dancer from the National Dance Theatre Company was offered a position in a small dance company in New York which could guarantee three paid weeks a year for performances with perhaps an additional six weeks of paid rehearsal time. The dancer had mixed feelings about the offer: despite the benefits of working with a New York company, the net value of that experience would be offset by having to work at something else for supplemental earnings and to spend a grueling three-hour train ride each day to and from classes and rehearsals. In a reflective letter to the artistic director of the National Dance Theatre Company the dancer expressed strong misgivings about the professional involvement: "I am one of those crazy people who have always said that the day the NDTC becomes a job and not a commitment to dance, then I'll stop. I don't really want to dance for a salary. Now I may really be crazy, but during rehearsals and performances with our own Company the benefit I get is many times what this company [in New York] or another dance company could pay me. I believe in what we are doing and I believe that the joy and honor of belonging to a movement greater than 'dance' as a word far outweighs any traumas one goes through in our Company." This point of view has prevailed among the majority of the people who have worked for the Company during its first twenty-one years. They have often acknowledged the advantages of personal development as well as the psychic benefits gained from participation in the creative process offered by a group like the National Dance Theatre Company.

There are a number of economic options open to theater companies. The two that immediately come to mind are state support and support from the private sector. State support is common in many European nations, countries in the Socialist bloc, and a few African states. In the United States private support comes from corporations, foundations, and rich patrons. In some cases a company may receive a combination of both kinds of assistance. In the United States, for example, many theater companies are given grants by the National Endowment for the Arts and grants-in-aid from state and local governments as well as by private funds from foundations and individuals seeking tax exemptions. The Arts Council in Great Britain and other dominions of the Commonwealth is the organization through which public funds are channeled for national opera, dance, and drama companies. Since public and private funding is not as commonplace in Jamaica, the National Dance Theatre Company has had to function without such guaranteed core support. Direct subsidization by the artists themselves was therefore regarded as the solution.

Gate receipts, small donations, advertisements in program brochures, and corporate commissions of dance works provide cash flow for operating expenses. But economic advantages come in other ways: government goodwill in facilitating overseas tours; fare reductions offered by Air Jamaica, the national airline; donated professional services, such as doctors, chiropractors, and lawyers; and anonymous scholarships set up for Company members.

The Company's management made a conscious decision to utilize whatever limited public funds were available to establish and maintain a national School of Dance because of the important influence the school would have on dance education and on the cultural sensibilities of the community. This priority seemed appropriate since providing salaries for the more than sixty members as paid professionals would have put the Company out of business within a year. Through this kind of investment in dance training Company members were able to acquire skills that helped promote separate professional careers in teaching, research, and freelance choreography. Enterprising members, drawing on their educational and performing experience, are thus able to find appropriate methods of satisfying their material welfare. Despite its principle of confidentiality, the Company should regularize these methods and consciously develop new ones. Otherwise, we face the risk of attracting only those members who can afford to make the sacrifices of time and money needed to guarantee excellent work.

The fact that none of the Company leaders is paid remains a critical point. In Jamaica a theater director who plans to make a living off the work of unpaid voluntary performers cannot expect the group to survive for long. Also the pretense that pocket expenses offered actors and dancers constitute real wages for these performers, many of whom may be otherwise employed, simply distorts the reality of the Caribbean situation. The frequent demise of professional theater groups in Kingston during the 1970s was due in part to the refusal by many organizers to face the constraints hampering the development in Jamaica of fully salaried performers. The Musical Theatre Company and the National Chorale—which have endured —are nonprofit unpaid ensembles, although the former hires directors and orchestras for a fee, while the conductor and some guest artists of the latter have received honoraria. The Jamaican Folk Singers have survived through the voluntary efforts of its singers and musicians.

Short of a windfall of private donations or the unlikely prospect of making the ensemble a public enterprise supported by public funds, the National Dance Theatre Company of Jamaica must find appropriate means of attracting other funds for its continuing survival.

The Future: A Question of Organization

Another critical question for the future involves the management structure rationalizing the development of what Dennis Scott aptly describes as subsystems.[7] Scott generously prefaced his recommendations with a survey, as he perceived it, of the organizational history of a group like the National Dance Theatre Company, which progresses from one stage of organization, where one person as the leader makes everything come together, to a second stage, where subdivisions emerge that are based on delegation of authority to others who not only relate to each other but also refer back to the leader. The Company has been operating on the level of the second stage for well over a decade. But Scott also described a third stage of growth in which there is an "integration of the subsystems . . . so that they form new organisms themselves"; in this type of situation the "subsystems start dictating the growth of the organisation itself."[8] The National Dance Theatre Company in fact has now become one entity in a network of dance-related activities: education and training (Jamaica School of Dance), community dance development (Cultural Development Commission), research (African Caribbean Institute of the Institute of Jamaica), and actual dance theater performance (not only the Company itself but other Jamaican dance groups as well). Within the Company's organizational structure the subsystems of music, design, technical direction, and administration provide their own independent points of view to the overall output.

The linear progression from one organizational stage to the next is perhaps too tidy a concept for such a naturally contradictory and complex organism as a dance company. What usually happens is that aspects of all three stages tend to coexist in dialectical relationships, although a particular stage may be more dominant at any given time. In artistic organizations such subsystems usually interact informally rather than formally, and the National Dance Theatre Company is no exception.

A voluntary arts organization must operate with tolerance, common sense, and compassionate understanding as well as a certain tough-mindedness. It requires of its members dedicated commitment, artistic integrity, a sense of purpose, a capacity for balancing personal ambitions against collective goals, and aspirations for which everyone is willing to work. Good intentions alone do not lead to the moral authority, that such an organization must acquire in order to survive or to develop even further. Any attempts to rob the organization of this authority, whether by intentional distortion of its history or by the denigration of its achievements, must be resolutely resisted in the interest not only of its own survival but also of the efforts that have catalyzed other cultural activities.

Such an arts organization cannot afford to debase the currency of its creative output primarily in the interest of building an efficient machine that may be adept at making money but incapable of producing significant work. This is not an argument for casual administration or mismanagement, nor an argument against profits. But a dance company is known by the quality of its artistic achievements. The administrative structures were best devised to serve this end.

The Future: A Question of Mirroring Society

As previously stated, the Company has been an important model for other arts groups operating in the Caribbean, but there remains a question about whether it should continue in its role of mirroring the cultural realities of Jamaican society. For there is nothing in the twenty-one-year history of the country's independence to suggest that Jamaicans are yet guaranteed a cultural certitude based on their creative output. There is no logical indication that the products of the imagination have yet become an organic part of an ethos that will not only define the new society but also embolden its people to articulate its collective wisdom through its proven abilities. One is forced to state this despite the achievement of those who introduced to the musical world the calypso and reggae forms or have given style and purpose to Caribbean dance theater through the work of the National Dance Theatre Company following the examples of the Ivy Baxter Creative Dance Group and the Little Carib Dancers of Trinidad. Doubts about cultural significance seem to persist despite the contributions of Caribbean novelists, poets, and playwrights to world literature, particularly since 1945, or of the seminal conceptions of the Rastafarians, who by means of religious synthesis have created alternative ways for the society to perceive its own humanity and its God. Caribbean society is yet to mirror in any deep sense the philosophy of its own thinkers, who have made valuable contributions to twentieth-century conceptions about freedom and liberation, racial tolerance and equality, human dignity, and the possibilities of new economic, social, and cultural orders. There is nothing to convince this author that these achievements have yet earned for the Caribbean peoples the general respect they deserve. It is against this background of continuing uncertainty that the National Dance Theatre Company must examine its future if it is to accomplish more than mere survival. It must insist on holding a mirror up to the society and must constantly question why and for whom the Company exists.

This challenge must be taken seriously without undue solemnity; self-assertion about set goals should be pursued without debilitating rancor. Unswerving commitment to excellence must not allow oneself to be intimidated into inaction by the desire to be worthy imitators of others. Above all, the job must be tackled with discipline and a sense of order without losing the flexibility and spontaneity of the creative spirit evident among the people at large; this common source of energy for cultural action must be nurtured to effect genuine social change. In the developing world anyone who runs any kind of institution—from the government to the village sports club—realizes how difficult it often is to overcome self-doubt inherent in a historically dependent people. Generosity and magnanimity of spirit is required in defiance of self-negation; alienation and anomie, even when they are natural responses to historical disillusion, are hazards when building anything in new societies. The arts also entails risks, since there exists something akin to politics of the arts in which egos clash, envy gets mixed up with genuine perception, and fear of failure forces even daring innovators to go on the defensive. But the politics may also alleviate the anguish of emotional pain and uncertainty that attend the creation of a work of art, and it may enhance the satisfaction of being able to meet challenges. It is this hope of redemption that must inform both the aesthetic vision and the no-nonsense battle to forge new worlds of experience.

In this quest the challenges are compounded with every new milestone overtaken. For an organization like the National Dance Theatre Company there is the danger of being caught between the exaggerated claims of ancestral bliss and the facile pretentiousness of up-to-date modernity. People wedded to their ancestral roots will express nothing but interminable yearnings for atavistic rhythms, while those who have a taste for metropolitan mores will gratuitously, if not with doctrinaire arrogance, bemoan the fact that the cultural scene in the Caribbean is still way behind the avant-garde of New York, London, or Paris. In the world of dance ancestral bliss does not always mean the vigor and kinetic force of the Yoruba, Ibo, or Akan forefathers. Instead there are those who, insisting the Caribbean heritage is rooted in Eurocentric soil, accept as their ancestral icons the traditions that produced Pavlova, Nijinksy, Diaghilev, or Cecchetti and such institutions as Sadler's Wells and the Royal Ballet in the mother country.

The notion that the British heritage within the Caribbean deserves dance scenarios based on a world of dying swans, gallant princes, and sleeping beauties is by no means dead among many Caribbean people, although the prospect of these motifs dominating the region's cultural ethos seems remote at this point in history. The paradox of a Russian dispensation in the political and social organization of a transformed postcolonial Caribbean is ever so evident. Athough Soviet ideology may be taboo, Russian ballet is acceptable. One of the major gifts of technology being transferred from metropolitan Moscow to the peripheral allies in the region would undoubtedly be the technical training of Bolshoi or Kirov. It is a paradox that has worked miracles for the survival of Alicia Alonso, herself a product of Western ballet traditions. Alonso would have suffered professional demise after the cultural-cum-economic embargo of Castro's Cuba by the United States had it not been for the accessibility of one of the major sources of the tradition centered in Moscow and Leningrad. But the Caribbeanization of Alonso's company might prove a more important development, although the great tradition of European classical ballet, particularly the influences of its technical and aesthetic discoveries, does merit its place in Western dance theater, including facets of it that are seen in the Caribbean.[9]

The emergence of greater stylistic focus and aesthetic logic in the National Dance Theatre Company is no reason to believe it will automatically degenerate into complacency or chauvinistic monotony. Andrew Salkey, reviewing the book *Roots and Rhythms* for the BBC radio in 1969, saw the Company as making sense because of its maverick tendencies: "The brilliant success of the NDTC, for me at any rate, has its root and rhythm in the fact that it is forever experimental, restless, innovative, and richly diverse. Its quicksilver nature is of importance at a time when similar dance theatres, throughout the Commonwealth if not throughout the world, are narrowing their energies and scope into too sharply defined nationalistic 'art programmes' and 'tourist policies.'"[10]

Afterword

In the final analysis an organization stands or falls on the moral authority it can muster for itself. That authority will be judged on the effectiveness of providing opportunities for the growth and enrichment of individual members while keeping the dynamics of the group functioning. Experimentation with personal interactions—which demands constant reevaluation in terms of problem solving—reflects the particular style of organizational management. The creative arts, which is what the National Dance Theatre Company is involved in, offers the greatest potential for such continuing experimentation. Each new season of dance—like each new dance work to be lit, photographed, or provided with sound—is indeed a new experience; each show virtually starts from scratch despite the advantages of cumulative experiences from the past. But traditionally one is only as good as one's last work. The never-ending cycle of engaging in complex human interaction provides the creative artist, like the creative manager, with countless possibilities leading to frustration or to satisfaction. Success will come with faith in the collective power of the Caribbean spirit surviving from below. Future dance creators must be prepared not merely to discover, they must also invent frameworks in which new discoveries can be made. Even though much of the results of the experiments will turn out to be ephemeral, the search must go on.

Is the Caribbean capable of achieving a cultural synthesis out of its disparate elements? Jamaica's National Dance Theatre Company believes it is and therefore has pursued a course to demonstrate this in earnest. To the joy of hundreds of thousands of viewers all over the globe the Company has sometimes taken flight. In the future, contact with the implosive energy of ancestral hearths and the vigor of contemporary reality must be continually renewed so that even greater heights can be reached.

The Jamaican dance theater must be able to put these challenges into perspective and to continue its efforts to discover forms that faithfully reflect the movement patterns and cultural sensibilities of a region that is not only rich in movement vocabulary but also capable of shaping that vocabulary into a dance theater language that will carry both the magic of myth and the logic of cultural significance. Joseph Brodsky, in an article published in 1983 in *The New York Review of Books,* pointed out that the language of Derek Walcott's poetry has shown a "way to gain an identity superior to the confines of class, race, and ego."[11] The Company's founders and leaders envisage their task in dance theater as similar to Walcott's in literature. It has been difficult for some individuals in the past, and even at this time, to grasp the import of this vision. But the Company must be prepared to stick to its belief that such vision will open the way for profound social changes, changes that Jamaica, the Caribbean, and all of humanity obviously will continue to need for a long time. The Company has been accused in the past of being either too bourgeois or too ghetto-oriented, too black or not black enough, too brown or not white enough. Nor has it been possible to satisfy the egos of all Company members. This is a situation that is not likely to change overnight. It is part of the democratic structure inherent in the theater arts that such contradictions are accepted with equanimity. In the end the tension that is nurtured must be creative rather than disintegrative. It will be up to all participants—the dancers, singers, musicians, and technicians as well as the many supporters of the dance—to work relentlessly together. If the National Dance Theatre Company of Jamaica wishes to continue to meet the challenge of making sense of reality for the people of the Caribbean, then the Company's future role will be tied in with the awesome task of shaping a new society on the basis of self-definition and artistic discovery.

Appendix 1. The Tours

DATE	YEAR	PLACE	PRESENTER
Aug. 23–31	1963	Stratford, Ontario	Stratford Festival
Feb. 11–13	1965	Nassau, Bahamas	Nassau Civic Ballet
Sept. 10–Oct. 10	1965	London; Cardiff; Liverpool; Coventry; Bournemouth	Commonwealth Arts Festival
Jan. 31–Feb. 8	1966	Berlin; Düsseldorf; Munich	Jamaica Tourist Board
Aug. 1–8	1967	Montreal	Expo '67
Apr. 23–29	1968	Nassau, Bahamas	Nassau Civic Ballet
Apr. 11–16	1969	Saint George's, Grenada; Bridgetown, Barbados	Carifta Expo '69
Aug. 12–19	1969	Mexico City; Guadalajara	Palacio de Bellas Artes
Dec. 2–6	1969	Atlanta	Spelman College, Atlanta University
May 9–14	1970	Miami	*Miami Herald*
Sept. 28–Oct. 3	1970	Miami	*Miami Herald*
Aug. 15–25	1971	Port of Spain, San Fernando, Trinidad	Nicholas Symonette
Aug. 26–29	1971	San Juan	University of Puerto Rico
Apr. 30–May 3	1972	Miami	*Miami Herald*
June 27–July 1	1972	Hamilton, Bermuda	Bermuda Arts Council
Aug. 24–28	1972	Georgetown, Guyana	Carifesta '72
Sept. 17–23	1972	London	Sadler's Wells Foundation
Apr. 8–16	1973	Brooklyn	Brooklyn Academy of Music
Apr. 4–14	1974	Brooklyn; Philadelphia	Brooklyn Academy of Music; Temple University

VENUE	SPONSORS
Avon Theatre	Government of Jamaica
Dundas Civic Centre	Government of Jamaica
Scala Theatre; New Theatre; Royal Court Theatre; Belgrade Theatre; Winter Garden	Government of Jamaica
Various concert halls and small theaters	Jamaica Tourist Board; Lufthansa Airlines
Théâtre Port-Royale	Expo '67; Government of Jamaica
Paradise Island Theatre	Nassau Civic Ballet
Nutmeg Theatre; Combermere High School	Government of Jamaica
Palacio de Bellas Artes; Teatro Degollado	Mexican Airlines; Government of Jamaica
Spelman Arts Theatre	Spelman College, Atlanta University
Dade County Auditorium	*Miami Herald*; Air Jamaica; Jamaica Tourist Board
Dade County High Schools	*Miami Herald*
Queens Hall; Naparima Bowl	Nicholas Symonette; Jamaica Tourist Board
University Theater, Río Piedras	University of Puerto Rico
Dade County Auditorium	*Miami Herald*
Rosebank Theatre	Bermuda Arts Council
Guyana Cultural Centre	Government of Jamaica
Sadler's Wells	Sadler's Wells Foundation; British Overseas Airways; Jamaica Tourist Board
Brooklyn Academy of Music	Brooklyn Academy of Music; Air Jamaica
Brooklyn Academy of Music; Temple University	Brooklyn Academy of Music; Air Jamaica

DATE	YEAR	PLACE	PRESENTER
Aug. 31–Sept. 8	1974	Havana; Santiago	Government of Cuba
Apr. 18–20	1975	New Orleans	Ninth-Ward Neighborhood, Inc.
May 16–19	1975	Toronto; Ottawa	Jamaica National League
June 15	1975	Yellow Springs, Ohio	Ohio Festival
June 30–July 3	1975	Mexico City	Government of Jamaica
Apr. 1–4	1976	Washington, D.C.	Howard University
Aug. 14–28	1976	Sydney; Canberra; Melbourne	Elizabethan Theatre Trust
Aug. 21–Sept. 14	1977	West Berlin; Bonn; Aachen; Hamburg; Munich; Frankfurt	Government of Germany
July 29–Aug. 4	1978	Havana	Government of Cuba
Apr. 9–13	1979	Port of Spain, Trinidad	Jamaica Trinidad Association
Apr. 14–16	1979	Bridgetown, Barbados	Government of Barbados
Aug. 21–Sept. 2	1979	Moscow; Leningrad; Kiev	Government of Jamaica
Sept. 30	1979	New York	Visual Arts Research and Resource Center Relating to the Caribbean
Nov. 27–30	1980	Brooklyn	Visual Arts Research and Resource Center Relating to the Caribbean
Aug. 12–19	1981	Toronto; Kitchener–Waterloo	Organization of Caribbean Canadian Initiatives
Sept. 30–Oct. 4	1982	San Juan	Inter-American Festival of Arts
Dec. 3–5	1982	Miami	Hospital Relief Fund
Jan. 10–17	1983	Caracas	Government of Venezuela
Sept. 14–18	1983	New York	Caribbean Educational and Cultural Institute

VENUE	SPONSORS
Teatro Lorca; Teatro Oriente	Government of Jamaica; Government of Cuba; Cubana Airlines
Theater of Music and Performing Arts	Ninth-Ward Neighborhood, Inc.
O'Keefe Centre; National Arts Centre	Jamaica National League; Air Jamaica
Antioch College	Government of Jamaica
Palacio de Bellas Artes	Government of Jamaica
Cramton Auditorium, Howard University	Inter-American Foundation; Howard University
Theatre Royal; Canberra Theatre; Princess Theatre	Government of Australia
Urania; Beethovenhalle; Eurogress-Halle; Congress Center; Zircus Krone; Offenbach Theater	Government of Germany; Air Jamaica
Cathedral Square; Teatro Lorca	Government of Cuba; Government of Jamaica
Queens Hall	Grace Kennedy Ltd., Jamaica
Combermere High School	Government of Barbados
Tchaikovsky Concert Hall; Lidnij Theater; Palace of Culture	Government of Jamaica; Government of USSR
Carnegie Hall	Visual Arts Research and Resource Center Relating to the Caribbean
Brooklyn Academy of Music	Visual Arts Research and Resource Center Relating to the Caribbean; Jamaica Tourist Board
Ryerson Theatre; Centre in the Square Theatre	Organization of Caribbean Canadian Initiatives
Performing Arts Center, Santurce	Government of Puerto Rico
Villa Viscaya Museum; Orange Bowl	Caribbean Central America Committee, Washington, D.C.
Teatro Municipal; Central University	Government of Venezuela
City Center Theater	Caribbean Educational and Cultural Institute

Appendix 2. The Repertoire

1962

LEGEND OF LOVERS' LEAP
Choreography: Eddy Thomas
Music: Oswald Russell
Costumes/decor: Eddy Thomas

A TIME TO REJOICE
Choreography: Eddy Thomas
Music: Oswald Russell
Costumes/decor: Eddy Thomas

FOOTNOTES IN JAZZ
Choreography: Eddy Thomas
Music: Leonard Bernstein, Dave Brubeck
Costumes: Eddy Thomas

AFRICAN SCENARIO
Choreography: Rex Nettleford
Music: traditional West African
Costumes/decor: Eddy Thomas

AFRO–WEST INDIAN SUITE
Choreography: Rex Nettleford,
   Eddy Thomas, Eyrick Darby
Music: traditional (Mapletoft Poulle, arr.)
Costumes: Eddy Thomas and others

FRENCH WEST INDIAN SUITE
Choreography: Eyrick Darby, Lavinia Williams
Music: traditional (Mapletoft Poulle, arr.)
Costumes: Eddy Thomas and others

1963

DIALOGUE FOR THREE
Choreography: Rex Nettleford
Music: Joaquín Rodrigo
Costumes: Eddy Thomas
Decor: Eugene Hyde

PLANTATION REVELRY
Choreography: Rex Nettleford
Music: traditional
Costumes: Eddy Thomas

POCOMANIA
Choreography: Rex Nettleford
Music: Jamaican poco (Rex Nettleford, arr.)
Costumes/decor: Eddy Thomas

GALLANDAR LA PAVA
Choreography: Rex Nettleford
Music: traditional Colombian
Costumes: Eddy Thomas

GAMES OF ARMS
Choreography: Eddy Thomas
Music: Oswald Russell
Costumes: Eddy Thomas
Decor: Milton Harley

LIZA
Choreography: Eddy Thomas
Music: Eddy Thomas
Costumes: Eddy Thomas

JAZZ FANTASIA
Choreography: Sheila Barnett
Costumes: Eddy Thomas

1964

AND IT CAME TO PASS
Choreography: Eddy Thomas
Music: Darius Milhaud
Costumes: Eddy Thomas

CONCERT SUITE
Choreography: Eddy Thomas
Music: Lennox Berkely
Costumes: Eddy Thomas

TWO DRUMS FOR BABYLON
Choreography: Rex Nettleford
Music: Aaron Copland, Gene Gutche
Costumes: Eddy Thomas
Decor: Rex Nettleford

DIARIST IN SAND
(Solo)
Choreography: Rex Nettleford
Music: Aaron Copland
Costumes: Eddy Thomas

FOILED ENCOUNTER
Choreography: Sheila Barnett
Music: Eddy Thomas
Costumes/decor: Eddy Thomas

COUNTRY WEDDING
Choreography: Eddy Thomas
Music: traditional
Costumes/decor: Eddy Thomas

DANCE TIME IN CASCADE
Choreography: Joyce Campbell
Music: traditional
Costumes: Eddy Thomas

1965

KAS KAS
Choreography: Rex Nettleford
Music: traditional
Costumes: Eddy Thomas
Decor: Rex Nettleford

RECOLLECTIONS
Choreography: Rex Nettleford
Music: Norman Dello Joio
Costumes/decor: Eddy Thomas

DANCE ANDANTE
Choreography: Rex Nettleford
Music: Franz Schubert
Costumes: Eddy Thomas
Decor: Maria LaYacona, George Carter

PARADE KINGSTON 13
Choreography: Eddy Thomas
Music: Eddy Thomas
Costumes: Eddy Thomas
Decor: Lloyd van Pitterson

RITES
Choreography: Neville Black
Music: Silvestre Revueltas
Costumes/decor: Neville Black

WALTZ SUITE
Choreography: Neville Black
Music: Sergei Prokofiev
Costumes/decor: Neville Black

1966

MASQUES OF GOD
Choreography: Rex Nettleford
Music: Béla Bartók, Sergei Prokofiev
Costumes: Eddy Thomas
Decor: Howard Parchment

JAMAICAN PROMENADE
Choreography: Eddy Thomas,
  Eyrick Darby, Rex Nettleford
Music: Eddy Thomas,
  traditional (Adrian Clarke, arr.)
Costumes: Eddy Thomas

OMEGAN PROCESSION
Choreography: Eddy Thomas
Music: Darius Milhaud
Costumes: Eddy Thomas
Decor: Moira Small

HOMECOMING
(Solo)
Choreography: Sheila Barnett
Scenario: Denis Scott
Music: Anatoliavov
Costumes: Eddy Thomas

THE AWAKENING
(Love Duet)
Choreography: Neville Black
Costumes: Eddy Thomas

1967

MISA CRIOLLA
Choreography: Rex Nettleford
Music: Ariel Ramírez
Costumes: Eddy Thomas
Decor: Howard Parchment
Dedicated to Richmond Barthe

NIGHT SHELTER
Choreography: Neville Black
Music: traditional
Costumes: Neville Black

FABLES
Choreography: Neville Black
Costumes/decor: Susan Alexander
Based on James Thurber tales

SONATA
Choreography: Neville Black
Music: Paul Hindemith, Walter Piston,
   Igor Stravinsky, Pablo de Sarasate
Costumes: Neville Black
Decor: Eddy Thomas (conception: Neville Black)

1968

THE KING MUST DIE
Choreography: Rex Nettleford
Music: Art Blakey
Costumes/decor: Howard Parchment

FOLKFORM
Choreography: Rex Nettleford
Music: traditional (Marjorie Whylie, arr.)
Costumes: Moira Small

RING HUNT
(Duet)
Choreography: Sheila Barnett
Music: Charlie Mingus
Costumes: Sheila Barnett
Decor: Tom Cook

LEGENDARY LANDSCAPE
Choreography: Neville Black
Music: electronic score (Neville Black, arr.)
Costumes/decor: Moria Small

BACH, BRUBECK, AND COMPANY
Choreography: Neville Black
Music: Johann Sebastian Bach, Dave Brubeck
Costumes: Moira Small

BREAD
(Vignette)
Choreography: Dennis Scott

1969

ALL GOD'S CHILDREN
Choreography: Rex Nettleford
Music: Cannonball Adderley
Costumes/decor: Easton Lee

CANTOS
Choreography: Neville Black
Music: traditional (Marjorie Whylie, arr.)
Costumes: Neville Black

NIGHT DANCES
Choreography: Neville Black
Music: Maurice Ravel
Costumes: Neville Black

AIRS AND GRACES
(Interlude—Vignette)
Choreography: Neville Black
Music: Georg Philipp Telemann
Costumes: Neville Black

IMAGES
Choreography: Sheila Barnett
Music: Claude Debussy
Costumes/decor: Tom Cook

1970

LUCIFER LUCIFER
Choreography: Rex Nettleford
Music: Charles Gross
Costumes/decor: Colin Garland

MARRIED STORY
Choreography: Rex Nettleford
Music: traditional (Marjorie Whylie, arr.), Don Mills
Costumes: Easton Lee

SHADOWS
Choreography: Sheila Barnett
Music: Marjorie Whylie
Costumes/decor: Richard Montgomery

IN THE SPIRIT
Choreography: Sheila Barnett
Music: American spirituals
Costumes: Bert Rose

SYNTHESIA
Conception: Rex Nettleford
Improvisations by Company dancers
   with a sequence by Frank Ashley

1971

JOURNEYS
Choreography: Rex Nettleford
Music: Howard Roberts
Costumes: Bruce Jones
Decor: Richard and Sally Montgomery
Commissioned by Eastern Airlines

KUMINA
Choreography: Rex Nettleford
Music: traditional Jamaican
Costumes/decor: Donat Buckner
Commissioned by House of Dunhill

MURALS
Choreography: Sheila Barnett
Music: Johann Sebastian Bach, Heitor Villa-Lobos, and others
Costumes/decor: Richard and Sally Montgomery

BALLOT
Choreography: Thomas Pinnock
Music: Miles Davis, Yussef Lateef
Costumes: Bruce Jones

1972

CELEBRATIONS
Choreography: Rex Nettleford
Costumes: Bert Rose
Decor: Jerry Craig
Commissioned by Jamaican Heritage

BALLAD OF A LADY
Choreography: Rex Nettleford
Costumes/decor: Donat Buckner

MOUNTAIN WOMEN
Choreography: Sheila Barnett
Music: Marjorie Whylie
Costumes/decor: Richard and Sally Montgomery
Commissioned by Texaco Caribbean Inc.

A QUESTION OF BALANCE
Choreography: Sheila Barnett
Music: Bob Sinicrope
Costumes/decor: Michael Bryne

RESURRECTION
Choreography: John Jones
Costumes: John Jones
Commissioned by Bank of Nova Scotia (Jamaica) Ltd

DESPERATE SILENCES
Choreography: Thomas Pinnock
Music: reggae selections

1973

THURSDAY'S CHILD
Choreography: Bert Rose
Costumes/decor: Bert Rose

I'VE BEEN BUK'D
(Solo with NDTC Singers)
Choreography: Rex Nettleford, Sheila Barnett

HOMAGE
Choreography: Rex Nettleford
Costumes: Donat Buckner
Decor: Richard Montgomery

STREET PEOPLE
Choreography: Rex Nettleford
Music: reggae selections
Costumes: Bruce Jones
Decor: Richard Montgomery

WINDSONG
Choreography: John Jones
Costumes/decor: John Jones

1974

MYAL
Choreography: Rex Nettleford
Music: traditional (Marjorie Whylie, arr.;
  Louise Bennett, consult.)
Costumes: Rex Nettleford

TRIBUTE TO CLIFF
Choreography: Rex Nettleford
Music: Jimmy Cliff
Costumes: Claudia Robinson

GLORY ROAD
Choreography: Bert Rose
Music: American spirituals
Costumes/decor: Bert Rose

THE ROPE AND THE CROSS
Choreography: Sheila Barnett
Costumes/decor: Sheila Barnett

1975

BACKLASH
Choreography: Rex Nettleford
Music: Toots Hibbert, Marjorie Whylie
Costumes/decor: Donat Buckner

COURT OF JAH
Choreography: Rex Nettleford
Music: Bob Marley
Costumes/decor: Colin Garland

REFLECTIONS
Choreography: Bert Rose
Costumes: Bert Rose, Denise Francis

SUPERNOVA
Choreography: John Jones
Music: Sun Ra
Costumes/decor: John Jones

1976

PEACE OFFERING
Choreography: Rex Nettleford
Music: Keith Jarrett
Costumes: Rex Nettleford

CHARACTER SKETCHES
Choreography: Rex Nettleford
Music: traditional
Costumes: Rex Nettleford

NI—WOMAN OF DESTINY
Choreography: Sheila Barnett
Music: Marjorie Whylie
Costumes/decor: Kofi Kayaga

CARO
(Love Duet)
Choreography: Bert Rose
Costumes: Denise Francis

JUBILATE
Choreography: Bert Rose
Costumes: Denise Francis

MOODS
(Solo)
Choreography: Bert Rose
Costumes/decor: Bert Rose

SOMEDAY
Choreography: Patsy Ricketts
Costumes: Patsy Ricketts

1977

WONDER LOVE AND RAISE
Choreography: Rex Nettleford
Music: Stevie Wonder
Costumes: Garth Robinson
Decor: Richard Montgomery

I NOT I
Choreography: Sheila Barnett
Music: Marjorie Whylie
Costumes/decor: Kofi Kayaga

SWITCH
Choreography: Bert Rose
Music: Hubert Laws
Costumes: Garth Robinson

1978

THE CROSSING
Choreography: Rex Nettleford
Music: Quincy Jones
Costumes: Denise Robinson
Decor: Bert Rose

ELEMENTS
Choreography: Rex Nettleford (conception), Bert Rose,
    Patsy Ricketts, Jackie Guy
Music: traditional (Marjorie Whylie, arr.)
Costumes: Barbara Requa, Pansy Hassan, Rex Nettleford

THE BROTHERS
Choreography: Patsy Ricketts
Music: Ernest Bloch
Costumes: Patsy Ricketts
Decor: Pansy Hassan

EBB FLOW
(Love Duet)
Choreography: Bert Rose
Costumes/decor: Bert Rose

WOMAN SONG
(Solo)
Choreography: Sheila Barnett
Music: Keith Jarrett

1979

DRUMSCORE
Choreography: Rex Nettleford
Music: traditional (Marjorie Whylie, arr.)
Costumes: Rex Nettleford, Pansy Hassan

BACK TO BACH, VIVA BACH
Choreography: Rex Nettleford
Music: Johann Sebastian Bach, Antonio Vivaldi
Costumes: Claudia Robinson
Decor: George Carter

CHAINLINKS
Choreography: Sheila Barnett
Music: Cedric "Im" Brooks
Costumes: Garth Robinson

1980

TWO DRUMS FOR BABYLON
(New Production)
Choreography: Rex Nettleford
Music: Peter Ashbourne
Costumes: based on original designs by Eddy Thomas
Decor: Rex Nettleford

CARIBBEAN SUITE
Choreography: Rex Nettleford
Music: traditional, Marjorie Whylie
Costumes: George McGann

SULKARI
Choreography: Eduardo Rivero
Music: traditional Cuban Yoruba (Marjorie Whylie, arr.)
Costumes/lighting: Eduardo Rivero
Courtesy Danza Nacional de Cuba

ROMANCE
(Love Duet)
Choreography: Eduardo Rivero
Costumes: Eduardo Rivero

1981

ROCKSTONE DEBATE
Choreography: Rex Nettleford
Music: Bob Marley, Marjorie Whylie
Costumes: Pansy Hassan
Decor: Rex Nettleford

THE GOSPEL ACCORDING TO
Choreography: Rex Nettleford
Music: American spirituals (Don Shirley, arr.)
Costumes: Rex Nettleford, Pansy Hassan
Decor: David Boxer
Commissioned by Alcan Jamaica Ltd

SOLITUDE
(Solo)
Choreography: Jackie Guy
Music: Tomaso Albinoni (lyrics: Morgana King)
Costumes: Jackie Guy

1982

LITANY
Choreography: Rex Nettleford
Music: Marjorie Whylie (theme: Peter Ashbourne)
Costumes: Gabrielle Harban

THE VISITOR
Choreography: Rex Nettleford
Music: Aaron Copland
Costumes/decor: Susan Alexander

FANTASY
Choreography: Barbara Requa
Music: Chick Corea
Costumes/decor: Barbara Requa

PHASES
Choreography: Tony Wilson
Music: Leonard Bernstein, Duke Ellington, Herbie Hancock
Costumes: Denise Robinson

JUST TIME
Choreography: Tony Wilson
Music: Two Tops of Fun

1983

GERREHBENTA
Choreography: Rex Nettleford
Music: traditional (Marjorie Whylie, arr.)
Costumes/decor: Donat Buckner

SOULSCAPE
Choreography: Rex Nettleford
Music: George Gershwin
Costumes: Denise Robinson, Gabrielle Harban

SUMMER IS
Choreography: Sheila Barnett
Costumes: Paulette Cousins
Decor: Pansy Hassan

TRIO
Choreography: Barbara Requa
Music: Fritz Kreisler
Costumes: Barbara Requa
Decor: Bert Rose

PROGENY
Choreography: Tony Wilson
Music: Tomaso Albinoni
Costumes: Denise Robinson

RECOLLECTIONS
Choreography: Clive Thompson
Music: Ramsey Lewis
Costumes: Charles Schoonnaker

NOTE: All lighting designs, beginning with the first season in 1962, have been executed by George Carter.

Appendix 3. The Members

FULL MEMBERS

DANCERS

Founders

Sheila Barnett
Audley Butler
Joyce Campbell
Shirley Campbell
Bridget Casserly
Yvonne daCosta
Pansy Hassan
Maureen Holder
Rosalie Markes
Monica McGowan
Rex Nettleford
Barbara Requa
Bert Rose
Gertrude Sherwood
Mavis Stoppi
Eddy Thomas

Others

Neville Black
Samuel Bailey
Madge Broderick
Fredericka Byfield
Noelle Chutkan
Yvonne Ffrench
Dorothy Fraser
Melanie Graham
Alaine Grant
Jackie Guy
Noel Hall

Gabrielle Harban
Fitzroy Hunt
Duran Hylton
Beverly Kitson
Dorothy McFarlane
George McGann
Carol Miller
Sandra Minott
Barry Moncrieffe
Sandra Monroe
Andrea Nash
Judith Pennant
Thomas Pinnock
Arlene Richards
Michael Richardson
Patsy Ricketts
Denise Robinson
Cheryl Ryman
Dennis Scott
Jacqueline Smith
Jean Summers
Neil Summers
Alison Symes
Judith Wedderburn
Derek Williams
Tony Wilson

Provisional/Supporting

Joye Abraham
Frank Ashley
Hyacinth Beckford
Michael Binns
Oswald Blackwood
Loretta Breakspeare
Glenford Brown
Victor Brown
Desmond Caesar-Brown

Ernest Cromwell
Carson Cumberbatch
Milton Dawes
Glen Dhyll
Sita Dickson
Merril Dunstan
Nancy Epinat
Eleanor Ferguson
Adrian Fletcher
Bunny Heron
Barbara Kaufmann
Pauline Khan
Dennis Lindo
Catherine March
Diane March
Calvin McDonald
Junior McGlashan
Carole McLaren
Paula Monroe
Christopher Morrison
Carol Murdock
Hillary Phillips
Monica Potts-Lawrence
Lois Requa
Delroy Rose
Karlene Samuels
Marilyn Sanguinetti
Hugh Williams

SINGERS

Carl Bliss
Marlene Buckeridge
Marie Cunningham
Vivienne Dewdney
Robert Dunkley

Louraine Emmanuel
Hope Foreman
Carmen Gordon
Lloyd Hall
Noel Heron
Stan Irons
Vin James
Paula Johnson
Joyce Lalor
Carole Reid
Wesley Scott
Vibart Seaforth
Leo Tyson
Marjorie Whylie
Cleonie Whyte

Provisional Singers

Claudette Allen
Lurline Bennett
Dave Buchanan
Sonia Campbell
Cecil Cooper
Vernon Darby
Pauline Davis
Winston Ewart
Connie Fraser
Roy Hall
Henrick Hamilton
Linda Hamilton
Purcess Mattheson
Sandra McKenzie
Hazel Sinclair
Martha Thompson
Charles Wright

MUSICIANS

Barbara Boland
Jeffrey Cobham
Steve Golding
Desmond Ivey
Minky Jefferson
Leighton Johnson
Lloyd Mason
Keith Reid
Marjorie Whylie

DRUMMERS

Ronan Critchlow
Richard Cunningham
Earl Edwards
Antonio Henry
Irvine Jarrett
Billy Lawrence
Obadiah Lewis
Leaford McFarlane
Carl Messado
Milton Osbourne
Lloyd Patterson
James Walker
John Walker
Horace Wedderburn

STAGE MANAGERS

Felix Barnett
Frederick Hickling
Tony Locke
Noel Vaz

LIGHTING DIRECTOR

George Carter
Rufus McDonald (asst.)

MUSICAL DIRECTOR

Majorie Whylie

BALLET MISTRESS/MASTER

Yvonne daCosta
Audley Butler

LEADER, NDTC SINGERS

Joyce Lalor
Marjorie Whylie

SOUND DIRECTORS

Clyde Cunningham
Baldwin Lennon

ARTISTIC COORDINATOR

Barry Moncrieffe

COSTUME COORDINATOR

Pansy Hassan

WARDROBE

Shirley Campbell
Barbara Kaufmann

PHOTOGRAPHER

Maria LaYacona

MANAGEMENT COMMITTEE

Chairmen

Joseph Cools-Lartigue
John Cooke
Maurice Stoppi

Secretary

Verona Ashman

Treasurer

Baldwin Lennon
Paul Breen
Carl Bliss

Public Relations Officer

Roy Burns
Heather Royes
Barbara Gloudon

Little Theatre Movement

Greta Fowler
Larry Shadeed

Others

Sheila Barnett
Wycliffe Bennett
Carmen Bishopric
Harold Brady
Ronan Critchlow
Melanie Graham
Patrick Lynch

Kay Lyons
Carmen Manley
Owen Minott
Hugh Morrison
Barbara Requa
Pat Rosseau
Elsie Sayle
Barry Watson
Dorothy Wells

Ex Officio

Artistic director
Lighting director
Stage manager
Musical director
Sound director
Ballet mistress
Artistic coordinator
Photographer
Leader, NDTC Singers
Public relations officer

CHOREOGRAPHERS

Sheila Barnett
Neville Black
Rex Nettleford
Barbara Requa
Bert Rose
Eddy Thomas

Supporting Choreographers

Joyce Campbell
Jackie Guy
Thomas Pinnock
Patsy Ricketts
Tony Wilson

OTHER VOLUNTARY CONTRIBUTORS

SET DESIGNERS

Donat Buckner
Eugene Hyde
Colin Garland
Milton Harley
Howard Parchment
Moira Small
Kofi Kayaga
Richard Montgomery
Seymour Leichman
David Boxer
Jerry Craig

COSTUME DESIGNERS

Richard Montgomery
Sally Montgomery
Easton Lee
Donat Buckner
Bruce Jones
Claudia Robinson
Colin Garland
Kofi Kayaga
Maria Smith
Grace Hamilton
Garth Robinson
Tom Cooke
Michael Bryne
Billy Dumont (accessories)

COMPOSERS

Oswald Russell
Carlos Malcolm
Noel Dexter
Bob Sinicrope
Peter Ashbourne

ARRANGERS

Carlos Malcolm
Mapletoft Poulle
Adrian Clarke
Ernest Ranglin

GUEST CHOREOGRAPHERS

John Jones
Eduardo Rivero
Clive Thompson

GUEST PERFORMERS

Clive Thompson
Namron
Celia Holten
Jennifer Muller & Co.
Ann Lake
Paul Jurek
Nicole Taylor
Patsy Barnett
Rona Barnett
The Frats Quintet
Winston White
Granville Lindo
R. Henry Richards
Sydney Clarke
Wilfred Warner
Altamont Wilson
Joye Thompson
Alston Bair
Paul Bicknell
Barbara Wilkin
George Wedderburn
Micky McGowan

COURTESY TUTORS

Barbara Fonseca
May Soohih
Betty Rowe
Punky Facey

TECHNICAL

Emma Crooks
Donat Buckner
David Ashley
Vin McKie
Philip Morris
Norman Cunningham

DRUMMERS

Sonny Bethelmy
Ivan Harban

MUSICIANS

Bryon Lee
& the Dragonnaires

MAKEUP

Elizabeth of Sweden
Sheila Burke (Max Factor)

SECRETARIAL

Peggy Greaves
Louise Carter

Daphne Headley
Mildred Brooks
Doreen Barrow
Claudette James
Mignonette Peters
Joy Blake
Janet Liu-Terry
Dorothy Hollingsworth
Oscar Carwin

PHOTOGRAPHY

Amador Packer
Sam Hillary
Roy Cruise
Owen Minott
Jamaica Tourist Board
Jamaica Information Service

FILM & VIDEO

Jamaica Information Service
Jamaica Broadcasting
 Corporation
Natalie Thompson
CBS (United States)
NBC (United States)
BBC (Great Britain)
Telstar (West Germany)
ABC (Australia)
Harvey Films
Mediamix
CBC (Canada)

PAID FREELANCE CONTRIBUTORS

MUSICIANS

Piano

Mapletoft Poulle
Adrian Clarke

Violin

Flo Wilson
Pete Stewart
Noel Peck

Flute

Carol Bacon Harty
Cedric "Im" Brooks
Alphonse Clarke

Trumpet

Winston Turner
Ossie Wilkins
Winston Graham
David Madden
Elnathan Brackenridge

Clarinet/Saxophone

Peter Hudson
Bertie King
Neville Graham

Guitar

Janet Enwright
Rupert Bent
Wallace Wilson
Ernest Ranglin
Jimmy Steele
Irvine Lloyd
Johnny Grant

Bass

Herbert Nelson
Trevor Bitter
Boris Gardiner
Henry Miller
Maurice Gordon

Drums

Eric Phillips

Congas

Larry McDonald

LIGHTING OPERATORS

Ainsley Wright
Leslie Dawkins
Donovan Tomlinson
Derrick Tomlinson
Patrick Tomlinson
Marcel Blackburne
Gillian Hickling
David Samuels
Roy Thomas

STAGE CREW

Stanley Dawkins
Lloyd Schloss
Kenneth Morgan
Terrence Marriott
Donald Thomas
Derek Shaw
Michael Locke

SCENE BUILDER

Donald Howell
Philip Morris

COSTUMES

Mrs. Caesar-Brown
Millicent Matthie
Aston K. Levy
Audrey Mantock
Claudia Robinson
Violet Guy
Jean Lee
Sally Thompson
Kay McFarlane
Grace McIntosh
Dennis Lindo
Enid Rattray
Arnold Kerr
Gem Williams

COSTUME MAINTENANCE

Lucille Graham
Melva Riley

FRONT HOUSE & BOOKING

Celia Carter
Inez Hibbert
Mavis Virtue
Christine Passmore
Janet Matalon
Stanley White
Aston White

SIGN PAINTER

Joseph Williams

PRINTERS

United Printers
Lithographic Printers
Offset Printing
Stephenson's Printery

Appendix 4. Government and Corporate Sponsors

JAMAICA

ALCAN JAMAICA LTD
AIR JAMAICA
ALCOA MINERALS OF JAMAICA INC.
BANK OF NOVA SCOTIA (JAMAICA) LTD
JAMAICAN HERITAGE
TEXACO CARIBBEAN INC.
KEY HOMES LTD
NATIONAL CONTINENTAL CORPORATION
BRITISH OVERSEAS AIRWAYS CORPORATION
BARCLAYS BANK INTERNATIONAL LTD
EDWIN CHARLEY LTD
GENERAL MANAGEMENT SERVICES
INDUSTRIAL COMMERCIAL DEVELOPMENTS LTD
DESNOES AND GEDDES LTD
J. WRAY AND NEPHEW LTD
JAMAICA CITIZENS BANK
EASTERN AIRLINES
HOUSE OF DUNHILL
SAVILLE ROWE HOUSE OF FASHIONS
GRACE KENNEDY LTD
ROYAL BANK FOUNDATION
LITTLE THEATRE MOVEMENT

GOVERNMENT OF JAMAICA:
   Office of the Prime Minister
   Ministry of Development and Finance
   Ministry of Foreign Affairs
   Jamaica Tourist Board
   Jamaica Cultural Development Commission

OVERSEAS

STRATFORD FESTIVAL, ONTARIO
ORGANIZATION FOR
   CARIBBEAN CANADIAN INITIATIVES, TORONTO
JAMAICAN NATIONALS LEAGUE, TORONTO
NATIONAL ARTS CENTRE, OTTAWA
BROOKLYN ACADEMY OF MUSIC
MIAMI HERALD
JAMAICA PROGRESSIVE LEAGUE, NEW YORK
SPELMAN COLLEGE, ATLANTA UNIVERSITY
VISUAL ARTS RESEARCH AND RESOURCE CENTER,
   NEW YORK
HOWARD UNIVERSITY, WASHINGTON, D.C.
MEXICANA AIRLINES, MEXICO CITY
SYMONETTE ENTERPRISES, PORT OF SPAIN
COMMONWEALTH ARTS FESTIVAL, LONDON
SADLER'S WELLS, LONDON
INSTITUTE OF PUERTO RICAN CULTURE, SAN JUAN
UNIVERSITY OF PUERTO RICO, SAN JUAN

GOVERNMENT SPONSORSHIP:
   MEXICO
   CUBA
   BARBADOS
   GRENADA
   GUYANA
   AUSTRALIA
   FEDERAL REPUBLIC OF GERMANY
   USSR

Notes and References

CHAPTER 1

1. Rex Nettleford, *Caribbean Cultural Identity—The Case of Jamaica: An Essay in Cultural Dynamics* (Kingston: Institute of Jamaica, 1978), 183.
2. Commonwealth Caribbean replaces the term West Indies, the earlier designation for the English-speaking Caribbean, which comprises thirteen independent islands and the mainland territories of Guyana and Belize. Starting with the colonization of Saint Christopher and Barbados in the early sixteenth century, Britain held imperial sway until the 1960s, when Jamaica and Trinidad, followed by other Caribbean territories, became independent. They all joined the Commonwealth of Nations—a club of former British colonies formally presided over by the British monarch, who is also the formal monarch of several member states.
3. Nettleford, *Caribbean Cultural Identity*, 183.
4. See Richard Price, ed., *Maroon Societies: Rebel Slave Communities in the Americas*, 2nd ed. (Baltimore: John Hopkins University Press, 1979), for historical background on the concept of marronnage, used here as a figurative term for the sensibility that employs cunning, secrecy, resistance by camouflage as strategies of survival forged from the historical experiences of the Maroons, or fugitive rebel slaves. See also Robert Charles Dallas, *The History of the Maroons*, 2 vols. (London: Longman and Rees, 1803).
5. Nadine Gordimer, "Living in the Interregnum," *The New York Review of Books* (January 20, 1983), 21.
6. Theodor Adorno, quoted in ibid.
7. Czeslaw Milosz, quoted in ibid., 24.
8. Mervyn Morris, foreword to *Focus 1983* (Kingston: Caribbean Authors Publishing Company, 1983).
9. Gordimer, "Living in the Interregnum," 26.
10. John Stewart, *An Account of Jamaica and Its Inhabitants* (London: Longman, Hurst Rees and Orme, 1808), 263.
11. Hans Sloane, *A Voyage to the Islands of Madera, Barbados Nieves, S. Christophers, and Jamaica with a Natural History of the Herbs and Trees, Four-footed Beasts, Fishes, Birds, Insects, Reptiles, and of the Last of Those Islands,* 2 vols. (London: The author, 1707–25), 1:vi.
12. James M. Phillipo, *Jamaica: Its Past and Present States* (London: John Snow, 1843), 242; reprint, introduction by Philip Wright (Freeport, N.Y.: Books for Libraries Press, 1971).
13. Peter Marsden, *An Account of the Island of Jamaica; with Reflections on the Treatment, Occupation, and Provision of the Slaves* (Newcastle: S. Hodgson, 1788), 33–34.
14. Ibid.
15. James Kelly, *Voyage to Jamaica and Seventeen Years Residence in That Island . . .* (Belfast: James Wilson, 1838), 21.
16. William James Gardner, *A History of Jamaica from Its Discovery by Christopher Columbus to the Year 1872* (London: E. Stock, 1873), 184.
17. See Robert D. Abrahams and John H. Szwed, eds., *After Africa: Extracts from British Travel Accounts and Journals of the Seventeenth, Eighteenth, and Nineteenth Centuries Concerning Slaves, Their Manners, and Customs in the British West Indies* (New Haven: Yale University Press, 1983), especially Chapters 5–6.
18. Edward Brathwaite, *The Development of Creole Society in Jamaica, 1770–1820* (Oxford: Clarendon Press, 1971), 220 (the bracketed interpolation is Brathwaite's). Brathwaite's quotation regarding philosophy is by Derek Walcott, from the sequence "Tales of the Islands" in his collection of poems *In a Green Night* (London: Jonathan

Cape, 1972), 26: "Teach our philosophy the strength to reach / Above the navel; black bodies, wet with light, / Rolled in the spray as I strolled up the beach."

19. See Judith Lynne Hanna, *To Dance Is Human: A Theory of Nonverbal Communication* (Austin: University of Texas Press, 1979).

20. Ibid., 3.

21. The term jonkonnu (also John Canoe or jonkanoo) is used in Jamaica and the Bahamas for masquerade bands of revelers that emerged in plantation history and were active during the three days' festivities at Christmastime. See Abrahams and Szwed *After Africa*, Chapter 5, for eighteenth- and nineteenth-century commentators on the ceremony. See also two unpublished master's theses—Sheila Barnett, "Jonkonnu and the Creolization Process in Jamaica: A Study in Cultural Dynamics" (1977); Cheryl Ryman, "Dance as a Major Source and Stimulus for Communicating Africanisms in Order to Effect a Process of Self-Actualization" (1983), both Institute of Jamaica—for in-depth analyses of the development and cultural significance of jonkonnu in Jamaican history.

22. The Haitian set-girls—named for a set of dancers and also known as French set-girls—were featured in the jonkonnu ceremonies from the end of the eighteenth century to the 1840s. These women revelers were organized in costumed groups, or sets, of reds and blues, and vied for audience attention through their fine dress and dancing. See bibliographic works cited in notes 17 and 21. Joyce Campbell's choreography for the National Dance Theatre Company's 1964 piece *Dance Time in Cascade* used the Haitian set-girls designs left by Isaac Mendes Belisario, the nineteenth-century Italian painter and etcher working in Jamaica.

23. Slavery was legally abolished on August 1, 1834, but an apprenticeship period, lasting until 1838, was set by the Abolition Act as a timetable for ultimate liberation.

24. Arthur Lewis, "Striving to Be West Indian," *The Sunday Gleaner* (February 20, 1983), 18.

25. All of these names refer to African-derived rituals extant in Jamaica. Kumina embraces the dominant elements of music, dance, spirit possession, healing, and the use of herbs; as a rite it is practiced on auspicious occasions (see discussion of the National Dance Theatre Company's repertoire in Chapter 3) mainly in the parish of Saint Thomas and to a lesser extent in the parishes of Portland, Saint Mary, Saint Catherine, and Saint Andrew. Pukkumina and Zion together represent the syncretized cults of Jamaica religious worship. The former has retained African elements of worship; the latter is more Euro-Christian in orientation, sharing with orthodox Christianity the authority of the Bible. Closely related to pukkumina are bongo, convince, and flenkee cults. Zion, which has its historical roots in Christian revivalism known as the Great Revival movement of 1860, deals with heavenly spirits such as angels, archangels, and apostles. Pukkumina involves ground spirits regarded as evil by the Zionists. The distinction between the two movements reveals the persistent dialectical relationship in the society between Africanisms and the culture of the colonizing power. Since the 1970s Zion revivalism has again inspired evangelicalism.

Tambu is a recreational rite derived from African customs, and in terms of dance it bears strong resemblances to kumina, which, it is believed, is a secular variant of it. Tambu is danced in Trelawny in the Wakefield and Friendship districts. Etu is claimed to be Yoruba-derived and danced at wakes in the parish of Hanover. Etu is also danced on festive occasions such as weddings and dinner parties. African cuisine is featured and the most proficient performers in the circle are rewarded with shawls; hence the shawling dance in the National Dance Theatre Company's 1983 work *Gerrehbenta*. Gerreh is another recreational dance best known in western Jamaica. As a "deadyard ceremony," which was performed at wakes, gerreh utilizes ring games and dances of skill; for example, the calembe stick dance, featuring a dancer walking on two poles horizontally held by two men while in motion. Dinkimini, also a deadyard ceremony, is recreational, offering the dancers a wide range of innovation. According to Cheryl Ryman, "the aim is to defy death by life—great activity with marked sexual overtones, a prelude to new life is a display of man's re-creative capacity" (see *NDTC Newsletter* [July 1983], 11c).

Rastafarianism is a popular religious movement flourishing in Jamaica since the early 1930s; it has spread throughout the world by means of its music and a life-style that appeals to nature. Its beliefs are centered on human dignity and the brotherhood of man as well as on the divinity of the former emperor of Ethiopia Haile Selassie and the repatriation to Africa of the uprooted black man. Rastafarianism has been a source of energy for creative expressions in language, music, art (painting and ceramics), dance, fashion (clothes and hairdos), and diet (natural foods). See the excellent article by Cheryl Ryman, "The Jamaican Heritage in Dance," *Jamaica Journal* 44 (June 1980), 2–14.

26. For information on voodoo see Harold Courlander, *The Drum and the Hoe: Life and Lore of the Haitian People* (Los Angeles: University of California Press, 1960); Lavinia Williams, *Haiti-Dance* (Frankfurt: Brönners Druckerei, 1959); Fradique Lizardo, *Danzas y Bailes Folklóricos Dominicanos* (Santo Domingo: Editora Taller, 1974); Fradique Lizardo, *Apuntes: Religiosidad Popular Dominicana* (Santo Domingo: Museo del Hombre Dominicano, 1982). For santeria see William Bascom, "A Focus of Cuban Santeria," in *Southwestern Journal of Anthropology* 6, no. 1 (1950): 64–68. For shango see George Eaton Simpson, *Religious Cults of the Caribbean: Trinidad, Jamaica, and Haiti*, rev. ed., Caribbean Monograph Series No. 7 (San Juan: Institute of Caribbean Studies, University of Puerto Rico, 1970). For cumfah see Frank Pilgrim, "Some Folk Dances of Guyana," paper presented at the UNESCO Cultural and Conservation Conference, July–August, 1970, Kingston, University of the West Indies.

27. Quoted in Wycliffe Bennett, "The History of Dance Theatre in Jamaica," paper presented at the symposium on the Collaboration Between the National Dance Theatre Company and the Jamaica School of Dance, May 25–26, 1982, Kingston, Cultural Training Centre. See also Ivy Baxter, *The Arts of an Island: The Development of the Culture and of the Folk and Creative Arts in Jamaica, 1494–1962* (Metuchen, N.J.: Scarecrow Press, 1970), especially Chapter 20, "The Dance Renaissance."

28. Rastafarianism is a modern theological invention, which gives to its adherents a black God hailing from Ethiopia. Reggae refers to the music that emerged from the ghettos of urban Kingston in the late 1960s and spread throughout the world as an international pop music form, largely through the work of Bob Marley, considered the superstar of the form, and Jimmy Cliff, Peter Tosh, Toots Hibbert, and Gregory Isaacs and bands such as Black Uhuru and Third World. The music—with an emphasis on a heavy four-beat rhythm, using bass, electric guitar, and drum with the scraper coming in at the end of the measure—accompanied songs rejecting establishment culture. For information on Rastafarianism, see bibliographic references cited in note 11 to Chapter 3. For a fuller description of reggae, see Stephen Davis, *Reggae Bloodlines: In Search of the Music and Culture of Jamaica*, photographs by Peter Simon (Garden City, N.Y.: Anchor Press, 1977).

29. Hanna, *To Dance Is Human*, 9.

30. See Bennett, "Dance Theatre in Jamaica," who quotes Joan McCulloch as follows: "I am in touch with Miss Ninette de Valois, director of the Sadler's Wells Ballet, who has shown great interest in our movement, and it is likely that one or two of our students will go to Sadler's Wells Ballet for their training." Barbara Fonseca was the one chosen. Others went to Toronto, where they studied with Boris Volkoff. Ivy Baxter went to London to study with Sigurd Leeder (see note 36 below).

31. H. V. Ormsby Marshall, "Native Dances of Jamaica, B.W.I.," *The Dancing Times* (June 1939), 287.

32. Ibid. (my emphasis).

33. Quoted in Bennett, "Dance Theatre in Jamaica."

34. See Martha Warren Beckwith, *Black Roadways: A Study of Jamaican Folk Life* (Chapel Hill: University of North Carolina Press, 1929; New York: Negro Universities Press, 1969).

35. See Katherine Dunham, *Katherine Dunham's Journey to Accompong* (New York: Henry Holt and Company, 1946). Dunham's fieldwork took her to Trinidad and Haiti as well. See also Ruth Beckford, *Katherine Dunham: A Biography,* foreword by Arthur Mitchell (New York: Marcel Dekker, 1979).

36. See Baxter, *Arts of an Island.* In Baxter's book, Chapter 20, entitled "The Dance Renaissance," traces the work in Jamaican dance theater from the 1920s to independence. Considered the founder of Jamaican creative dance, Baxter studied first with Hazel Johnston in Jamaica and later in London with Sigurd Leeder—who directed the School of European Dance there during and after World War II—before returning to Jamaica to lead the Ivy Baxter Creative Dance Group to national and wider Caribbean prominence.

37. See Molly Ahye, *Cradle of Caribbean Dance: Beryl McBurnie and the Little Carib Theatre* (Port of Spain, Trinidad: Heritage Cultures, 1983).

   According to the Jamaican journalist Ulric Simmonds, "there is intricate variety in the art forms of Beryl McBurnie, the result of the cosmopolitan origins of the West Indies —the minuet and glissando of the French, the flamencos of Andalucia, the fatalism of the Ganges, the proud high step of Northern Europe, and above all the vigour of the African forest intermixed in a bewildering variety of beauty and expression. Here and there, you get a glimpse of the Aboriginal West Indian—the savage Carib, the gentle Arawak, the fierce Owiarria, the wrestling Warrus." See Ulric D. Simmonds, "Spirit of the Past with Art of Modern Theatre," *The Sunday Gleaner* (August 14, 1955).

38. Baxter refers to the work of Johnston as monumental and avers that it "coincided with the general awakening of the arts in the island." See Baxter, *Arts of an Island,* 288.

39. *Rat Passage,* composed by Eddy Thomas and scored by Mapletoft Poulle, was the featured work in *Creations in Dance*; choreography was by Baxter herself. The piece was remounted by Nettleford for the show *Sun over the West Indies,* performed in Washington and Baltimore in 1961.

40. Eyrick Darby, who worked for the most part in tourist entertainment, was a talented dancer and dance creator. He studied for a summer at Jacob's Pillow in Massachusetts and did most of the choreography for the show *Danse Moderne,* which was presented under the auspices of the Baxter company.

41. Quoted in Bennett, "Dance Theatre in Jamaica." Orford St. John, a journalist and theater enthusiast originally from England, founded the Repertory Players, based in Kingston; he directed and acted in several of their plays.

42. Edward Brathwaite dealt with the theme of fragmentation in his keynote address to the Caribbean Dance Seminar, December 6, 1979, at the Jamaica School of Dance, Kingston. George Lamming also stressed the theme in his address at the annual dinner of the Press Association of Jamaica, December 12, 1981, in Kingston.

43. For a discussion of cultural imperatives relevant to the self-government movement, see Rex Nettleford, ed., *Norman Washington Manley and the New Jamaica: Selected Speeches and Writings, 1938–1968* (London: Longman, 1971), 98–122.

CHAPTER 2

1. The memorandum, composed as a position paper by the codirectors, was sent in September 1962 to members of the National Dance Theatre Company, NDTC Archives.

2. The Little Theatre Movement encouraged the use of dance in the pantomimes (pantomusicals) of 1959 *(Jamaica Way),* 1960 *(Caribe Gold),* and 1961 *(Banana Boy)* in

order to give them a sense of energy and movement. Eddy Thomas and Rex Nettleford choreographed *Jamaica Way*, while Nettleford choreographed and codirected, with Louise Bennett, *Carib Gold* and choreographed and directed *Banana Boy*, which included the core members of the future National Dance Theatre Company and marked a watershed in the use of dance as an integral part of the plot of a musical play.

3. "National Dance Company," *Spotlight 23*, no. 12 (December 1962), 24–26.

4. This was the first tour outside the Caribbean region by a group of Jamaican dancers working in a creative dance style. The repertoire was derived from the Ivy Baxter Creative Dance Group with most of the works choreographed by Baxter. Rex Nettleford and Noel Vaz were directors of the show, which in Washington, D.C., was performed in the Cramton Auditorium at Howard University. Eddy Thomas and Clive Thompson, both studying at the Martha Graham school in New York, joined the Company in Washington.

5. See Alma Mock Yen, "What Is a National Venture?" *The Daily Gleaner* (May 20, 1963), 12.

6. Andrew Hope, "A Tendentious Offering," *The Daily Gleaner* (February 5, 1983), 4.

7. See "From the Artistic Director," NDTC Souvenir Program (1982).

8. Edward Seaga, letter to Rex Nettleford, October 2, 1962.

9. See Michael Manley, *Politics of Change* (London: Andre Deutsch, 1974), especially 155–57. The first public commission Manley set up in 1972, when he formed the government, was the Arts Exploration Committee chaired by Rex Nettleford.

10. Edward Seaga resumed many of his cultural programs begun in the 1960s, with special concentration on national heritage projects—archaeology and conservation of the plantation homes (Great Houses) such as Devon House—arts and crafts development, cultural tourism, and national festivities. The archaeology projects include a government-sponsored dig at a site at New Seville, where Columbus first landed; there were underwater digs at Port Royal in the 1960s.

11. See note 8 above (my emphasis).

12. Nettleford choreographed for every major theater production in Oxford between 1957 and 1959, including the first performance in England of Maurice Ravel's one-act opera *L'Enfant et les Sortilèges*.

13. Nettleford worked with Alan Bennett and Dudley Moore on the Fringe show at the 1959 Edinburgh Festival. In 1961 he choreographed the revue *Pieces of Eight* staged at the Lyric Hammersmith in London. Both Bennett and Moore later became internationally famous for their review *Beyond the Fringe*. Moore subsequently has established a distinguished film career in Hollywood.

14. The Hungarian-born teacher Rudolf Laban devised a notation for dance and invented a new system of dance involving creative rhythms and the supremacy of motion. His great influence on European modern dance was through two of his pupils—Mary Wigman and Kurt Jooss—and his influence on movement theory resulted from his method of teaching corrective exercise to factory workers in England. The Jamaican dance received its Laban influences from Ivy Baxter, Sheila Barnett, and Barbara Requa.

15. Herma Díaz, who introduced Hazel Johnston to the ballet, was an important pioneer in promoting the classical ballet tradition in Jamaican dance theater. See Ivy Baxter, *The Arts of an Island: The Development of the Culture and of the Folk and Creative Arts in Jamaica, 1494–1962* (Metuchen, N.J.: Scarecrow Press, 1970).

16. See Wayne Brown, *Edna Manley: The Private Years, 1900–1938* (London: Andre Deutsch, 1975).

17. For more information on this poet, see Louise Bennett, *Jamaica Labrish*, introduction by Rex Nettleford (Kingston: Sangster's Book Stores, 1966), and *Louise Bennett: Selected Poems*, introduction by Mervyn Morris (Kingston: Sangster's Book Stores, 1982).

18. See Leroy Leatherman, *Martha Graham: Portrait of the Lady as an Artist*, photo-

graphs by Martha Swope (New York: Alfred A. Knopf, 1966).

19. Both Vin James and Paula Johnson performed in the 1962 *Roots and Rhythms* show as members of the Canboulay Singers, led by Trinidad-born Marina Maxwell.

20. See Rex Nettleford, *Roots and Rhythms: Jamaica's National Dance Theatre,* photographs by Maria LaYacona (London: Andre Deutsch, 1969; New York: Hill and Wang, 1970).

21. Derek Walcott, "Superfluous Defence of a Revolutionary: Focus on the Jamaican Dance Company," *Trinidad Express* (August 20, 1971), 4.

22. Winnifred Risden, review of *Roots and Rhythms* by Rex Nettleford, *Caribbean Quarterly* 16, no. 3 (September 1970), 71–74.

23. See Norman Rae, "Where'ere We Wander?" *The Daily Gleaner* (July 30, 1963), 7. *Public Opinion* criticized the Company's 1964 season as a "mixed bag of dance" and its "many variant styles . . . as hotch potch" (see "Mixed Bag of Dance," *Public Opinion* [August 14, 1964], 13).

24. See Alejandro Alonso, "Folklore as the Original Source," *Juventud Rebelde* (September 4, 1974), 1.

25. Deborah Jowitt, "Dance," *The Village Voice* (April 26, 1973), 42.

26. William Littler, "Jamaica Dance: Good Intentions, Bad Art," *The Toronto Star* (May 18, 1975).

27. See William Littler, "Jamaicans Are Fine Diplomats," *The Toronto Star* (August 14, 1981), 4.

28. Maud Fuller, "Seen Twice: Notes from the North," *NDTC Newsletter* (February 1982), 3.

29. Dick Klund, quoted in Souvenir Program for the Miami Herald Travel Show, Dade County Auditorium, Miami (May 11–12, 1970), 3. Klund, who was the public relations director for *The Miami Herald,* had seen the Company in Jamaica.

30. Walcott, "Superfluous Defence of a Revolutionary," 4.

31. Hector Campos-Parsi, quoted in "The NDTC and the Wider Caribbean," NDTC Souvenir Program (1976), 4.

32. See George Beckford, "Reflections on the National Dance Theatre Company," *NDTC Newsletter* 3 (1968), 1–3.

33. Keith W. Calhoun, "The Role of Culture in a Developing Nation: The National Dance Theatre Company of Jamaica in a Case Study Analysis" (master's thesis, Program in International Relations, Stanford University, 1977), Chapter 3.

34. Dennis Scott, "Dance and This Society," *The Sunday Gleaner* (April 12, 1970), 27. See note 4 to Chapter 3.

35. The full details of the Company tours outside Jamaica are given in Appendix 1.

36. See "Pro Pourri," *Gameday* (December 1982), 172; *Gameday* is the Orange Bowl Souvenir Program.

37. The Caribbean Basin Initiative project comprises twenty-eight developing countries in Central America, the northern part of South America, and the Caribbean, which are offered "innovative one-way free trade providing duty-free access to the United States market for twelve years." See supplement to *The Daily Gleaner* (November 11, 1983), devoted to the Caribbean Basin Initiative.

38. The Expo was a trade exhibition of the Caribbean Free Trade Association (Carifta), which preceded the Caribbean Community (Caricom). The exhibition was hosted by Eric Gairy, Grenada's prime minister at the time.

39. See Walcott, "Superfluous Defence of a Revolutionary."

40. Franz Guenther Buescher with his daughter, Tiana Buescher-Wigle, and her husband, James E. Wigle, as the two assistants.

41. Spelman College is a constituent college of the Atlanta University system. Albert Manley, Spelman's president in 1969, instituted the college's artist-in-residence program. The Jamaican painter Barrington Watson also participated in the program.

42. This organization, which is housed at the Caribbean Cultural Center in New York City, is devoted to the development of Caribbean

arts and culture among the various Caribbean nationalities residing in the United States.

43. On the previous visits to New York the Jamaica Tourist Board, the Jamaican Consulate General, and the commercial agency responsible for Jamaica's public relations in the United States were active in promoting the Company's appearances. They were less active on the 1983 visit.

44. The letter by the exiled Bolívar was written on September 6, 1815, from Kingston to Henry Cullen, an Englishman living in Falmouth. The letter outlined Bolívar's plans for the liberation and for the political development of Venezuela and all of Hispanic America. See Aurelio R. López Williams, "The Jamaica Letter," *Jamaica Journal* 7, no. 3 (September 1973), 2–5, for a discussion of Bolívar's letter.

45. See "From the Artistic Director," NDTC Souvenir Program (1970), 10.

46. See "Company Highlights, 1974–1975," NDTC Souvenir Program (1975), 4–5.

47. Organización Latinoamericana de Energía (OLADE).

48. Jimmy Cliff, one of the great Jamaican reggae song writers, also starred in *The Harder They Come,* a cult movie about Kingston's depressed masses during the 1960s.

49. Parish competitions in dance and music are held annually in Jamaica from May to August. At the end of this period, during the independence celebrations, the prize-winning performers—the gold and silver medalists—participate in the annual presentation known as *Mello-Go-Round.* The inclusion in the show of the Company work *The Crossing* was unique because of the special nature of this particular event, which celebrated the nation's "coming of age" on its twenty-first birthday.

50. The segment of the videotape devoted to the National Dance Theatre Company showed their *Afro–West Indian Suite.* The tape of the Commonwealth Arts Festival was directed by John Furness.

51. In Rastafarian protest language "Babylon" refers to the imperialist West in general and socially oppressive Jamaican society in particular. The police are usually earmarked for the nomenclature, as the agents of "downpression."

52. "Roots and Rhythms" (editorial), *The Daily Gleaner* (December 9, 1972), 8.

53. Based in Washington, D.C., the Inter-American Foundation works in grass roots and other community development programs throughout Latin America and the Caribbean. Its innovative approach to development assistance under the presidency of Bill Dyal, Jr., won for the foundation, as well as for the United States, friends in the Caribbean and Latin America along with some detractors among the more conservative elements on Capitol Hill.

CHAPTER 3

1. For a complete list of the Company's active repertoire for the years 1962–83, see Appendix 2.

2. For a description of jonkonnu and set-girls, see notes 21 and 22 to Chapter 1.

3. In 1968 *Plantation Revelry* was slightly reworked; another returning lady was added, and there was a finer texture to the piece.

4. Dennis Scott, "Dance and This Society," *The Sunday Gleaner* (April 12, 1970), 32. This is the first section of a three-part article by Scott that discusses at length four Company works: *Plantation Revelry, Two Drums for Babylon, The King Must Die,* and *All God's Children.* The article was serialized in the *Gleaner* on April 12, 19, 26, 1970.

5. In the late 1960s the American black power protest movement spread to the Caribbean. Company dancers studying in New York were not unaffected by events in the United States, and they returned with a new sensitivity to the treatment of black themes in art. The "minstrelsy" in *Plantation Revelry* was of course delineated deliberately as a sarcastic comment on a quirk of black history. Dennis Scott was among the few critics of the piece who understood the irony of the deceptively simple pantomime.

6. Norman Rae, "Where'ere We Wander?" *The*

Daily Gleaner (July 30, 1963), 7. Harry Milner also criticized the piece: see "Embarrassment of Riches," *The Sunday Gleaner* (August 4, 1963), 12.

7. "Ballet Satire on Arms Race," *The Times* (London) (September 25, 1965), 6.

8. Scott, "Two Drums for Babylon," *The Sunday Gleaner* (April 19, 1970), 36. See note 4 above.

9. See Frantz Fanon, *Les Damnés de la Terre,* preface by Jean-Paul Sartre (Paris: François Maspero, 1961); *The Wretched of the Earth,* translated by Constance Farrington (New York: Grove Press, 1965; Evergreen Black Cat Edition, 1968), especially Chapter 1, "On Violence." At the beginning of his three-part article for the *Gleaner,* Dennis Scott quoted a passage from Fanon's book (Black Cat Edition, p. 57) about the circle of the dance as a means of protection: "Symbolic killings, fantastic rites, imaginary murders—all must be brought out." See *The Sunday Gleaner* (April 12, 1970), 27; see also note 4 above.

10. After the text was completed, the United States invaded strife-torn Grenada, where the prime minister of the new revolutionary Marxist regime had been killed by rival factions accusing him of being deviationist. The so-called rescue mission of President Ronald Reagan was purportedly to liberate American students attending an off-shore medical school there and the Grenadians from the threat of a Communist takeover. Reagan found support for the mission from the members of the Organization of Eastern Caribbean States, as well as Barbados and Jamaica, which together encouraged the United States to intervene. The invasion was believed to have been on the agenda of U.S.-Caribbean relations for a long time because of United States fear of Cuban and Soviet influence in the area.

11. Haile Selassie, who became emperor of Ethiopia in 1930, is regarded as divine in the belief system of the Rastafarians. In 1974 Haile Selassie was deposed by an army coup and died in captivity the same year. See Leonard E. Barrett, *The Rastafarians: A Study in Messianic Cultism in Ja-* maica (San Juan: Institute of Caribbean Studies, University of Puerto Rico, 1968); Rex Nettleford, *Identity, Race, and Protest in Jamaica* (New York: William Morrow, 1972); Leonard E. Barrett, *The Rastafarians* (Kingston: Sangster's Book Stores; Boston: Beacon Press, 1977).

12. See *Caribbean Quarterly* 26, no. 4 (December 1980), a special issue devoted to the subject of Rastafari.

13. *Bongo Divertimento,* played by the symphony orchestra of Saint Paul-Minneapolis, was introduced to the choreographer of the work by Hugh Morrison of the University of the West Indies.

14. Sartre's "fable," which Scott alludes to, is a philosophic anecdote Sartre invokes to present an existential dilemma involving the problem of choice and will. In the early part of World War II one of Sartre's students in Paris was anguished over the question of joining the Free French Forces to avenge his older brother's death in the German offensive of 1940 or remaining with his mother, who would be plunged into helpless despair without him. The relevant passage from Sartre reads: "Ainsi, en venant me trouver, il savait le réponse que j'allais lui faire, et je n'avais qu'une réponse à faire: vous êtres libres; choisissez, c'est-à-dire inventez. Aucune morale générale ne peut vous indiquer ce qu'il y a à faire; il n'y a pas de signe dans le monde." ("Therefore, in coming to see me he knew the answer I was going to give him, and I had only one answer to give: 'You're free, choose, that is, invent.' No general ethics can show you what is to be done; there are no omens in the world.") See Jean-Paul Sartre, *L'Existentialisme est un Humanisme* (Paris: Nagel, 1946), 46–47; *Existentialism,* translated by Bernard Frechtman (New York: Philosophical Library, 1947), reprinted in *Existentialism and Human Emotions* (New York: Philosophical Library, The Wisdom Library, 1957), 27–28.

15. Scott, "Two Drums for Babylon," *The Sunday Gleaner* (April 19, 1970), 29. See note 4 above.

16. The term "dread" is used to describe the

typical mood, even sensibility, of the Rasta-farian commitment; often it defines a state of contained anger. A Rastafarian wearing locks—uncut matted hair—is sometimes referred to as a "dread."

17. Ska, a type of popular music that emerged during the mid-1950s from the urban mass population in Jamaica, had its roots in American pop music, Caribbean traditional music (Zion revival and pukkumina), and Rastafarian drumming popularized by a musician known as Count Ossie. Rock-steady, intermediate between ska and reggae and greatly influenced by American rhythm and blues, was popular in Jamaica about 1960.

18. Scott, "So, to All God's Children," *The Sun-cay Gleaner* (April 26, 1970), 29. See note 4 above.

19. The colors green, red, and gold universally appear in the flags of countries liberated from colonialism after World War II. In con-trast, red, white, and blue are predominant in flags of imperial nations—such as, Great Britain and France—or in flags of former colonies of Britain and Spain which gained their independence in the eighteenth and nineteenth centuries—such as, the United States, Canada, and many countries of Latin America. Red, white, and blue sug-gest colonialism to many Third World peoples.

20. Ole Hige is the mythical figure of the old hag in both Jamaican and Guyanese lore. Usually depicted as witch and sorceress, she can also bring good luck to those she fancies.

Annie Palmer is the legendary witch of the Rose Hall sugar plantation who reput-edly killed her husbands and suffered re-tributive justice at the hands of one of her trusted slaves. The figure is clearly a repre-sentation of the historical power and op-pression suffered at the hands of the planter during slavery. The figure is made famous in H. G. DeLisser's novel *The White Witch of Rose Hall.*

Nanny, the historical heroine of the Ja-maica Maroons who flourished in the early eighteenth century, was feared by the Brit-ish, whom she defied even after the 1739 treaty of peace between them and the rebel slaves. Nanny is now a national heroine of Jamaica and is the subject of Sheila Bar-nett's dance *Ni—Woman of Destiny.*

21. Anna Kisselgoff, "The Dance: Jamaica Life," *The New York Times* (April 13, 1973), 48.

22. *Lucifer Lucifer,* discussed more fully under "Caribbean Themes of Religion and Ritual," was never performed after its first season. In the absence of film and video records of them, some works of a dance company are virtually lost.

23. The choreographer insisted on beating the gong himself.

24. Don McDonagh, "Dance: Jamaica Warmth," *The New York Times* (April 9, 1974), 36.

25. See Anna Kisselgoff, "Dance: Jamaica Company," *The New York Times* (April 5, 1974), 26.

26. Wycliffe Bennett, "NDTC at 20," *Jamaica Journal* 16, no. 1 (February 1983).

27. Ibid. (my emphasis).

28. "Kaya Katumbe" and "Anjooma," the two chants from *Ni—Woman of Destiny,* are Maroon songs collected by Marjorie Whylie. The first is a work song, the second is the word for stranger in the Maroon dialect.

29. See Errol Hill, *The Trinidad Carnival: Man-date for a National Theater* (Austin: Uni-versity of Texas Press, 1972), as well as *Caribbean Quarterly* 4, no. 3–4 (March–June 1956), a special issue devoted to the Trinidad Carnival.

30. Scott, "Dance and This Society," *The Sun-day Gleaner* (April 12, 1970), 32. See note 4 above.

31. Edward Kamau Brathwaite, "Caribbean Perspective: Historical Framework," paper presented at the Caribbean Dance Semi-nar, December 6–8, 1979, Kingston, Ja-maica School of Dance.

32. Some scholars consider pukkumina—rather than pocomania—as the correct

spelling since it shows the links with the ancestral kumina. The second spelling is misleading because it can be read as a little (*poco*) madness (*mania*). Edward Seaga has written in the insert notes for his album on Jamaica's folk music: "The customary spelling of this word has always been pocomania. However, I have altered the spelling to suit the phonetics of the word as it is pronounced by cult members and their associates themselves. There appears to be no evidence to establish this term as being of Spanish origin as the customary spelling indicates." *Folk Music of Jamaica*, Ethnic Folkways Library P453 (1956).

33. Kisselgoff, "Dance: Jamaica Life," 48.
34. For an explication of Annie Palmer's place in Jamaican legend, see note 20 above.
35. See also note 20 above for background on the heroine Nanny.
36. For an in-depth discussion on the creation of *The Crossing,* see Shirley Maynier-Burke's interview with Rex Nettleford in *Jamaica Journal* 43 (March 1979), 2–11.
37. Kisselgoff, "Dance: Jamaica Company," 26.
38. Clive Barnes, "Dance: Local Debut for Jamaica National Company," *The New York Times* (April 12, 1973), 58.
39. Grace Djabaki Djabatey, visiting instructor at the Jamaica School of Dance in October 1977, defined "agbadza" in the following manner: "Agbadza is danced by an ethnic group of Ghana known as the Anlos or Ewe. It . . . uses the upper part of the body. There may be rotation or upward and downward movements of the shoulders or expansion of the chest along with certain arm movements and contraction and release of the shoulder blades." (Notes transcribed by Cheryl Ryman.)
40. According to the Company's musical director, Marjorie Whylie, who chose the songs, they depict love in a humorous vein, as if Caribbean men are embarrassed by expressions of love. The songs in the suite were entitled "Me Mumma Mi Darling," "True Lover," "Amanda Grant," "Darling, No Tell Nuh Lie," and "Lion Heart."

CHAPTER 4

1. Pamela O'Gorman, "The Music of the NDTC," paper presented at the symposium on the Collaboration Between the National Dance Theatre Company and the Jamaica School of Dance, May 25–26, 1982, Kingston, Cultural Training Centre.
2. William Littler, "Jamaicans Are Fine Diplomats," *The Toronto Star* (August 14, 1981), 4.
3. O'Gorman, "Music of the NDTC."
4. Ibid.
5. Marjorie Whylie, notes for lecture demonstration at the Conference of the Association of Caribbean Historians, April 18, 1983, Kingston, Creative Arts Centre, University of the West Indies. See Michael Reckord, "Historians Lectured on NDTC," *The Daily Gleaner* (April 30, 1983), 4.
6. For the following discussion on Caribbean music, I am deeply indebted to Marjorie Whylie, particularly to her notes for the lecture demonstration she presented at the 1983 Conference of the Association of Caribbean Historians at the University of the West Indies (see note 5 above). Not only does Whylie possess a profound knowledge of music style and forms indigenous to the Caribbean, she also has a firm grasp of the relationship of this music to the native dances.
7. Skin drums are drums whose heads are made of animal skin held in place by hardwood pegs—Haitian and Cuban arada drums—or by wooden or metal hoops—congo and kumina drums from Jamaica and elsewhere. The sound apparently was anathema to the planters throughout the region. As late as the period 1915–35, during the military occupation of Haiti by the United States, Haitian drums were banned by the American occupation army.

The stomping tube is known as vaccine in Haiti and bamboo-tamboo in Trinidad. (Tambu, tamboo, and tambou are alternate spellings in the Caribbean, the result of orthographic variants for the same sounds from African languages and dialects.) The vaccine is made from a piece of bamboo with a mouthpiece cut into one end at a joint membrane. The bamboo-tamboo consists of pieces of hollow dry bamboo cut at various lengths so that they can be played in musical thirds, fifths, and so forth. See Harold Courlander, *The Drum and the Hoe: Life and Lore of the Haitian People* (Los Angeles: University of California Press, 1960), especially Chapter 18. See also liner notes to the record album, recorded in Trinidad, *Bamboo-Tamboo, Bongo, and the Belair,* Road Recordings, Cook Laboratories 5017.

8. "Nine-night" and "last prayers" are Jamaican terms for a wake.

CHAPTER 5

1. A welcome exception to this approach was the enlightened perspective of Bengt Häger, a member of the International Dance Council, who is a moving spirit in the development of modern dance in his native Sweden. Following years of dedicated work in contemporary dance, Häger induced UNESCO to sponsor a museum in Stockholm devoted to preserving world dance on film. All national dances were to be included in the museum, not only those from Europe and the United States but also forms indigenous to Africa, the Orient, and the rest of the Americas, including the Caribbean. Amadou-Mahtar M'Bow, UNESCO's director general, was present when the museum's collection was dedicated. Tapes of some of the dances of the National Dance Theatre Company of Jamaica have been deposited in the collection.

2. The technique that informs the expressive Company work *Sulkari,* which Eduardo Rivero choreographed in 1980, points directions for Caribbean dance art in its formal and classic presentation while it also draws conscious inspiration from pre-1959 Graham and from yoga breath control. Despite the grandeur of classical ballet posturing, the soul of the piece is the majesty of African sculpture. Rivero had to find the technical means of progressing from one figure to the next, just as early modern dance and neoclassical pioneers, including Nijinsky, did with figures from Grecian urns and classic friezes.

3. Sheila Barnett, "Jamaica Dance Theatre: Influences, Sources, Content, Performance, Social Index," paper presented at the seventh Commonwealth and International Conference on Sports, Physical Education, Recreation, and Dance, September 23–28, 1982, Brisbane, Australia.

4. Kaiso, regarded as the original term for calypso, is discussed by Errol Hill in *The Trinidad Carnival: Mandate for a National Theater* (Austin: University of Texas Press, 1972), especially 60–63. For a more popular account of the pre-Lenten festivity, see Keith Warner, *The Trinidad Calypso: A Study of the Calypso as Oral Literature* (London: Heinemann, 1982).

5. For a relevant discussion of reggae, see note 28 in Chapter 1. See also Sebastian Clarke, *Jah Music: The Evolution of the Popular Jamaican Song* (London: Heinemann, 1980).

6. Cheryl Ryman's codified vocabulary list has been duplicated in mimeographed form but has not been formally published.

7. Until the 1950s mento was the most popular folk music of Jamaica. As a traditional song and dance style, mento is characterized by a strong syncopation on the last beat of each bar. The songs often ridicule or censure individuals within a group in veiled or symbolic terms.

8. Hector Campos-Parsi, quoted in "The NDTC and the Wider Caribbean," NDTC Souvenir Program (1976).

9. Derek Walcott, "Superfluous Defence of a Revolutionary: Focus on the Jamaican

Dance Company," *Trinidad Express* (August 20, 1971), 4.

10. Clive Barnes, "Local Debut for Jamaica National Company," *The New York Times* (April 12, 1973), 58.

11. See Anna Kisselgoff, "The Dance: Jamaica Life," *The New York Times* (April 13, 1973), 48.

12. Deborah Jowitt, "Dance," *The Village Voice* (April 26, 1973), 41.

13. See William Littler, "Good Intentions, Bad Art," *The Toronto Star* (May 18, 1975).

14. Maud Fuller, "Seen Twice: Notes from the North," *NDTC Newsletter* (February 1982), 5–7.

15. William Littler, "Jamaicans Are Fine Diplomats," *The Toronto Star* (August 14, 1981), 4 (my emphasis).

16. Peter Williams, "Caribbean Return," *Dance and Dancers* (November 1972), 41.

17. Norman Rae, "Where'ere We Wander?" *The Daily Gleaner* (July 30, 1963), 7.

18. Archie Lindo, "NDTC Dance: High Standards," *The Star* (July 21, 1975), 21.

19. See William Moore, "Dance Beat: Jamaica National Dance Company," *The Black American* 22, no. 40 (October 1983).

20. Quoted in Selma Jeanne Cohen, ed., *The Modern Dance: Seven Statements of Belief* (Middletown, Conn.: Wesleyan University Press, 1966), 6.

21. Alan Kriegsman, "Caribbean Cant," *The Washington Post* (April 3, 1976).

CHAPTER 6

1. For a complete list of Company members see Appendix 3.

2. Peter Williams, "The National Dance Theatre of Jamaica in London," *Dance and Dancers* (November 1965), 27.

3. Harry Milner, "A Wide Range," *The Sunday Gleaner* (December 7, 1975) 5.

4. Williams, "National Dance Theatre of Jamaica in London," 27.

5. Ibid., 52.

6. Deborah Jowitt, "Dance," *The Village Voice* (April 26, 1973), 42.

7. Peter Williams, "Caribbean Return," *Dance and Dancers* (November 1972), 41.

8. According to one Jamaican newspaper, it was "sheer delight." See Archie Lindo, "Continuity, a Link with the Past," *The Star* (July 26, 1983), 6.

9. See Harry Milner, "NDTC Opening Night," *The Sunday Gleaner* (March 12, 1972), 5.

10. Jowitt, "Dance," 42.

11. Dennis Scott has been published widely as a poet and is also the author of many plays, including *Echo in the Bone* and *Dog*.

12. See Lenore Weiss, "Jamaica Ensemble Projects Vivid Reality," *Daily World* (New York) (April 20, 1973), 8. In the early 1970s the average age of the Company dancers was thirty-two, and the reviewer for the *Daily World* felt that this accounted for a sense of "maturity which New York troupes often lack."

13. Clive Barnes, "Jamaicans Open Dance Season," *The New York Post* (September 16, 1983), 48.

14. William Littler, "Jamaicans Are Fine Diplomats," *The Toronto Star* (August 14, 1981), 4.

15. Anna Kisselgoff, "Dance: Jamaica Troupe," *The New York Times* (September 15, 1983), C17.

16. See Charles H. Fowler, "Music of the Americas," *High Fidelity/Musical America* (July 1981), 18–20 (*Musical America*).

17. The real estate package comprises an apartment block, a cottage, and a triplex located at Old Rich Road in Saint Andrew, one of Jamaica's corporate area parishes.

18. Robert Charles Dallas, *The History of the Maroons* (London: Longman and Rees, 1803), 2:453–54; cited in Gordon K. Lewis, *Main Currents in Caribbean Thought: The Historical Evolution of Caribbean Society in Its Ideological Aspects, 1492–1900* (Baltimore: Johns Hopkins University Press, 1983), 106.

19. James Anthony Froude, *The English in the*

West Indies; or, The Bow of Ulysses (London: Longmans, Green and Company, 1888), 286–87. Even though paternalistic views resembling colonialism are still present in many social, economic, and political relationships, it is difficult today to comprehend the distorted way these views were rationalized in the nineteenth-century under the guise of ethics and moral rectitude. Froude, writing in the same passage cited in our text, makes even bolder claims about racial certainty: "We have a population to deal with, the enormous majority of whom are of an inferior race. . . . They are docile, good-tempered, excellent and faithful servants when they are kindly treated; but their notions of right and wrong are scarcely even elementary; their education, such as it may be, is but skin deep, and the old African superstitions lie undisturbed at the bottom of their souls."

CHAPTER 7

1. These women, the first diploma graduates of the Jamaica School of Dance, were strategically placed in the school system to encourage the development of dance in education. They were students at the Contemporary Dance Centre before it was incorporated into the School of Dance.
2. Moira Logan, "The International Conference on Dance and the Child," *Dance Magazine* (December 1972), 88.
3. Derek Walcott, "The Muse of History—An Essay," in Orde Coombs, ed., *Is Massa Day Dead?—Black Moods in the Caribbean* (Garden City, N.Y.: Doubleday, Anchor Books, 1974), 4.
4. Cheryl Ryman, "Dance Research Activities, 1974–1982," African Caribbean Institute, Institute of Jamaica (November 1982), 2 (unpublished mimeographed notes). As an institutional framework, the African Caribbean Institute nurtures dance research by such investigators as Cheryl Ryman and

Sheila Barnett and is also a repository for their findings.
5. Cheryl Ryman, *NDTC Newsletter* (July 1983), 11a–11c.
6. See Rosalie Smith McCrea, introduction to catalog *Art and Dance* (Kingston: National Gallery of Jamaica, 1983), 1–3. McCrea, the museum's assistant curator, also organized the exhibition.
7. Pantomime musicals choreographed by Rex Nettleford include *Jamaica Way* (1959), *Carib Gold* (1960), *Banana Boy* (1962), *Bredda Buck* (1964), *Anancy and Pandora* (1967), *Anancy and Doombay* (1968), *Dickans for Fippance* (1974), *Brashana Oh* (1976), *The Witch* (1975), *Tantaloo* (1982). Sheila Barnett choreographed *Queenie's Daughter* (1963); Bert Rose *Twelve Million Dollar Man* (1977); Joyce Campbell *Rockstone Anancy* (1970); and Jackie Guy *Music Boy* (1971), *Mansong* (1980), *Johnny Reggae* (1978), *Pirate Princess* (1981), *Ginneral B* (1983).
8. See Leebert Bethune, "Song for the Dancers—Kumina," and Mervyn Morris, "Mother of Judas, Mother of God," in NDTC Souvenir Program (1976), 22. See also Mervyn Morris, "Dialogue for Three," in Rex Nettleford, *Roots and Rhythms: Jamaica's National Dance Theatre*, photographs by Maria LaYacona (London: Andre Deutsch, 1969; New York: Hill and Wang, 1970), 111.

CHAPTER 8

1. See Edward Kamau Brathwaite, "Caribbean Perspective: Historical Framework," paper presented at the Caribbean Dance Seminar, December 6–8, 1979, Kingston, Jamaica School of Dance. The seminar was sponsored by the Organization of American States and the Jamaica School of Dance.
2. It was Pearl Primus, in "African Dance: Eternity Captured," *Caribe* 7, no. 1–2: 21–28, who pointedly noted the importance of rhythm to African life in general.

3. "Harry Milner Looks at Two Decades of Theatre Music and the Dance," *The Sunday Gleaner* (August 1, 1982). In a special supplement to the *Gleaner,* commemorating the twenty-first anniversary of Jamaican independence, the critic Harry Milner seems to hold himself virtually as guardian of the European balletic tradition, to the point that he christened a fledgling dance ensemble as the antidote to the assertive heresies of the National Dance Theatre Company. See *The Daily Gleaner* (July 30, 1983), 21.
4. Dennis Scott, "So, to All God's Children," *The Sunday Gleaner* (April 26, 1970), 29. See note 4 to Chapter 3.
5. See Derek Walcott, "Superfluous Defence of a Revolutionary: Focus on the Jamaican Dance Company," *Trinidad Express* (August 20, 1971), 4.
6. See Wycliffe Bennett, "NDTC at 20," *Jamaica Journal* 16, no. 1 (February 1983), 59–61.
7. There is a subtle point in Littlewhite's analysis which is best appreciated by citing the relevant section of his letter: "It is important at this stage to examine the Marley profile, especially to his devotees. From as far back as 1964 Marley has been seen as a singer and composer, heavy with social commentary. With the greater acceptance of Rastafari in our society some people are anxious that Rastafari should be accorded the praise they have been denied for years. To many *Court of Jah* was supposed to provide this. Instead, and I speak for myself here, what we saw was not a subjective, sympathetic profile but rather something resembling an outsider's view of the movement. When you set this against the three earlier works, it gives the impression that Marley's music is the least important."
8. Norman Rae wrote many critiques of the Company for *The Daily Gleaner* between 1963 and 1967, but see especially "Where'ere We Wander?" (July 30, 1963), 7.
9. See Rex Nettleford, *Roots and Rhythms: Jamaica's National Dance Theatre,* photographs by Maria LaYacona (London: Andre Deutsch, 1969; New York: Hill and Wang, 1970). The remarks the critics took such offense at are on pages 112–13.
10. Winnifred Risden, review of *Roots and Rhythms* by Rex Nettleford, *Caribbean Quarterly* 16, no. 3 (September 1970), 74.
11. Ibid.
12. Andrew Salkey, review of *Roots and Rhythms* by Rex Nettleford, in BBC radio broadcast, transcript reproduced in *NDTC Newsletter* 10 (1969), 24.
13. Peter Williams, "The National Dance Theatre of Jamaica in London," *Dance and Dancers* (November 1965), 23.
14. Ibid., 27.
15. Peter Williams, "Caribbean Return," *Dance and Dancers* (November 1972), 39.
16. Ibid.
17. Marius Liepa, "Dancers from Jamaica," *Soviet Culture* (August 31, 1979).
18. Clive Barnes, "Jamaicans Open Dance Season," *The New York Post* (September 16, 1983), 48.
19. Anna Kisselgoff, "Dance: Jamaica Troupe," *The New York Times* (September 15, 1983), C17.
20. Jane Rigney, "Jamaica Dance Troupe a Visual Feast," *The New York Tribune* (September 7, 1983).
21. Rod Baker, "Dance: A Stumbling Beginning," *The New York Daily News* (September 15, 1983), 12.
22. Such heretical views in neocolonial Jamaica have been regarded in some quarters as insolent. Ironically a poet, whose work is not generally known to be the victim of amateurish cant or ignorant reporting, wrote in an article in Kingston's *Sunday Sun* that criticism of the Company, unless favorable, was deemed to be a high-risk affair. Naturally this precipitated a debate, which attempted to place in perspective our objections to a certain mode of journalistic criticism and prove that our daring to insist on critical excellence does not contradict the encouragement of frank views about the

Company's work and achievements. The subsequent debate, as well as the original article, also appeared in the *Sunday Sun:* see Mervyn Morris, "Criticism and the NDTC" (August 1, 1982), 14, 26; Rex Nettleford, "NDTC: Excellence and Su-Su" (letter to editor, August 8, 1982), 19; Mervyn Morris, "NDTC: Su-Su and Truth" (August 15, 1982), 15, 26; Rex Nettleford, "A Thirst for Salacious Fare" (letter to editor, August 22, 1982), 16.

23. Edward Kamau Brathwaite, letter to Rex Nettleford, May 22, 1969. The Caribbean Artist Movement (CAM), founded in London in 1966 by Brathwaite and others, was responsible for the publication of the literary journal *Savacou.*

CHAPTER 9

1. During the 1970s the policy of worker participation in industry became a matter of national concern for the government, trade unions, and employers in Jamaica. The chairman of the national committee making recommendations for greater worker participation was Rex Nettleford. Mervyn Morris in his queries about the NDTC's administration scored a neat point in the ensuing debate by inquiring about the degree of "worker participation" in the operation of the Company.

2. In cases of economic hardship there have been pressures on fulfilling basic needs, but the problem has been solved without compromising the ethos of the group. Each case has been handled confidentially without embarrassment to the individual. The fact that no Company member, including the leadership, is paid also instills mutual trust. Petty cash expenses are provided annually, but these fall below the individuals actual expenditures.

3. See James MacGregor Burns, *Leadership* (New York: Harper and Row, 1978), particularly Chapter 1, "The Power of Leadership."

4. Ibid., 19 (Burns's emphasis).

5. Ibid.

6. Ibid., 20.

7. Dennis Scott, "The Future Perspectives for Jamaican–Caribbean Dance," paper presented at the symposium on the Collaboration Between the National Dance Theatre Company and the Jamaica School of Dance, May 25–26, 1982, Kingston, Cultural Training Centre.

8. Ibid.

9. Of great significance, although less well known, is the work of Ramón Guerra, which in style and content is rooted in Afro–Cuban folklore but draws on the configurations of early Graham for its technical base. Another successful result of such cross-fertilization of traditions is *Sulkari* by Eduardo Rivero, a disciple of Guerra.

10. Andrew Salkey, review of *Roots and Rhythms* by Rex Nettleford, in BBC radio broadcast, transcript reproduced in *NDTC Newsletter* 10 (1969), 24.

11. Joseph Brodsky, "On Derek Walcott," *The New York Review of Books* (November 10, 1983), 40.

Index

R

Rae, Norman, 28, 69, 109, 186, 254, 259–60
Ramírez, Ariel, 151, 163, 227
Ranglin, Ernest, 228
Rastafarianism (Rastafari), 21, 24, 32, 36, 49, 96, 110, 116, 118–23, 124, 126, 160, 189, 193, 204, 252, 256, 259, 276
Rastaman, 95
Rat Passage, 29, 35, 54, 56, 231
Ravel, Maurice, 163
Reckord, Verena, 260
Recollections (Thompson), 153, 161, 194, 205, 218, 220
Reflections, 133, 192, 195, 196, 197
reggae, 24, 32, 71, 81, 118, 124, 127, 163, 167, 181, 190, 193, 204, 226, 230, 254, 259, 276
Reid, Carole, 223, 226
Reid, Keith, 231
Repertory Players, 238
Requa, Barbara, 58, 62, 66, 84, 91, 97, 99, 100, 105, 129, 173, 193, 195, 196, 245, 246, 247
Requa, Lois, 220
Resurrection, 133, 194, 196, 205
Revelations, 93, 264
revivalism (Zion revivalism), 21, 126, 127, 141, 181, 255
Revueltas, Silvestre, 158, 163
Reynolds, Malachi (Kapo), 251
rhumba, 180
Richards, Arlene, 212, 215, 216, 217
Richardson, Michael, 210, 211
Ricketts, Patsy, 66, 67, 91, 100, 105, 131, 154, 193, 200, 202, 203, 205, 212, 246, 254
Rigney, Jane, 264
ring games, 20, 21
Ring Hunt, 143, 159, 161, 191
Risden, Winnifred, 69, 260–61
Rites, 144, 158, 192, 204, 207, 209
Rivero, Eduardo, 105, 186, 194, 220, 227
Robbins, Jerome, 143, 159, 194
Robinson, Barbara, 245
Robinson, Claudia, 252
Robinson, Denise, 212, 215, 216, 251
Robinson, Garth, 252
rocksteady, 24, 167
Rockstone Debate, 111, 116, 181, 190, 214, 215
Rodgers, Rod, 204, 210
Rodney, Carl, 86
Rodrigo, Joaquín, 129, 163, 169
Romance, 194
Roots. See Jones, Quincy

Roots and Rhythms (book), 67, 236, 260, 261, 278
Roots and Rhythms (show), 42, 54, 55, 97, 137, 208, 221, 234
Rope and the Cross, The, 90, 116–17, 131–32, 150, 151, 182, 191, 196, 200, 202, 205, 233
Rose, Bert, 59, 60, 66, 97, 99, 100, 105, 126, 129, 152, 156, 173, 192, 195, 197, 213, 215, 244, 246, 251, 253
Rose, Delroy, 219
Rousseau, Pat, 239
Rowe, Betty, 65
Rowe, Punky, 30, 65
Rowe School of Dancing, 29, 202
Royal Academy of Dance (London), 248
Royal Ballet, 25, 171, 248, 277
Royal Ballet School, 221
Royes, Heather, 88, 236
Rumsey School of Ballet, 213
Russell, Oswald, 66, 164, 253
Ryerson Theatre, 85
Ryman, Cheryl, 66, 67, 102, 180–81, 206, 209, 210, 212, 249–50, 253, 255

S

Sadler's Wells (ballet), 25, 26, 248, 277
Sadler's Wells (theater), 75, 76, 81, 82, 193, 196, 262
Saint Andrew High School, 215
Saint Andrew Scots Kirk, 50, 90, 91, 94
Saint Andrew Singers, 221, 222
St. John, Orford, 30, 238
Saint Joseph's Teacher Training College, 245
Saint Lucia, 169
Salkey, Andrew, 261–62, 278
samba, 180
Samuels, Karlene, 210
Sanguinetti, Marilyn, 211
santeria, 21, 180
Santo Domingo, 21, 31
Sartre, Jean-Paul, 123, 263
Scala Theatre (London), 84, 262
schottische, 20
Schubert, Franz, 142, 163
Scott, Dennis, 66, 67, 73, 108, 114, 121, 142, 202, 204, 209, 210, 257, 258
Scott, Wesley, 223, 226
Seaforth, Vibart, 151, 223, 224, 226, 227
Seaga, Edward, 46, 47, 48, 49, 65, 81, 88

Seaton, Isobel, 43
Self-Theatrical Group (dance company), 218
set-girls. *See* Haitian set-girls
Seven Stages, 54
Shadows, 116, 165, 191, 200, 202, 228
shango, 21
Shawn, Ted, 219
Shearer, Hugh Lawson, 44
Shearer, Sybil, 41, 192
Sherwood, Gertrude, 59, 66, 99, 129, 195, 197
Silvera, Pansy. *See* Hassan, Pansy
Simpson, Fay, 41, 57, 196, 213
Sinicrope, Bob, 165, 253
Sistren Theatre, 213
Six and a Trumpet, 157
ska, 24, 167
Skatalites, 254
slavery, 13, 16, 18–19, 20, 23, 26, 30, 31–33, 109–10, 247; plantation America, 28, 109, 126, 138, 152, 155–57, 190; slave dances, 12, 16, 17–18, 34
Small, Moira, 252, 253
Smith, Jacquie, 212, 215, 216
Smith, Jean, 65
Smith, Lew, 41
Smith, Maria, 245
Sokolow, Anna, 203
Solitude, 133, 193, 205
Soltau, Penny, 30
Someday, 193, 210
Sonata, 192
Soohih, Anatole, 41
Soohih, May, 31, 41, 65, 205
Soohih School of Dance, 56, 58, 59, 196, 220
Soulscape, 141, 161, 190, 214, 216
Soyinka, Wole, 259
Spelman College, 86
Spotlight (magazine), 42–43
Star, The (Kingston), 260
stomping tube, 168
Stoppi, Maurice, 73, 238
Stoppi, Mavis, 58, 62, 206, 207, 209, 238
Stratford Festival (Ontario), 77, 81, 88, 236
Stravinsky, Igor, 163
Street People, 113, 123, 190, 196, 205, 206, 207, 208, 214, 215, 237, 259
Sulkari, 121, 139–40, 148, 160, 167, 181, 186, 194, 213, 214, 215, 216, 227, 228
Sullivan, Kay, 237, 248, 251
Summer Is, 153, 154, 161, 192, 205, 207, 215, 216, 217, 219, 233
Summers, Jean (Jean Binns), 66, 67,

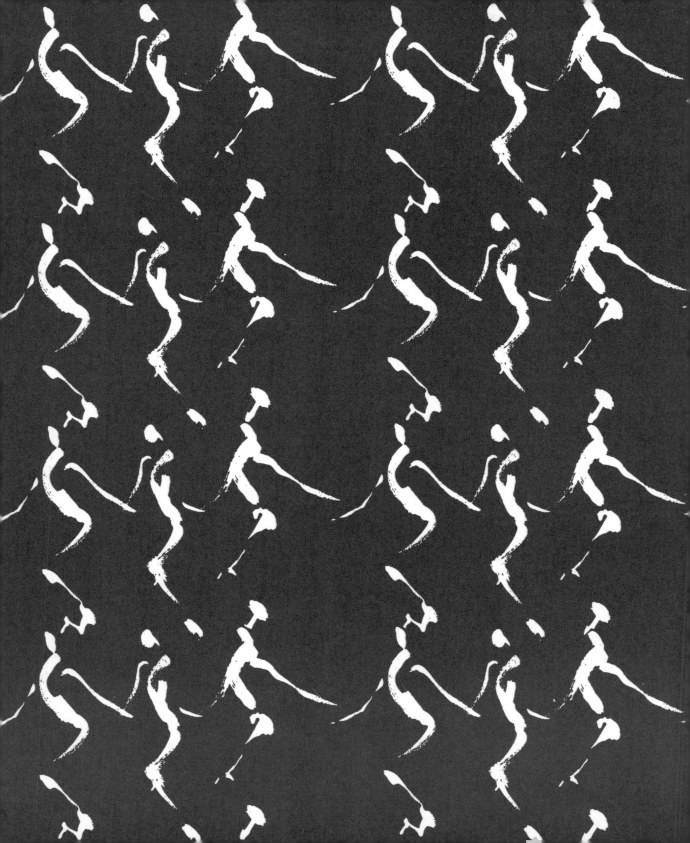